IRISH 'INGLESES'

The Irish Abroad

GENERAL EDITOR: RUÁN O'DONNELL, UNIVERSITY OF LIMERICK

The series publishes short biographies and collected writings studying Irish men and women who made their mark outside their native country. Accounts of those who settled permanently overseas are published along with the life stories of temporary residents and involuntary emigrants. Expatriates of all types are considered whether explorers, travellers, military personnel, colonial pioneers, members of religious orders, professionals, politicians, revolutionaries, exiles or convicts. Most titles concern the Irish in North America, the former territories of the British Empire (including Australasia) and Great Britain, although biographies of those who journeyed to Spanish America, the West Indies, Africa, Continental Europe and other non-English speaking sectors will form part of the series.

Already published in the Irish Abroad series from Irish Academic Press:

Thomas Francis Meagher
The Making of an Irish-American
John M. Hearne and Rory T. Cornish (Eds)

Through American and Irish Wars
The Life and Times of Thomas W. Sweeny
Jack Morgan

Bishop in the Dock
The Sedition Trial of James Liston in New Zealand
Rory Sweetman

Irish Republicanism in Scotland 1858-1916
Fenians in Exile
Máirtín Seán Ó Catháin

Ireland, Australia and New Zealand
History, Politics and Culture
Laurence M. Geary and Andrew J. McCarthy (Eds)

After the Flood
Irish America 1945–1960
James Silas Rogers and Matthew J. O'Brien (Eds)

IRISH 'INGLESES'

The Irish Immigrant Experience in Argentina
1840–1920

HELEN KELLY

Trinity College, Dublin

IRISH ACADEMIC PRESS
DUBLIN • PORTLAND, OR

First published in 2009 by Irish Academic Press

2 Brookside,
Dundrum Road,
Dublin 14, Ireland

920 NE 58th Avenue, Suite 300
Portland, Oregon,
97213-3786, USA

This edition © 2009 Helen Kelly

www.iap.ie

British Library Cataloguing-in-Publication Data
An entry can be found on request

978 0 7165 3007 7 (cloth)
978 0 7165 3008 4 (paper)

Library of Congress Cataloging-in-Publication Data
An entry can be found on request

Printed in Great Britain by the MPG Books Group, Bodmin and King's Lynn

Contents

List of Figures

List of Tables

List of Appendices

Acknowledgements

This book is the result of doctoral research and as such, I would like to begin by thanking my supervisor, David Fitzpatrick, for his meticulous appraisal of chapters, particularly in regard to statistical analysis, and for his invigorating supervision. In addition, David N. Doyle generously provided an insightful and detailed commentary on an earlier draft for which I am extremely grateful. I am also greatly indebted to a number of scholars who, over the course of this study, have generously contributed to its development: Juan Pablo Alvarez, Ciaran Brady, Terry Barry, David Dickson, Patrick J. Garrahan, James Heaney, Tom Kelly, Richard Kirwan, Michael Laffan, Oliver Marshall, Jonathan Moore, Edmundo Murray, William Murray, Micheál Ó Siochrú, Hilda Sábato, Bill Vaughan, Anne Walsh and Edward Walsh.

There are a number of institutions and individuals both in Ireland and Argentina that provided consistent and generous support. In Argentina: Archivo General Nacional; The *Southern Cross* newspaper – especially Luis Delaney and Alicia; Centro Argentino Irlandés de San Pedro; Father Tom O'Donnell, Pallottine Fathers, San Antonio de Areco; The Christian Brothers; The Jockey Club; Father Ambrose Geoghegan, Passionist Fathers; The Rattigan family; and to my friends in Rosario, especially Javier Garaghan and María Luisa Gutiérrez Peart, who were my first introduction to the Irish community in Argentina through my Uncle, Father Bernard Kelly, who himself provided much of my initial inspiration.

In Ireland: Trinity College Library, especially Anne Walsh and Mary Higgins who generously agreed to allocate precious financial resources for the purchase of the *Southern Cross* archive; Juergen Barkhoff and John McPartland for facilitating leave from Trinity to complete this manuscript; Greg Harkin, All Hallows College, for allowing me such unprecedented access to correspondence held in its archive; Noelle Dowling, Dublin Archdiocese Archive; Fr. Dolan McCarthy, Pallottine Fathers, Dublin; and to Pamela Hilliard and Jill Walsh in the Department of History, Trinity College, for all their assistance and kindness.

Finally, I owe immeasurable gratitude to my family for the unflinching support and love received from them. I continue to look to them for the important things in life. This book is dedicated to the heads of that family, Tom and Bridie Kelly, who have selflessly given to all of us and who are both so precious.

Helen Kelly
March 2009

List of Illustrations
(All illustrations courtesy of the Centro Argentio Irlandés de San Pedro)

1 Bernard Fox, married to Mary Robbins on 24 January 1872.

2 José O´Neill and Margarita Harrington with their childrenDolores, Santiago, Delia, Manuel, Eduardo and Daniel, 1918.

3 Margarita and Brígida Young Fennon c. 1885.

4 Fr. Pío Walsh, sometime in charge of St. Patrick's chapel.

5 Station at Arrecifes parish church, 17 March 1922 (a 'station' being a mission by Catholic priests in the countryside or in a rural town).

6 Teresa Porta Young at the storehouse.

7 Celtic crosses at the cemetery of Carmen de Areco, Buenos Aires province. Photo Edmundo Murray 2003.

8 Elena Kehoe Tyner and Tomás O´Riordon Young, c. 1910.

9 Luke Doyle and Catalina Gaynor with their children Santiag and Eduardo in Estancia Santa Catalina, 1875.

10 Station at St. Patrick's Chapel of Santa Lucía, 1890s.

11 Juan, Cristobal and Thomas Young Doran.

12 Juancito Young in his sulky.

13 Maria Kennedy, Carlos, Eduardo, Patricio, Marcos and Tomás, José Feeney of Co. Longford.

Introduction

Between 1801 and 1921 no less than eight million Irish men, women and children emigrated from Ireland.[1] Of these, approximately two thirds went to the United States, one tenth to Australia[2] and, from 1822 to 1929 an estimated 7,159 Irish immigrants arrived at the port of Buenos Aires.[3] The history of this mass exodus of the Irish populace has been the object of study and interpretive controversy for decades, and the resulting literature has been of extraordinary value both for the countries hosting the new immigrants and for the history of Ireland itself. Yet, with the notable exceptions of Eduardo Coghlan's pioneering work in the 1980s and the more recent contribution of Edmundo Murray, both of which are discussed below, Irish migration to Argentina has been largely neglected. Two features immediately distinguished Argentina as an Irish immigrant destination: the first was its Spanish vernacular; the second, that it was the only predominantly Catholic nation that attracted significant levels of Irish immigrants. Consequently, the experience of the Irish in Argentina was qualitatively different from that in Australia or the United States. Viewed in these terms, Argentina presents not only a fascinating case study in its own right, but also provides a valuable point of comparison in Irish emigration studies.

Of all Latin states, Argentina demonstrated an early awareness of the benefits European immigrants could offer its economy, its society and its racial composition. Drawing on roots in the progressive liberal policies of Bernardo Rivadavia's early political leadership, Argentina, from the fall of Juan Manuel Ortiz de Rosas in 1852 to the presidential election of Hipólito Yrigoyen in 1916, underwent a process of development and consolidation. By encouraging immigration and foreign investment, the economy experienced rapid growth and infrastructure development, which, most importantly, facilitated population expansion. Thus, as it embarked upon what was to become a faltering path to political stability and nationhood, Argentina was, from the outset, uniquely shaped by the presence and influence of European immigration.

Although early twentieth-century historiography of Argentina referred in brief to immigration, it was not much concerned with the impact that ethnic differentiation had had on social and cultural change. Instead, scholarly historical discourse addressed the separation of Argentina from Spain and the political and economic development of the independent republic. In the 1930s, for example, Ricardo Levine edited a collection of diverse historical essays, *Historia de la nación argentina,* which examined political and ecclesiastical history.[4] But it was José Maria Rosa who, over the course of several decades, produced one of the earliest and most renowned accounts of Argentina. Born in Buenos Aires in 1906, Rosa, the grandson of a Spanish immigrant, published thirteen volumes of *Historia argentina,* in which theories of liberalism and conservatism, federalism and centralism, were examined within the context of Argentina's political and cultural history. This approach was supplemented in the 1940s and 1950s by a number of studies by economic historians such as Miron Burgin and Ricardo Ortiz, which examined the economic consequences of divergent political thought.[5]

One of the earliest scholars to successfully combine political, cultural and economic history was Tulio Halperín-Donghi. His seminal study, *Historia contemporánea de América Latina,* is an assured exposition of the history of the entire continent from Spanish conquest to postcolonial independence and postwar economic and political administrations. First published in 1969, it was revised and expanded over several editions and translated into English in 1973. Although addressing European immigration within the broader context of social and economic change, the sheer scale of the study necessarily resulted in a broad discourse on immigrant flows. However, from the 1970s, as emigration studies attracted wider scholarly attention, so the historiography of immigration in Latin America became more detailed and expansive.

Studies emerged examining specific ethnic groups, presenting detailed analysis of regional structures within homelands and peculiarities of settlement within Argentina. Amongst these were two edited collections on Spanish and Italian immigration: the first by Fernando Devoto and Gianfranco Rosoli, *La inmigración italiana en la Argentina;* the second by Hebe Clementi, *Inmigración española en la Argentina.*[6] Both gave expression to a rich, diverse body of essays and are invaluable for comparative scholarly analysis of immigration from both Italy and Spain as well as from Europe in general. Perhaps the most ambitious study to emerge is the recently published work of Fernando Devoto, *Historia de la inmigración en la Argentina.*

Devoto impressively charts the arrival and development of all immigrant communities in nineteenth and early twentieth-century Argentina and contextually positions their contribution to the development of the republic.

Although this subject is largely dominated by Spanish-language works, there are exceptions. Two notable examples are those of Herbert S. Klein and Samuel L. Baily. Klein's comparative approach to Italian immigration in Argentina and the United States demonstrated the importance of homeland regionalism when assessing social progression of immigrant communities within disparate host countries.[7] Baily's more extensive study, also on Italian immigration, continued in the same vein by examining specific Italian settlements in the cities of Buenos Aires and New York. Baily concluded that diverse adjustments to native societies were a result of 'what they brought with them, what they found abroad, and what developed over time'.[8] Regionalism as a key component of the immigration process was also recognised by José Moya in his text *Cousins and Strangers: Spanish Immigrants in Buenos Aires, 1850–1930*. This is perhaps of particular relevance in relation to Spain: Basque immigrants had a distinct character from that of Spanish immigration in the broader sense, both in terms of homeland differentiation and settlement within Argentina. However, evidence from the German community suggests a different view. Ronald C. Newton's study, *German Buenos Aires, 1900–1933: Social Change and Cultural Crisis*, does not place any particular emphasis on regional origin and, despite the occasional dispute between various immigrant associations extolling conflicting republican and socialist ideology, the general impression of a community comprising largely of a 'prosperous middle class' was one of 'egalitarian conviviality'.[9]

These individual ethnic studies reflect both the importance of addressing each ethnic group separately, as well as the sheer scale of migratory movement that flowed outward from old Europe to this corner of the New World. Abundance of land, urban expansion, labour shortage and the promise of a more just society, real or imagined, provided an attractive and necessary alternative to the misery of overpopulation, economic stagnation and social wilderness experienced in native homelands. Argentina thus presented a viable and significant option for nineteenth-century émigrés. In this regard, the unique movement of English-speaking, and in particular Irish, immigrants must be examined within the broader milieu of European immigration as a whole. Although not attracting significant numbers from across the island of Ireland, the regional nature of Irish immigration in Argentina demonstrates how, from small beginnings, family members aptly conveyed the benefits of being part of this wider European flow to a receptive audience within specific Irish town-lands.

The general historiography of the Irish in Argentina has, until recent years, comprised mainly of literature that is both impressionistic and anecdotal, in which the lives of singular individuals were examined. Amongst the most famous examples of these is William Brown. Born in Foxford, County Mayo, in 1777, Brown first arrived in the River Plate in 1809, returning two years later at the height of the War of Independence with Spain. Despite territorial advances by republican forces, Spanish warships had blockaded the port of Buenos Aires, commandeering arriving vessels and cargoes. His own ship falling victim to such a fate, Brown avenged himself by boarding and seizing a Spanish cruiser and triumphantly sailing her into port. This endeavour was viewed within Buenos Aires as the defiant act of a patriot and Brown was duly appointed commander of a small fleet of sailing boats, which became the nucleus of the Argentine navy.[10] Though he was historically accredited as its founder and heralded as a national hero, there are, nonetheless, scholarly attempts to provide a more balanced account of the man from Foxford. Evidence of privateering and piracy as well as rumours of desertion suggest a darker, more complex character than many historical works have portrayed.[11]

Other studies of the Irish include family histories such as that of the Lynches. The son of a mercantile family in Galway, in the eighteenth century Patrick Lynch arrived in Argentina via Spain. Through an advantageous marriage with Rosa de Galayan de la Camara, the heiress to a large cattle estate in Mendoza, Lynch rapidly acquired wealth and social respectability. Although falling foul of the political regime of Rosas and losing much of its land to confiscation, the family survived to recover lost capital in the aftermath of the dictator's rule. The Lynch bloodline produced an illustrious array of descendants, including the nineteenth-century Chilean naval hero, Admiral Patricio Lynch; the twentieth-century novelist, Benito Lynch; and, perhaps most notoriously, the revolutionary Ernesto 'Che' Guevara, born in Rosario in 1928.[12]

Although valuable in their own right, these studies fail to place Irish immigration in the context of economic, demographic and cultural change in Ireland, as well as in the wider environment of immigration to Latin America in general. Of contemporary works, Thomas Murray's *The Story of the Irish in Argentina*, published in 1919, is perhaps the earliest offering of the nineteenth-century community and, although presenting an at times jaundiced appraisal, provides a useful source of analysis for assessing a distinct Irish identity. All these books and articles, of course, form part of the general historiography of later works, which more accurately depict the Irish community against the broader backdrop of social history.

Juan Korol and Hilda Sábato's 1981 study, *Cómo fue la inmigración irlandesa en Argentina*, presents quantitative analysis of the Irish sheep faming community. Although its decidedly Marxist narrative is now somewhat dated, it nonetheless imparts excellent empirical analysis of primary data and contributes significantly to the historical discourse of the community. Also, Edmundo Murray's *Devenir irlandés*, translated into English in 2006, is a compilation of immigrant letters, which affords valuable insight into the motivations, experiences and cultural development of the nineteenth-century Irish immigrant in Argentina. However, of all more recent works, Oliver Marshall's *English, Irish and Irish-American Pioneer Settlers in Nineteenth-Century Brazil* is perhaps the first published etymological and contextual study of English-speaking immigration to the Latin continent.

When examining Irish immigration in Argentina, all studies are confronted with the generic difficulty of distinguishing the Irish from the broader '*Inglés*' group. The same can be said, of course, for Welsh and Scottish communities. And failure to navigate, or at least appreciate, this interpretative and archival dilemma is hugely problematic in relation to quantitative and empirical analysis. The official collectivism of '*Inglés*' creates an ambiguity whereby any attempt to translate the term from the Spanish vernacular as either 'English' or 'British' ignores important ethnic subtleties regarding those persons of 'British Isles origin'.[13] Matters are further compounded when later generations are considered. Donald Akenson is rightly critical of studies that do not differentiate between first generation – Irish born – and subsequent generations.[14] Indeed, J.J. Lee has observed that, in not clarifying the composition of a 'multigenerational ethnic group', scholars may simply 'find the Diaspora they want'.[15] Although both commentators express valid criticisms, the application of a rigorous empiricist approach in Argentina is severely hampered by the quality of official records. But, most significantly, official statistical representation of the Irish as '*Inglés*' limits both the precision of ethnic comparison within Argentina as well as against the broader backdrop of Irish immigration history.

The adoption and application of the term 'Inglés' by the Irish community was fundamental to its cultural and social development. The subjective and at times contradictory nature of an Irish 'Inglés' identity frequently fractured the community and highlighted ideological and aspirational divisions within its ranks:

> That some Irishmen should conform to English ways at home is natural enough. It is frequently the only path by which they may reach honours, wealth or prosperity. But why the sons of Irishmen should ape the ways of the English life in this country, when they gain nothing by it but contempt, is a psychological problem, which is difficult to solve.[16]

Appearing in 1882 in the Irish-Argentine newspaper *The Southern Cross*, this editorial comment offered a singular view of the Irish community as a consequence of complex and entwined features of Irish immigration. The editorial expressed the bewilderment and irritation felt across segments of the community from the 1880s, as political shifts both in the homeland and Argentina demanded that lines of ethnic identity be redefined. Lee has contested that within host countries of Irish immigrants it was not whether the correct or incorrect ethnic delineator was applied that is of prime importance, but the reconstruction of emigrants' and host countries' perception of ethnicity as related to by both parties.[17]

This is particularly apt in Argentina, where Irish immigrants uniquely entered what was an elite social climate for 'Ingleses' and one that facilitated social and economic mobility. In the decades following independence, consecutive political leaders had espoused a distinct Anglophile attitude.[18] Although it was not subject to the direct influence of British colonialism, its cultural and economic forces had nevertheless shaped the emerging republic. Economic strength, political dominance and the perceived cultural superiority of England were particularly exalted and the Irish strategically fostered an 'Inglés' identity as a result. This functioned on two levels: first, in regard to the individual, it differentiated the immigrant as being from superior ethnic stock; and, second, it facilitated integration of the broader 'Inglés' group into elite native society. Thus, an 'Inglés' identity assumed huge significance in terms of how natives viewed 'Ingleses' and how immigrants presented themselves as 'Inglés', manifestations of which permeated the entire fabric of the Irish community institutionally, culturally, economically and socially.

Although presenting an advantageous environment, as a recipient of Irish immigrants Argentina was not consistent with other destinations of choice. An important feature of Irish out-migration in the nineteenth century, as defined by Akenson, was the selection of destination. He argued that immigrants elected market economies in which they could deal successfully and where the primacy of the English language was accepted. This model, whilst applying to outposts of British colonialism, does not fit Argentina. On the one hand, evidence certainly signifies that immigrants were able to negotiate and deal successfully within the native market economy.[19] Paradoxically, however, they were able to thrive in a nation where English was not the dominant language and where arriving immigrants were linguistically disadvantaged.[20] That this potential hurdle was overcome so skilfully is an indication both of the organisation of the Irish community and of the structure of Argentine society itself.

It would be impossible to study the course of Irish immigration and settlement in Argentina without also addressing the background whence they came, and here, in contrast to the retarded development of the subject in Argentina, there is a wealth of literature underlying Irish emigration from Ireland. These studies have grown from an understanding of Irish social and economic history. Thanks to historians such as Louis Cullen and Cormac Ó Gráda, amongst whose many works are Cullen's *The Emergence of Modern Ireland, 1600–1900* and Ó Gráda's *Ireland: A New Economic History, 1780–1939*, we now have an understanding of regionalism. Complex economic and geographical variations coloured the landscape of nineteenth-century Ireland. No province or county responded uniformly to environmental or economic change, while factors such as population density and industrial development diversely affected regional emigration levels. Surface similarities and differences in regional culture within the principal areas sending emigrants to Argentina, for example, disguise subtleties about social class in the nineteenth century. Analysis of this phenomenon has greatly benefited the history of Irish emigration into other countries, exemplified by the work of David Fitzpatrick in *Irish Emigration 1801–1921* and *The Irish in Britain, 1871–1921*, as well as Kerby Miller in his ambitious study of Irish immigrants in North America, *Emigrants and Exiles*. Of particular relevance to the current work, however, is the contribution of Donald Akenson.

Akenson's work on Irish immigrant communities is particularly valuable as a point of reference for Argentina owing to the paucity of studies relating to the Irish in Latin America in general. His book, *The Irish in South Africa*, is of peculiar significance, as not only were immigrant numbers low, but the Irish culturally integrated into a broader 'British' community. Nonetheless, further parallels are limited since Irish immigrants in South Africa were predominantly non-Catholic, of urban settlement and accounted for less than one-fifth of the total 'Anglo-Celtic' group.[20] Furthermore, although incomplete, official data provided a record of Irish immigrants as a distinct ethnic group. Thus, the major conceptual and methodological problem encountered as a result of the obscurity of 'Irish' within the *'Inglés'* classification is unique to Latin America. Be that as it may, in Argentina the difficulty of ethnic identification in turn provides a means of understanding the process of change experienced by the Irish. Arriving as an unidentified mass within English-speaking *'Inglés'* immigration, the community emerged as a distinct Irish-Argentine ethnic group.

But only by examining the movement of Irish migrants to Argentina within the broader context of European immigration does the Irish ethnic group emerge from the margins of Latin American immigration studies. Furthermore, by employing a comparative methodology against the broader context of Irish emigration history, a significant contribution can be made to the general historiography. Too frequently viewed through the heroic, or controversial, exploits of central historical figures, the origins and development of the Irish in Argentina have been largely overlooked and widely undervalued. However, in moving away from a character driven interpretation of the community, the Irish immediately and paradoxically become obscured by the generic *'Inglés'* classification. In turn, this results in the dilution of a sense of Irishness – which studies of individuals undeniably foster – once more hampering assessment of the community as a distinct immigrant group.

The separation of Irish from *'Inglés'* is thus the central aim of this study precisely because it reflects the cultural, social and economic equation that confronted Irish immigrants in Argentina. This process of differentiation from *'Inglés'* marks the Irish-Argentine experience as distinctive and separates it from models elsewhere. It is reflective of a cultural presumption that prevailed amongst the Argentine governing elite that no distinction should be made between Irish and *'Inglés'* because they were all English speaking. This not only represents the societal conditions into which Irish immigrants arrived but, for the historian, it is also closely related to a methodological problem whose roots lie in the character of the Argentine historical archive itself.

Researchers of Irish immigration to Argentina immediately encounter the acute archival dilemma of Irish separation from '*Inglés*'. And this challenge to the historian's investigative and interpretative skills is largely compounded by the scarcity and intractability of supplemental documentation. Thus the resulting process of compilation and analysis of sources in what are, at times, problematic and indeed dangerous archival waters is both an invigorating, exciting and pioneering experience. And as a counterpoint to such difficulties a number of near contemporary memoirs, reminiscences and surveys have contributed invaluably to the development of this study, as have the files of newspapers. In addition, important and hitherto unused evidence in the Dublin diocesan archives made a significant contribution, as did the as yet largely uncatalogued records of All Hallows College.

In the midst of all the archival impediments the cultural and conceptual confusion between Irish and '*Inglés*' endures. This study cannot hope to unravel all problems encountered and contradictions revealed. It seeks to offer only a pilot historical analysis of factors influencing the Irish immigrant community in nineteenth-century Argentina.

NOTES

1. See David Fitzpatrick, *Irish Emigration 1801–1921* (Dublin, 1984), p.1.
2. Ibid., p. 5.
3. Calculation based on the analysis of Eduardo Coghlan, *El aporte de los irlandeses a la formación de la nación Argentina* (Buenos Aires, 1982), Table 1, p.16, and Centro de Estudios Migratorios Latinamericanos [hereafter CEMLA], transcribed by Edmundo Murray, 2003.
4. Ricardo Levine (ed.), *Historia de la nación Argentina* (Buenos Aires, 1936)
5. See Miron Burgin, *The Economic Aspects of Argentine Federalism, 1820–1852* (Cambridge, Mass., 1946) and Ricardo M. Ortiz, *Historia económica de la Argentina* (Buenos Aires, 1955).
6. Fernando J. Devoto and Gianfranco Rosoli (eds), *La inmigración italiana en la Argentina* (Buenos Aires, 1988); Hebe Clementi (ed.), *Inmigración española en la Argentina* (Buenos Aires, 1991).
7. See Herbert S. Klein, 'The Integration of Italian immigrants into the United States and Argentina: A Comparative Analysis' in *American Historical Review*, vol. 88, no. 2 (1983), pp. 306–329.
8. See 'Italian Immigrants in Buenos Aires and New York City, 1870–1914: A Comparative Analysis of Adjustment' in Samuel L. Baily and Eduardo José Míguez (eds), *Mass Migration to Modern Latin America* (Wilmington, 2003), pp. 69–80. This article was based on Samuel L. Baily, *Immigrants in the Lands of Promise: Italians in Buenos Aires and New York City, 1870–1914* (New York, 1999)
9. Ronald C. Newton, *German Buenos Aires, 1900–1933: Social Change and Cultural Crisis* (Austin and London, 1977). See Newton's discussion on 'Before 1914: the Old Colony', pp. 3–31, esp. pp. 9 & 11.

10. For a narrative on Brown see John de Courcy Ireland, *The Admiral from Mayo: A Life of Almirante William Brown from Foxford* (Dublin, 1995); ibid., 'Admiral William Brown' in *The Irish Sword*, vol. VI, no. 23 (1962), pp. 119–21; Hector R. Ratto, *Historia del Almirante Brown* (3rd ed., Buenos Aires, 1985); Thomas Murray, *The Story of the Irish in Argentina* (New York, 1919), esp. ch. II

11. For a discussion in this regard see Micheline Walsh, 'Unpublished Admiral Brown Documents in Madrid' in *The Irish Sword*, vol. III, no. 23 (1957), pp. 7–19; Ricardo R. Caillet-Bois, *Nuestros corsarios: Brown y Bouchard en el Pacifico, 1815–1816* (Buenos Aires, 1930).

12. See Brian McGinn, 'The Lynch family of Argentina' in *Irish Roots*, no. 2 (1993), pp. 11–14; Alejandro Saez-Germain, 'Siempre al frente. Los Lynch: Casi mil años de historia' in *Noticias* (March, 1994), pp. 44–51; Ulises Petit de Murat, *Genio y figura de Benito Lynch*, (Buenos Aires, 1968).

13. Donald Akenson uses this group classification in relation to the Irish community in South Africa. See Donald Akenson, *The Irish in South Africa* (Grahamstown, 1991), p.14. Ibid.

14. Idem.

15. J.J. Lee, 'The Irish Diaspora in the Nineteenth Century' in Laurence M. Geary and Margaret Kelleher (eds), *Nineteenth-Century Ireland* (Dublin, 2005), pp. 182–222, esp. p. 185

16. *The Southern Cross*, 10 November 1882, p. 4.

17. See Lee (2005), pp. 204–206.

18. Tulio Halperín-Donghi, 'Economy and Society in Post-Independence Spanish America' in Leslie Bethell (ed.), *The Cambridge History of Latin America*, vol. III (*Cambridge, 1985*), pp. 299–345.

19. See Juan Carlos Korol and Hilda Sábato, *Cómo fue la inmigración irlandesa en Argentina* (Buenos Aires, 1981), pp. 81–118.

20. See Akenson (1991), pp. 42, 94.

CHAPTER ONE

Points of departure: demography, regionalism and the opening of Argentina

Between 1857 and 1897 it is recorded that some 32,501 'Inglés' immigrants arrived in Buenos Aires.[1] Although the failed invasion by British forces in 1806 brought 'Ingleses' to the River Plate earlier in the nineteenth century, a significant and sustained immigration process did not commence until the 1840s, peaking in the 1880s.[2] Cultural representations of Argentina as a destination for English-speaking immigration contributed, in part, to impressions of the southern hemisphere as an immigrant haven. However, as part of a larger European movement from the old world to the new, this process was subject to common psychological and economic factors, which determined a series of variables such as choice of destination and timing of emigration.

Amongst the 'Inglés' immigrants arriving in Buenos Aires was a sizeable contingent of Irish. Far from being a homogeneous society, nineteenth-century Ireland was clearly separated by geographical, economic, historical and cultural divides, which shaped the pattern of migration throughout the century. These complexities, obscured by Ireland's general reputation for over-population, poverty, high fertility and heavy emigration, were hugely diverse and regionally specific. It is within this context that all three counties that contributed most to immigration to Argentina are examined. Geographically situated within the relatively prosperous province of Leinster, Longford, Westmeath and Wexford had reasonably easy access to British markets. And yet each county experienced social and economic hardship before, during and after the Famine, which directly affected the composition of the migratory flow. Both class and occupational status will be assessed in Chapter 2 below, but what is most striking in relation to the current discussion is the extent to which a communication network, formed between

Buenos Aires and distinct Irish counties, supported and promoted what was ostensibly a process of chain migration.

Explanations of why Argentina became the focal point of migration for those persons from specific regions are complex, but two avenues of approach are obvious. First, that general demographics and economic forces operating in Irish society affected the character of immigration to Argentina. Second, that motivation for Irish departure must be examined within general theories of emigrant departures. It is to these areas that this chapter now turns.

RURAL LANDSCAPE IN NINETEENTH-CENTURY IRELAND

At the turn of the nineteenth century, Ireland, in line with a pan-European pattern, was undergoing a rapid increase in population. K.H. Connell's 1950 study estimated that between 1780 and 1840 the increase approximated 100 per cent, to total an overall figure of 8 million.[3] Connell attributed this increase to a low mean marriage age and a high mean fertility rate, arguing that early marriage was the 'only agency that could have given the impetus to any substantial increase in fertility'.[4] He further stated that the 'wretchedness of living conditions made marriage seem a welcome relief'.[5] Although many historical commentators have, in recent years, contested Connell's findings, the most influential challenge came through the pioneering work of Louis Cullen. Cullen's 1972 study, *An Economic History of Ireland since 1660,* has been described as 'the first coherent account of the long-run performance of the Irish economy'.[6] In it Cullen rejected Connell's hypothesis and calculated that Irish marital age and marital fertility were in line with European levels.[7] He contested that a more significant factor in population increase was a fall in the death rate from the 1750s as grain shortages and famines declined.[8]

Cullen's quantitative assessment has since been supplemented by a number of economic historians, notably Cormac Ó Gráda. Ó Gráda accepted that Irish population growth levels were exceptional in comparison to Europe during the latter half of the eighteenth century, but he argued that they were less so from 1821.[9] In questioning Connell's calculation of population growth, he nevertheless agreed that Ireland's massive increase was 'unsustainable without the sort of technical change and economic growth which results in ever-increasing demand for labour.'[10] But Ó Gráda computed that the decline in Irish birth rates post-Famine, although significant, was far more regionally erratic than across Europe, maintaining high comparative levels into the 1900s.[11]

Other studies concurred. Joel Mokyr stated that Connell's findings were based 'more on myth and prejudice than on facts'.[12] From the 1841 census Mokyr computed that only 3.3 per cent of all Irish marriages involved brides less than seventeen years of age and that, prior to the Famine, mean age did not vary significantly from the rest of Europe.[13] Research into European marriage patterns has identified two distinctive characteristics: first, a high age at marriage; and, second, a high proportion of persons who remained unmarried.[14] Indeed, it has been suggested that a desire to establish economic independence prior to marriage produced the European pattern of a higher mean age.[15] In arguing a comparable Irish marital age Moykr's contention is supported, at least in part, by research conducted by David Dickson and others into the hearth tax. This study contested that a fall in population growth from 0.9 per cent in the 1820s to 0.6 per cent in the 1830s, was evidence that living standards were under pressure and that the mean age at marriage was rising as early as the 1820s.[16]

In his evidence to the select committee on emigration in 1827, Malthus asserted that Ireland's over-population dilemma was indeed due to early marriage.[17] In its simplest terms, the traditional Malthusian model states that poverty and economic decline are a direct result of over-population, and that economic conditions limit population growth through a series of checks and balances. The 'positive checks' – wars, natural disasters, epidemics – served to drastically and brutally reduce population through increased death rates. The 'prudential checks' – postponement of marriage, curtailment of fertility – were more benign and restricted family expansion. Commenting on Malthus, T.W. Guinnane argued that such a correlation between birth rate and economic conditions required a severe economic downturn in order to bring about a corresponding decline in birth rate.[18] Guinnane found little evidence in support of this and computed that income had in fact doubled between 1850 and 1914. Furthermore, he identified that the low birth rate demographic of England and France established by 1900 was the result of a reduced family size, not a reduced propensity to marry.[19]

Guinnane's appraisal of Malthus was, to some extent, a continuation of Mokyr's earlier critique in which he challenged Malthus' theory of zero productivity of labour as a result of over-population. Moykr argued, rather, that the value of labour generally exceeded the cost of subsistence.[20] Guinnane largely reaffirmed this and maintained that the application of Malthus in nineteenth-century Ireland was rendered less credible as a consequence of Mokyr's findings.[21] But other historians, most notably David Fitzpatrick, have cast doubt over the accuracy of Mokyr's calculation of levels of income and employment. Fitzpatrick suggests that the average income arrived at by Mokyr cloaked the inequality of wealth distribution between farmer and labourer.[22]

The claim that regional variations contributed to forming a synthesis of unresolved discrepancies in relation to Irish migratory flows has been considerably substantiated by local research. David Fitzpatrick suggested that counties of heavier emigration had a markedly higher birth rate and that children were rendered more desirable by the future potential and economic benefit of emigration.[23] But Cullen identified the multiplication of agricultural labourers as the source of Ireland's pre-Famine population growth. In regions such as Galway, Clare, Mayo and Donegal, where the existence of smallholders was greatest, population increased rapidly.[24] Farming in these regions was overwhelmingly subsistence, with holders either subdividing existing land or colonising wasteland. But subdivision itself did not breed poverty: the practice was widely observed across the rich farming lands of Leinster, Munster and east Connaught, where farming was commercially profitable and from where came a surplus of livestock and grain for both the domestic and export markets.[25] While many holdings in northern counties were subdivided, incomes there were supplemented through textile output, although the decay of proto-industrialisation reduced poorer regions of the west, northwest and southwest to bare subsistence levels. Thus subdivision did not inevitably lead to disaster, but it was a significant destabilising factor within an economy vulnerable to exogenous shocks.[26]

As such, post-Famine Ireland witnessed a growing division between those regions that were to some extent integrated into the British economy, and those whose primary commodity was a cheap and mobile workforce.[27] It is within this context that the examination of Longford, Westmeath and Wexford acquires peculiar significance. Of all recorded Irish immigrants to Argentina, 73.43 per cent originated from these counties.[28] To take the case of Longford with its flat, low-lying pastures, it was regarded in 1886 as forming the central point of Ireland.[29] But its topography drew scant praise from

Samuel Lewis, who in 1837 described it as having 'little to attract the eye or excite the imagination'.[30] Yet, as one of the most densely pop-ulated regions in pre-Famine Ireland, registering higher levels than any corresponding Leinster county, Longford experienced severe land hunger.[31] Bog covered approximately one quarter of available land and the 1841 census recorded only 4 per cent of farms exceed-ing thirty acres.[32] Although Mokyr has argued that it was in the mid-dle range of county estimates for famine mortality, Kennedy has contested that, in relation to other Leinster regions, the Longford experience was indeed extreme.[33]

By contrast, Lewis described the beauty of Westmeath's rich landscape as ranking behind only that of Kerry, Wicklow, Fermanagh and Waterford.[34] Its fertile, arable land supported holdings given over to grazing as well as to agriculture, but its essentially rural economy was still incapable of sustaining pre-Famine population densities.[35] By 1911, population had contracted to 67 per cent of levels record-ed in 1861.[36] After the Famine, tenants with smallholdings produc-ing potatoes for home consumption and corn crops for sale did not long survive, and grazing farms that bought livestock from Ulster and Connaught rose to dominance.[37] Although the county showed little sign of industrialisation, its towns were centres of market activ-ity.[38] Rich soil encouraged the growth of dairy husbandry, much of the produce of which was sent to Dublin for export to the British market.[39]

The third county to send significant numbers to Argentina was Wexford.[40] Although generally regarded as one of the most fertile agricultural areas in the country, with high proportions of arable land yielding wheat, oats, barley and potatoes, its holdings along the sea-coast, particularly in the baronies of Forth and Bargy, were relatively modest, consisting typically of no more than 5–20 acres.[41] And yet contemporary observers commented that within these two town-lands 'indolence, idleness and want of employment for the people, is never heard'.[42] Arthur Young asserted that 'little farmers live very comfortably and happily, and many of them worth several hundred pounds'.[43] He later surmised that the 'cabins were gener-ally much better than I had seen in Ireland: large ones, with two or three rooms, in good order and repair, all with windows and chimnies. As well built as common in England.'[44] Although, in comparison with regions along the western seaboard, Young's com-ments may have been accurate, the reality of surviving on holdings of twenty acres or less was succinctly expressed by one Wexford farmer, who stated that living conditions were 'little removed from the labourers, always struggling for an increase and keeping one or two horses half fed and idle [for] a considerable portion of the year'.[45]

Thus, any analysis of character of the Irish rural economy in the mid-nineteenth century must pay acute attention to regional variations, in relation to which several indices are relevant, not least housing statistics. W.E. Vaughan's computation of rural housing statistics assessed second and fourth class housing levels by county. Vaughan assessed each of the thirty-two counties in rank order, the county with the highest percentage of second class housing and lowest percentage of fourth class ranking the highest. In 1851, Leinster and Ulster had the highest percentage of second class housing and the lowest percentage of fourth class. Across the three main sending areas to Argentina, Longford and Wexford were ranked fourteenth and eighth respectively both for second and fourth class housing, while Westmeath was ranked sixteenth for second class and eighteenth for fourth class. Both Westmeath and Longford witnessed an increase in second class housing from 10<20 per cent in 1841 to 30<40 per cent in 1861.[46] Numbers in fourth class cabins declined proportionately to less than 15 per cent of households.[47] County Down had both the highest level of second class housing and the lowest level of fourthclass, ranking first overall. At the opposite end of the scale, Connaught and Munster had the lowest level of second class dwellings and the highest of fourth class, with Kerry in the bottom two rankings of each category.[48] Mayo was ranked thirty-second and twenty-ninth respectively, with Cork positioned nineteenth for second class and twenty-eighth for fourth class. This would seem consistent with J.S. Donnelly's account of cottages in Cork, which he described as 'generally miserable excuses for dwellings; poorly thatched which sometimes even lacked doors and windows'.[49]

But it is generally agreed by historians that the regions most densely populated by smallholders were the worst hit by the Famine, with the agricultural labourer placed most at risk. The burden of immeasurable studies has been to differentiate the labourer from the farmer: labouring smallholders often occupying no more than a patch of land returning themselves as farmers, while farmers or their sons, through necessity, finding employment as labourers.[50] As J.W. Boyle remarked, 'labourers who survived or did not emigrate were joined by many thousands of the smaller tenants, who were now thrust down into their ranks'[51] The situation was further complicated by numbers of general labourers who should have been assigned to agriculture. In a report on the state of agricultural labour in 1909, census authorities stated that 'a large proportion of what are returned as general labourers may be assumed to be agricultural'.[52] Indeed, Fitzpatrick highlighted this when he identified the case of Thomas Gaughan, who returned himself as a 'landowner, mason, carpenter also'.[53] Thus an increasing number of farm workers, or farmers themselves, were forced to supplement their incomes as unskilled labour.[54]

It has been computed that on the eve of the Famine all counties outside Ulster sustained a ratio of at least two labourers to one farmer. By 1911 this was true of only four counties, three of which were in Leinster.[55] Emigration was generally greatest from regions dominated by agriculture. Connaught in particular suffered the most intense loss of its labouring class, with an over 60 per cent decrease in the ratio of male farm workers to 100 farms during the period 1851–1911.[56] In 1841, the most densely populated regions of the province were Sligo, Roscommon and Leitrim, averaging fifty persons per 100 acres.[57] Ten years later this density had fallen by 50 per cent to twenty-five persons. In comparison, Westmeath and Longford were in the modal belt of these changes from 1841 to 1871, Wexford similarly so. In 1841 in Westmeath and Wexford, the population density dropped from 30<40 (40<60 in Longford) to 20<30 in Westmeath and 30<40 in Longford and Wexford by 1851.[58] Regarding Famine mortality statistics the five highest counties were in Connaught; Westmeath and Longford were close to the national median and Wexford recorded very low levels, the lowest of all counties outside Dublin.[59] Nevertheless, it accounted for one of the highest proportions of male emigrants between 1851 and 1861.[60] Male cohort depletion rates continued stable in Westmeath and Longford from 1851 to 1871 (at 25 per cent and 40 per cent each decade).[61]

High levels of emigration among agricultural labourers facilitated the dispersal of an underemployed workforce. Between 1841 and 1901 it was calculated that the male population declined by approximately 38 per cent, while the number of rural labourers decreased by 73 per cent.[62] Donnelly's analysis of Cork suggests that the outpouring of landless labourers accounted for a 'greater intensity of emigration than any other county during the second half of the nineteenth century'.[63] Fitzpatrick demonstrated, however, that this did not indicate a corresponding shrinkage in the farming sector in regions most affected by emigration. He established a negative relationship between emigration and farming population depletion, in that emigration prone counties were least successful in diversifying labour opportunities. Consequently, sole reliance on overseas labour markets for employment dictated that short term peaks and troughs in emigration levels had little affect on long term employment prospects.[64]

And yet, the loss of the labouring class figured significantly in changing the post-Famine rural landscape. The area under tillage shrank steadily and the expansion of pasture farming necessitated a less labour-intensive workforce.[65] Tillage acreage fell by half in Cork between 1851 and 1891, with those areas where tillage declined most experiencing the highest emigration.[66] When counties are ranked according to loss of population, with those undergoing the greatest loss ranked highest, between 1841 and 1851 Cork ranked twelfth, registering a reduction of 23.98 per cent.[67] Longford recorded a loss of 28.7 per cent and ranked fifth. Westmeath was eighteenth with a decrease of 21.16 per cent, while Wexford recorded one of the lowest percentage falls in population at 10.83 per cent. These rankings altered significantly in the forty year period that followed (1851 to 1891), as Westmeath, Wexford and Longford all now ranked in the top fifteen counties for population decrease, with Westmeath positioned as high as fifth.[68]

Although all three regions comprised a number of smallholders within a community of larger holdings, the ratio varied significantly in distribution. This is illustrated in Table 1, which computes data from Agricultural Returns for 1851. A comparative analysis of land holdings is established for Longford, Westmeath and Wexford, as well as for three counties ranked amongst the lowest in Vaughan's analysis of housing statistics, in order to ascertain points of variation between eastern and western provinces.[69] Holdings have been expressed according to their acreage, beginning with those of less than five acres and ascending to those in excess of 200. The percentage of total holdings pertaining to each acreage category is then expressed for each county examined.

TABLE 1: DISTRIBUTION OF AGRICULTURAL HOLDINGS BY ACREAGE, 1852

County	Acres					Total
	0–5	5–30	30–50	50–200	200+	
Longford	1,907	5,593	1,034	637	61	9,232
% of total	20.66	60.58	11.20	6.90	0.66	100%
Westmeath	3,687	5,307	1,343	1507	315	12,159
% of total	30.32	43.65	11.05	12.39	2.59	100%
Wexford	4,516	8,143	3,094	2,854	1,507	20,114
% of total	22.45	40.48	15.38	14.19	7.49	100%
Cork	4,517	14,351	6,921	10,109	917	36,815
% of total	12.27	38.98	18.80	27.46	2.49	100%
Mayo	5,979	23,460	2,344	2,359	668	34,810
% of total	17.18	67.39	6.73	6.78	1.92	100%
Kerry	1,449	6,773	3,614	5,138	786	17,760
% of total	8.16	38.14	20.35	28.93	4.43	100%

Source: Calculated from Agricultural Produce Returns in Ireland in 1852.

Although the distribution of holdings by size is significantly different across each county, the frequent occurrence of subsistence farming is evident within all six regions examined. In Mayo, 84 per cent of dwellings occupied land of less than 30 acres. In Kerry, 66 per cent of holdings had less than 50 acres of farming land in a region of mountainous terrain. The percentage of fertile land within Kerry was significantly lower than in counties such as Westmeath or Wexford. In Wexford, the proportion of holdings with less than 30 acres was surprisingly high, at 67 per cent. Longford's and Westmeath's proportions were also high, at 81 and 75 per cent respectively. Even accounting for quality of land, many of these holdings would have been operating at subsistence.

But most significantly, the figures demonstrate serious inequalities of wealth, between counties and within counties. In each example, the occupation of land was decidedly top-heavy, with approximately 9 per cent of all holdings in Mayo occupying 61 per cent of available land. Longford and Westmeath faired slightly better with 8 per cent in Longford accounting for 45 per cent and 15 per cent in Westmeath accounting for 65 per cent. Wexford, although recording a somewhat more balanced ratio, was still notably top-heavy, with 26 per cent of holdings occupying 51 per cent of land. It would seem plausible to speculate, therefore, that the paucity of holdings exceeding 50 acres suggests that few emigrants, including those migrants choosing Argentina, were reared on large farms.

Thus, the rural economy in nineteenth-century Ireland indicated that people had to go; but other factors also applied. Economic considerations, although significant, were part of broader decision-making dynamics, which influenced both movement and timing. These additional influences, although assuming specific application in Ireland, had universal relevance to the process of emigration. As such, an examination of these issues must be addressed within the broader framework of international migration studies.

ECONOMIC AND PSYCHOLOGICAL MODELS OF EMIGRATION

Classical economic theories of migration see the movement of labour from low wage to high wage markets as an efficient use of labour tending to narrow inter-country wage disparities.[70] The migrant's decision to leave is thus subject to either the pull of unsatisfied markets in the receiving country, or the push of unsatisfied labour in the sending.[71] Such factors either constrain or facilitate emigration, depending on the individual's calculation of economic opportunity. Under neoclassical theory, this model is refined to incorporate the differentiation of labour and to acknowledge the importance of other contributing factors.[72] Quantitative analysts, such as Dudley Baines, translate human motivations into economic models by treating rates of migration as dependent variables determined by external factors (independent variables), which include growth of population, structural changes in agriculture, urban and industrial growth, and development of transport and communications. And the variation in emigration rates between countries is explained by the fluctuation of each independent variable within the individual market. Since the relative weight attributed by a given individual to each independent variable changes over time, the flow of emigration changes accordingly.[73] Thus, Baines concluded that the decision to emigrate had two key components: 'whether to go and when to go'.[74]

Although population increase, economic growth and transportation development have been identified as affecting rates of emigration across Europe, the significance of each factor varied considerably from country to country.[75] For example, some international studies have linked population growth to levels of emigration as a consequence of increased pressure on the supply of land.[76] John Kosa's study of Hungary found that during the 1880s, when emigration became notable, the bulk of emigrants were agricultural labourers without sufficient, or indeed any, land and with no anticipation of obtaining it.[77]

This was in direct contrast to the Southern Netherlands, which, although having a high population density, recorded consistently low rates of emigration.[78] Consequently, as with all contributing causes of emigration, it has been suggested that population pressure functioned in conjunction with several other factors.[79]

Amongst these were a variety of psychological issues. Primary fears are a loss of established structure and accommodation; insecurity as a result of perceived isolation and loneliness; and a weakened sense of belonging to a social group.[80] Whilst economic models assume that recovery in the home market stems emigration, this does not account for why, during times of severe economic downturn, some individuals remain, and during times of economic prosperity, others leave. Neither does it explain why, under improved political and economic conditions, some migrants return, while others do not. Fitzpatrick has argued that economic constraints merely affected the timing and destination of the move, the decision itself remaining constant, with the longer term outflow little changed by short term economic circumstances.[81]

A study conducted by Boneva and Frieze concluded that 'it is not always the poor that leave, it is often the wealthy'.[82] They argued that migrants had higher levels of achievement desire, power motivation and work centrality, with lower levels of familial ties and obligations. These have also been defined as 'achievement' and 'affiliation' motivation.[83] When existing conditions in the home country did not satisfy the designated criteria of success, the individuals high in 'achievement' motivation would seek better opportunities elsewhere, whereas those high in 'affiliation' motivation would elect to remain at home. In this regard, attachment to a community and culture directly affected the emigrants' decision, irrespective of work and income-related frustrations.

But J.J. Sexton attempted to synthesise the economic and psychological models and suggested that previous migratory trends were an influential variable, independently affecting the probability of emigration.[84] Family pressures and expectations functioned both as facilitating and constraining factors within an economic and social model. Support from the family and community smoothed the emigration transition from intention to reality, its absence acting as a constraint. Sexton argued that extensive migrant contact with the home family and neighbourhood created a favourable climate for emigration, increasing its probability irrespective of occupational or lifestyle fulfilment within the home market.[85] The sanctioning of migration by parents and family, and the influence of previous migrants, acted indirectly as a point of comparison for the non-migrant in assessing his social standing and economic prosperity.[86] Thus, 'emigration explains emigration'.[87]

The issues outlined above were central in shaping Irish emigration in the nineteenth century. Fitzpatrick stated that an 'obstinate desire to battle it out in one's own country' initially constrained Irish emigration, and that a mental transformation occurred to create a migrant population. It was this internal emotional battle, he contested, rather than an economic cost-benefit calculation, which ensured that 'the Irish would become an emigrant people'.[88] But Damien Hannan's 1970 study of a cohort of young persons in County Cavan stated that, of all the variables tested, income aspirations and social mobility were the most influential, irrespective of familial obligations or emotional constraints.[89] Hannan concluded that the three main factors affecting the decision to emigrate were occupational frustration, income frustration and family ties, which, although highly interrelated, had equally independent effects.[90]

The decision to emigrate was often based on employment conditions in destinations where previous kin had settled.[91] Bruce Elliott's study of Tipperary Protestants in Canada emphasised the importance and influence of 'clan' in determining the destination, although he argued that the actual timing of the decision was driven by economic and social conditions in the sending and receiving countries.[92] This would indicate an effective information flow between communities as to prevailing opportunities, and in part explains why emigrant numbers were higher in one year than another. Exchanged information not only provided a solid economic platform from which a rational cost-benefit evaluation could be made, but also allayed fears of change. Nevertheless, Becker stated that the decision, and indeed the timing of the decision, was not that of the individual alone but rather of the family unit operating as an economic unit.[93] Other commentators, including Elliott, have agreed that maximising family income was often the overall priority, with the interests of the individual best served through the collective prosperity of the entire family.[94]

But Elliott's study invokes an implicit challenge to conventional work, which suggests that chain migration was characteristic of impoverished Irish Catholics, who adopted a passive, traditional, communitarian approach to emigration, viewing it more as exile than opportunity.[95] Instead, Elliott linked Irish population movement and timing with strategies of inheritance.[96] He argued that avoiding ruinous subdivision and securing prosperity for future generations was a major motivating factor for both the decision and timing. And it is the concept of 'exile' versus 'opportunity' that is a useful hypothesis here. Amongst the general theorists of emigration, Grinberg and Grinberg have argued the importance of making a distinction between 'exile' as 'involuntary departure' and 'exiles' as those who 'did not travel toward something but were fleeing or expelled from something and are bitter, resentful, frustrated'.[97] And Faist sought to define the means by which the forces of forced and voluntary emigration might be identified. He questioned the differentiation between those fleeing drought and those escaping unemployment, concluding that the distinction was not a dichotomy but a graded scale.[98]

This conceptual distinction between emigration as exile and emigration as opportunity clearly requires further elaboration in the case of Irish emigration, not least in the case of Argentina. Significantly, in correspondence between Ireland and Australia, Fitzpatrick noted that only once did the term 'exile' appear and that letters expressed an 'affectionate affirmation of a voluntary emigrant'.[99] This is, in part, consistent with Miller's analysis, which suggested that nationalist rhetoric had distorted cultural and historical explanations for emigration, and that the majority of emigrants were not 'exiles' forced out by imperial tyranny, but had made rational and informed economic and social choices in the face of structural changes in Irish society.[100]

General models of emigration fail fully to explain Irish emigration, which was subject to widespread regional variations. But the dichotomy between emigration as exile or as opportunity, suggested by the indeterminacy of economic, social and geographic components, makes all the more pertinent an investigation into the origins and character of the Irish who emigrated to Argentina.

THE 'PULL' OF ARGENTINA

The size and success of British migration to South America has, in many ways, obscured its exceptional origins. South America as a 'British' immigrant destination was by no means an obvious choice. Oliver Marshall's recent study of Brazilian colonies stated that would-be immigrants were largely ignorant of what awaited them, able only to conjure mental images of either a 'land of mystery or a lush paradise'.[101]   Equally for Argentina, language, culture, climate and distance were obvious constraints. However, expanding British commercial interests in the River Plate facilitated cultural, economic and political commentary within the homeland. *The Times* in London contributed to this through the provision of general financial and political reports with respect to the leadership of the day and its impact on commerce and trade. Although acknowledging 'the most horrible, barbarous and cruel assassinations' under the diktat of Juan Manuel de Rosas, the newspaper espoused the benefits of immigration by unreservedly recognising Argentina as a 'vast and fertile region, [which] full of natural resources [was] one of the finest portions of the globe'.[102] In consistently tracking the republic's economy, its editorial remarked upon 'the liberal commercial system established since the fall of Rosas and the extraordinary augmentation of wealth and trade that has been consequent upon it'.[103]

First hand accounts of life in the River Plate contributed to exotic impressions of Argentina as a place of refuge. From the 1830s there was a substantial body of literary text published in England that, though not entirely reliable, offered various travel accounts.[104] Although the array of authors, ranging from diplomats to businessmen to agriculturists, had little in common, a number of allied themes emerged. General impressions of Argentina as a country of immigration were universally encouraging. Described as being comparable to either the United States or the English colonies of Australia or Canada, it was reported as offering particular advantage to 'younger sons, members of large families, whose parents are not blessed with large incomes; for with a small capital and moderate share of sound sense, they will be able to rear for themselves a comfortable home and a good living'.[105] This appraisal was tempered by the harsh realities of existence on the *campo* (plain) and the menace of unrealistic immigrant expectations. Although referring to the 'unquestionable "El Dorado" in the Rio de la Plata for the industrious [...] and the enterprising', one narrator commented on its illusive nature:

> The report of these extraordinary successes naturally creates, at a distance especially, the impression that the like is to be achieved now, that property can be acquired without capital, and that the industrial classes can become proprietors of land and stock by simply rounding a flock of sheep. Numbers arrive in this country, particularly those from Ireland, with this idea, much to their own prejudice; [...] 'El Dorado' become loafers in the campo addicted to caña (rum) drinking.[106]

This view was supplemented by cautionary tales that warned emigrants against arriving 'to commence sheep farming under the idea they can realise a fortune and retire in a few years. They must make-up their minds to rough it, and to persevere as they would have to do at home in a similar occupation.'[107]

Amongst the most renowned of these books was Sir Woodbine Parish's *Buenos Aires and the Provinces of the Rio de la Plata: From their Discovery and Conquest by the Spaniards to the Establishment of their Political Independence* and William Hadfield's *Brazil, the River Plate, and the Falklands Islands*. To take the first, Woodbine Parish had been *chargé d'affaires* in Buenos Aires from 1825 to 1832, and in offering a favourable account of Argentine society he recommended it as a suitable and attractive destination for British immigrants. His study devoted particular attention to trading and investment opportunities, which given his diplomatic background was unsurprising. The development of each province and the composition of European settlement was also charted. Parish enhanced his narrative through a series of accompanying illustrations, which beguilingly portrayed the city of Buenos Aires and Argentine life. These included the impressive main square, complete with the recently constructed Cathedral and Custom House; the derisory landing site at Buenos Aires port and peculiar transportation cart for arriving passengers; and the depiction of a beggar seated on horseback, explained as 'everything in this country is done on horseback [...] even beggars ride on horseback'.[108] Perhaps most exotic of all was the image of wild-looking gauchos riding sturdy steeds and lassoing strong, healthy cattle against the huge expanse of the pampas plains.[109]

The second author, William Hadfield, had arrived in South America as an employee of a Liverpool commercial house, progressing to the position of secretary to the South American General Steam Navigation Company at the time of his writing.[110] Although not including as many illustrations as Parish, Hadfield nonetheless presented a number of attractive vistas of lush valleys and dense forests. Whilst broadly agreeing with the earlier critic's appraisal of Buenos Aires, his account of port facilities was more explicit with regard to the experience awaiting passengers:

> What a landing! Worse even than what met the Spaniards on their first visit; for since that time heaps of mud have accumulated on the shore, which thus looks like rock and boats are obliged literally to grope their way through it, going as near as they can to the lands; but the usual process is for visitors to be bundled out of the boat into an open cart, drawn by two horses, like so many pigs or sheep, often at risk of being drenched. Indeed, nothing can be more wretched than this landing at one of the finest cities of South America, which does not possess a single jetty, wharf, pier or accommodation of any kind in this way.[111]

One of the most striking elements in the second editions of both books was commentary on the city's expansion.[112] Parish noted that 'with the influx of strangers, the value of property, especially in the more central part of the city, has been greatly enhanced and has led natives to add upper stories to some of the houses'.[113] This was reinforced by Hadfield in 1869, when he stated that the city now included 'two or three-storied [houses], large new hotels, fine shops and warehouses, and the great movement in the streets, all indicate a thriving place of business, which Buenos Ayres is'.[114] The former commentator progressed to approvingly remark on the 'English aspect' present in 'dwellings of the better classes', which now featured upholstered furnishings, wallpaper in place of whitewashed walls, and fireplaces instead of 'braziers and Spanish warming pans'.[115]

Flattering descriptions notwithstanding, institutional, in fact specifically municipal, inadequacies persisted. On his return to Buenos Aires in the late 1860s, Hadfield was dismayed to discover the continued absence of a sewerage system, which made the atmosphere 'very offensive to the olfactory nerves and [destroyed] the appellative "good airs", [...] there is no reason why the city should not be well drained and well paved'.[116] Perhaps even more hazardous was the difficulty in acquiring water:

> It is hardly credited that water is an expensive article within fifty yards of the Plata; but so it is. That obtained from most of the wells is brackish and bad, and there are no public cisterns or reservoirs, although the city is so slightly elevated above the river that nothing would be easier than to keep it continually provided by the most ordinary artificial means. As it is, those who can afford it, go to a considerable expense in constructing large tanks under the pavement of their courtyards, into which rain water collected from flat terraced roofs of their houses is conducted by pipes, and in general a sufficiency may thus be secured for the ordinary purposes of the family; but the lower orders are obliged to depend for a more scanty supply upon the itinerate water-carriers, who at a certain time of the day are to be seen lazily perambulating the streets with huge butts filled at the river, mounted on the monstrous cartwheels of the country, and drawn by a yoke of oxen: a clumsy and expensive contrivance altogether, which makes even water dear within a stones throw of the largest river in the world.[117]

Cost was not the only disadvantage as hot season droughts were a constant menace to livestock and increased the prevalence of human disease, most notably cholera.[118] Indeed, climate was identified as a primary foe, with humid conditions 'opening the pores of the skin, and inducing great liability to colds, sore throats, and consumptive and rheumatic affections'; the damp sufficient to 'rust keys in ones pocket'.[119] It was the unexpected and treacherous flash storms, however, that brought the most disastrous consequences:

Pomperos[120] are often accompanied by clouds of dust from the parched pampas, so dense as to produce total darkness, in which I have known instances of bathers being drowned ere they could find their way to the shore. [...] Day is turned to night, and nothing can exceed the temporary darkness produced by them, which I have known to last for a quarter of an hour in the middle of the day; very frequently they are laid by a heavy fall of rain, which mingling with the clouds of dust as it pours down, forms literally a shower of mud. [...] In the country whole flocks of sheep are sometimes overwhelmed and smothered. The landmarks separating one property from another are obliterated, and the owners are perhaps involved in law-suits to determine once more their respective possessions.[121]

Although winters in general were reported as relatively mild with, 'snow or ice [never] thicker than a dollar',[122] the threat of a dry cold season loomed yearly with potentially fatal results for livestock. One commentator lucidly portrayed the harsh realities of a 'desperately bad' winter by describing 'leagues and leagues of dried up herbage [that] lay along the north of the Buenos Aires Province [where cattle were] dropping off in their dozens, day by day'.[123] Most compellingly, in a stark summation of rural settlement it was stated that 'the desolation which lay so heavily on the face of nature took all the fun out of existence'.[124]

The publication of these various travel accounts informed, at least in part, the ideas of British literary society. But what was their effect on public opinion in Ireland? An intriguing article published in the *Dublin University Magazine* (*D.U.M.*) in 1854 offers some indication of how impressions of Argentina were transmitted to the Irish reading classes. In examining Hadfield's book, an anonymous reviewer described its author as a 'commercial or man of business'. With such credentials Hadfield was mercilessly dismissed as 'writing outside [of his] sphere of expertise' and, perhaps more importantly, found guilty of adopting 'a very incorrect and inelegant style'.[125] Although conceding that Hadfield's study had indeed provided 'information and instruction', the reviewer ungraciously concluded that its acquisition had been without 'pleasure or amusement'.[126]

In offering such a disparaging review, the *D.U.M.* not only distanced itself from the author's literary credentials and ability, but also from the subject matter in the more general sense. Despite the attractive portrayal of Argentina, the periodical did not encourage or endorse the destination as a consequence of Hadfield. Generally regarded as an organ of the conservative landholding class, the *D.U.M.* did not prompt any sustained general interest in Argentina.[127] Neither did the country receive any significant boost from ecclesiastical quarters. Although the Society of Jesus (the

Jesuits) had first arrived in Argentina from Brazil in 1587, it was the only religious order to have promoted it as a destination of immigrant choice within Irish society.[128] It is perhaps all the more remarkable, therefore, that from this limited institutional and cultural endorsement came the extraordinary development, albeit from small beginnings, of a sustained process of regional chain migration.

Although the germ of these beginnings is not easily explained, two things are clear. First, that Irish and in fact all English-speaking immigration to Argentina must be seen within the broader context of European arrival. From the time of independence, Argentina quickly became a magnet for European labour of which *'Inglés'* migrants were part, albeit distinct, of the overall flow. The consequences of this influx, framed within the political and economic development of the forming republic, will be discussed in Chapter 2 below, but it is sufficient here to note that, having arrived as components of a European phenomenon, Irish immigrants established a small but not insignificant foothold in emerging Argentine society. Second, that the consolidation and indeed expansion of that foothold was facilitated through the direct correspondence and encouragement of immigrant family members in seducing others to stake their future on Argentina.

Evidence of emigrant letters and chain migration casts significant light on migratory motivations. Correspondence between the homeland and Argentina has been identified as a prime contributor in establishing the nineteenth-century community, facilitating a 'kin' based support network for the newly arrived.[129] In Kathleen Nevin's semi-autobiographical account of a Longford girl's journey to Buenos Aires, *You'll Never Go Back*, important psychological insights are offered in relation to the migration process. The impetus to emigrate came from the return of an aunt who gave 'an astonishing account of Buenos Aires, a place we had never heard of and never expected to see'.[130] Family tales of independence and prosperity, coupled with economic and social dissatisfaction within the home community, combined to propel the decision, leaving the young girl determined to be 'off to that place in South America before the year is out'.[131]

Historical commentators such as Laura Izarra have argued that a persuasive recruitment network operated through immigrant correspondence, which enticingly described newly found prosperity.[132] This is apparent in Edmundo Murray's collection of immigrant letters, *Devenir Irlandés*, in which tales of affluence and adventure were recounted to friends and family in Ireland. The Murphy family letters in particular provided detailed accounts of socio-economic conditions found in Buenos Aires Province. The principal letter writer, John James Murphy, acquired several holdings and amassed 'considerable wealth' by the time of his death in 1909.[133] In their portrayal of financial and social independence, Murphy's letters provided a tantalising alternative to the stagnation of Irish society, describing a land that had 'all the comforts and happiness that any reasonable man might desire, [since] the Irish are now overrunning the country with their flocks'.[134]

Murphy had arrived in Buenos Aires in 1844 aged twenty-two, along with a number of 'friends and cousins'.[135] Murray suggests that his arrival was itself a result of chain migration instigated by James Petit, also from Wexford, who had emigrated to Argentina in c. 1831.[136] If so, once established Murphy continued the practice by instructing his brother to 'send out three men', as his holding was 'scarce of hands'.[137] In requesting labour he reassuringly and enticingly confirmed that remuneration would 'make labours [seem] light and toil an interesting object'.[138] Reportedly owning an *estancia* (ranch) 'ten times larger' than the family holding in Wexford, Murphy challenged those at home to contrast his experience in Buenos Aires with their own in Ireland, where 'holdings are a mere source of slavery'.[139] His comments, although perhaps imbued with a degree of self-satisfaction, nonetheless appear consistent with the findings in Table 1, which suggests small scale farming was the background of the majority of emigrants from County Wexford.

It has been contested that the extent to which Irish immigrants remained at the economic margin depended largely upon the degree of 'native' control over key sectors.[140] By arriving in Argentina at a time of national expansion, the Irish were advantageously positioned to benefit from an emerging rural economy, which held limited interest for native investment.[141] As an immigrant who had successfully taken full advantage of the gap in the market, Murphy confidently stated that 'the richest and most respectable natives can now see how money can be made. [...] And wherever a piece of land is up for sale, it's an Irishman is sure to get it, as no other dare go to the figure its now selling for.'[142] His eulogistic appraisal was tempered, however, by a cold reminder of the price success could exact in the harsh and alien conditions of the Argentine *campo*. Referring to the climate, Murphy expressed his own fear of sunstroke before confirming 'poor Robert Baggon's death from exposure to the weather in moving sheep'.[143]

Although fears of isolation and dislocation were a common immigrant experience, in Argentina such apprehension was compounded through language difficulties and cultural alienation. These worries were often dispelled upon arrival, however, as the community network eased initial discomfort and facilitated integration into broader society. Indeed, once settled, Murphy attributed his own 'fear of danger', which he had entertained at home, to a 'nervous weakness or fear'.[144] Nevertheless, William Bulfin, in his musings on life on the pampas, talked in the language of 'exile' and strongly lamented the circumstances in Ireland, which 'took away the strongest of the youths and maidens'.[145] As a staunch nationalist, Bulfin's choice of rhetoric was no doubt influenced by the prevailing political winds (as Miller has suggested), which encouraged this depiction of emigration.[146] Given that many within the Irish community in Argentina had benefited economically and socially from the process of migration, it is likely that Bulfin's appraisal did not represent the general view.

This is, in part, reflected in Murray's study. Drawing heavily on Fitzpatrick's collection of Irish immigrant letters in Australia, Murray assessed usage of the term 'home' – described as a most ambiguous term – by Irish immigrants in Argentina.[147] In available correspondence, 'home' appeared 129 times, of which 53.5 per cent referred to Ireland and 46.5 per cent to Argentina.[148] These proportions were altered when exact applications were introduced: actual dwelling, regional area, country – all of which on occasion were referred to as 'home'.[149] Other variables included 'home' as the place of birth, which within letters belonging to second or third generation descendants referred overwhelming to Argentina. Though limited conclusions can be drawn from this analysis, the relatively high proportion of references to Argentina as 'home' would not indicate an enforced exile or an acute longing to return.

The promise and scale of success in Argentina was certainly in direct contrast to the home farming experience. Although the emigrants did not hail from the famine stricken west, the preponderance of holdings occupying less than thirty acres within Longford, Westmeath and Wexford suggests that the majority of them came from farms supplying little more than subsistence. The enticing lure of an exotic and prosperous future, as told by those gone before, would surely have promised a welcome alternative. In easing cultural and economic transition for arriving immigrants, the already established community contributed both to the decision and timing of departure, allaying fears in the process. Literary impressions also contributed, being largely consistent with family accounts. Whilst both espoused the ample rewards hard work and perseverance could achieve, they equally provided stark reminders of the potentially fatal consequences the pioneering immigrant might face. In the absence of extensive and sustained general commentary on the benefits or desirability of Argentina, it was the direct correspondence of immigrants that provided the all-important incentive to travel. However, the effective functioning of this chain migration raises questions about the character of immigrant life within Argentine society itself, and it is with the answers to these that the rest of this study is concerned.

NOTES

1. *Segundo censo nacional de la República Argentina, 1895* [hereafter *Segundo censo nacional, 1895*]. See Chapter 2 below for statistical analysis.
2. For a discussion on early *'Inglés'* arrival see the introductory section of Thomas Murray, *The Story of the Irish in Argentina* (New York, 1919); see also Peter Pyne, *The Invasions of Buenos Aires, 1806–1807: The Irish Dimensions* (University of Liverpool: Institute of Latin American Studies, Research Paper 20, 1996).
3. K.H. Connell, *The Population of Ireland, 1750–1845* (Oxford, 1950), p. 25.
4. Ibid., p. 51.
5. Ibid., p. 59.
6. David Dickson and Cormac Ó Gráda (eds), *Refiguring Ireland: Essays in Honour of L.M. Cullen* (Dublin, 2003), see introduction, p. 12.
7. L.M. Cullen, *An Economic History of Ireland since 1660* (London, 1972), p. 118. See also Joel Mokyr, *Why Ireland Starved: A Quantitative and Analytical History of the Irish Economy, 1800–1850* (London, 1983), p. 60.
8. Cullen (1972), p. 117
9. Cormac Ó Gráda, *Ireland: A New Economic History, 1780–1939* (Oxford, 1994), p. 6
10. C. Ó Gráda, 'Demographic Adjustment and Seasonal Migration in Nineteenth-Century Ireland' in L.M. Cullen and F. Furet (eds), *Ireland and France 17th–20th Centuries: Towards a Comparative Study of Rural History* (Paris, 1980), pp. 181–193.
11. See Cormac Ó Gráda, *Before and After the Famine: Explorations in Economic History, 1808–1925* (Manchester, 1993), pp. 195–197.
12. Mokyr (1983), p. 37.
13. Ibid.
14. J. Hajnal, 'European Marriage Patterns in Perspective' in D.V. Glass and D.E.C. Eversley (eds), *Population in History* (London, 1965), pp. 101–143.
15. Ibid., p. 132.
16. D. Dickson, C. Ó Gráda and S. Daultrey, 'Hearth Tax, Household Size and Irish Population Change, 1672–1821' in *Proceedings of the Royal Academy*, vol. 82, c, no. 6 (Dublin, 1982), pp. 125–181, esp. p. 175.
17. See Ó Gráda (1994), p. 6.
18. T.W. Guinnane, *The Vanishing Irish* (Princeton, 1997), p. 14.
19. Ibid.
20. Mokyr (1983), pp. 39–42.
21. Guinnane (1997), p. 15.
22. See David Fitzpatrick, *Irish Emigration, 1801–1921* (Dublin, 1984), pp. 27–8.
23. Fitzpatrick (1985), p .40. Similar conclusions have been drawn in a study of German migration where fertility levels in regions of heavy out-migration declined at a slower pace, suggesting that heavy migration served as a counter balance to high fertility levels. See

J. Knodel, *The Decline of Fertility in Germany* (Princeton, 1974), esp. ch. 5. Moreover, it has been stated that, in Ireland, the practice of stem succession and the continuance of high fertility levels continued because unlimited emigration was possible. See R.E. Kennedy, *The Irish: Emigration, Marriage, and Fertility* (California, 1973), p. 200; Joel Mokyr and Cormac Ó Gráda, 'New Developments in Irish Population History, 1700–1850' in *The Economic History Review*, 2nd ser., vol. XXXVII, no. 4 (1984), pp. 473–488.

24. Cullen (1972), p. 117.
25. Ibid.
26. Mokyr (1983), p. 6.
27. David Fitzpatrick, 'The Disappearance of the Irish Agricultural Labourer, 1841–1912' in *Irish Economic and Social History*, vol. VII (1980), pp. 66–92
28. All three counties are in the Province of Leinster.
29. James P. Farrell, *Historical Notes of County Longford* (Dublin, 1886), p. 1
30. Samuel Lewis, *Topographical Dictionary of Ireland*, vol. II (London, 1837), p. 307
31. Liam Kennedy, Kerby A. Miller, with Mark Graham, 'The Long Retreat: Protestants, Economy, and Society, 1660–1926' in Raymond Gillespie and Gerard Moran (eds), *Longford: Essays in County History* (Dublin, 1991), pp. 31–61
32. T.W. Freeman, *Pre Famine Ireland: A Study in Historical Geography* (Manchester, 1957), p. 180
33. See Mokyr (1983), p. 267 and Kennedy et al. (1991), p. 50
34. Lewis (1837), vol. II, p. 696.
35. Mokyr (1983), p. 50.
36. Ibid.
37. Freeman (1957), p. 181.
38. Ibid.
39. Lewis (1837), vol. II, p. 697.
40. For a collection of essays on Wexford see Kevin Whelan (ed.), *Wexford: History and Society, Interdisciplinary Essays on the History of an Irish County* (Dublin, 1987).
41. Lewis (1837), vol. II, p. 703.
42. Robert Fraser, *Statistical Survey of the County of Wexford* (Dublin, 1807), p. 57.
43. Arthur Young, *A Tour in Ireland*, 2 vols (Dublin, 1780), vol. 1, p. 112
44. Ibid., p. 110.
45. Quoted in Freeman (1957), p. 58.
46. L. Kennedy, P.S. Ell, E.M. Crawford and L.A. Clarkson, *Mapping the Great Famine* (Dublin, 1999), map 30, p. 81.
47. Ibid., map 32, p. 83.
48. W.E. Vaughan, *Landlords and Tenants in Mid-Victorian Ireland* (Oxford, 1994), pp. 269–70, appendix 15. Despite Vaughan's findings, Alan Gailey has identified the limitations of using housing statistics as a measurement of wealth, arguing that localised discrepancies in housing category require an interdisciplinary approach in order to ascertain social and cultural significance. See Alan Gailey, 'Changes in Irish Rural Housing, 1600–1900' in P. Flanagan, P. Ferguson and K. Whelan (eds), *Rural Ireland 1600–1900: Modernisation and Change* (Cork, 1987), pp. 86–103.
49. James S. Donnelly, *The Land and the People of Nineteenth-Century Cork* (London and Boston, 1975), p. 17.
50. See Fitzpatrick (1980), pp. 67–69.
51. J.W. Boyle, 'The Rural Labourer' in *Threshold*, vol. 3, no. 1 (1959), pp. 29–40, esp. p. 31.
52. National Library of Ireland [hereafter NLI], Parliamentary Papers (1909, CII), p. 619.
53. Fitzpatrick (1980), p. 68.
54. Boyle (1983), p. 312.
55. Fitzpatrick (1980), p. 88, Table II.
56. Ibid., p, 85, map 4.
57. Kennedy et. al. (1999), p. 32.
58. Ibid., map 8, p. 34.
59. Ibid., maps 10, 11, pp. 37, 39.
60. Ibid., map 12, p. 41.
61. Ibid.
62. J.W. Boyle, 'The Marginal Figure: The Irish Rural Labourer' in S. Clark and J.S. Donnelly (eds), *Irish Peasants: Violence and Political Unrest, 1780–1914* (Wisconsin and Manchester, 1983), pp. 311–338.
63. Donnelly (1975), p. 229.

64. Fitzpatrick (1980), p. 74.
65. Boyle (1959), p. 33.
66. Donnelly (1975), p. 233.
67. Computed using the population statistics of W.E. Vaughan and A.J. Fitzpatrick (eds), *Irish Historical Statistics: Population, 1821–1971* (Dublin, 1978), pp. 5–15. For a table ranking all counties in order see Appendix I below.
68. Ibid., see Appendix II below.
69. See Vaughan (1994), pp. 269–270.
70. See B. Ghosh, 'Economic Migration and the Sending Countries' in J. Van Den Broeck (ed.), *The Economics of Labour Migration* (Cheltenham and Vermont, 1996), pp. 77–113.
71. N. Papasterigiadis, *The Turbulence of Migration* (Cambridge, 2000), p. 30.
72. Ghosh (1996), p. 83.
73. Dudley Baines, *Migration in a Mature Economy* (Cambridge and New York, 1985), p. 17.
74. Dudley Baines, *Emigration from Europe, 1815–1930* (Basingstoke, 1991), p. 21.
75. Baines (1985), p. 13.
76. In his analysis of Scandinavia, 1860–70, Baines demonstrated that a significant correlation existed between population increase and emigration levels. See ibid., p. 14.
77. J. Kosa, 'A Century of Hungarian Migration' in *American Slavic and East European Review*, vol. XVI (1957), pp. 501–514.
78. Baines (1985), p. 14.
79. Ibid., p. 15.
80. L. Grinberg and R. Grinberg, *Psychoanalytic Perspectives on Migration and Exiles* (New Haven and London, 1989), p. 19.
81. See David Fitzpatrick's discussion on 'Determinants' in Fitzpatrick (1984), pp. 14–30.
82. B.S. Boneva and I.H. Frieze, 'Toward a Concept of Migrant Personality' in *Journal of Social Issues*, vol. 57, no. 3 (2001), pp. 477–491.
83. W.A. Scott and R. Scott, *Adaptation of Immigrants: Individual Differences and Determinants* (Oxford, 1989).
84. J.J.Sexton, *The Economics and Social Implications of Emigration* (Dublin, 1991), p. 131
85. Ibid., p. 132.
86. For a discussion on migratory motivations see D. Hannan, *Rural Exodus* (London, 1970), pp. 237–264.
87. Baines (1985), p. 29.
88. Fitzpatrick (1985), p. 26.
89. Hannan (1970), p. 167.
90. Ibid., p. 200.
91. Baines (1985), p. 23.
92. See Bruce Elliott, *Irish Migrants in the Canadas* (Kingston and Montreal, 1988), p. 236.
93. G.S. Becker, *Altruism in the Family and Selfishness in the Market Place* (Discussion Papers, Centre for Labour Economics, London School of Economics, 1980), no.73, p. 5.
94. See also Guinnane (1997), in which he describes family households as economic enterprises where size and complexity reflected labour requirements.
95. For a discussion in this regard see Kerby A. Miller, *Emigrants and Exiles* (Oxford, 1985), pp. 131–135; see also Kerby A. Miller, 'Emigrants and Exiles: Irish Culture and Irish Emigration to North America, 1790–1922' in *Irish Historical Studies*, vol. XXII, no. 86 (1980), pp. 97–125. Although referring in the main to Catholic emigration, Miller also asserted that Protestant emigrants conformed to a variant of the 'exile' mentality.
96. Elliott (1988), p. 236.
97. Grinberg and Grinberg (1989), pp. 158.
98. T. Faist, *The Volume and Dynamics of International Migration and Transnational Social Space* (Oxford, 2000), p. 23.
99. David Fitzpatrick, *Oceans of Consolation: Personal Accounts of Irish Migration to Australia* (Cork, 1995), p. 617.
100. Miller (1980), p. 101.
101. Oliver Marshall, *English, Irish and Irish-American Pioneer Settlers in Nineteenth-Century Brazil* (Oxford, 2005), p. 7.
102. See as an example *The Times*, 29 June 1842, p. 5; 23 May 1849, p. 4.
103. Ibid., 24 November 1865, p. 6.
104. Ibid.
105. See as examples Sir Woodbine Parish, *Buenos Aires and the Provinces of the Rio de la Plata: From their Discovery and Conquest by the Spaniards to the Establishment of their Political Independence*

(London, 1838); William Hadfield, *Brazil, the River Plate, and the Falkland Islands* (London, 1854); Wilfrid Latham, *The State of the River Plate: Their Industries and Commerce* (London, 1866); Arthur Jeridein, *The Argentine Republic as a Field for the Agriculturist, the Stock Farmer, and the Capitalist* (London, 1870).

106. Jeridein (1870), p. 5.
107. Latham (1866), pp.177–8.
108. Hadfield (1854), 2nd ed. (1869), p. 247; see also pp. 160–1.
109. Parish(1838)], 2nd ed. (1852), p. 122.
110. Ibid., p. 147.
111. See *Dublin University Magazine* [hereafter *D.U.M.*], 'Hadfield's South America', vol. 44 (August 1854), pp. 204–22.
112. Hadfield (1854), p. 261.
113. The second edition of Parish was published in 1852; of Hadfield in 1869.
114. Parish (1852), p. 104.
115. Hadfield (1869), p. 104.
116. Parish (1852), p. 103.
117. Hadfield (1869), p. 104.
118. Parish (1852), p. 105.
119. Hadfield (1869), p. 136.
120. Parish (1852), p. 123.
121. Violently strong winds.
122. Parish (1852), p. 127.
123. Ibid., p. 123.
124. William Bulfin, *Tales of the Pampas* (London, 1900), p. 65.
125. Ibid., p. 66.
126. *D.U.M.*(1854), p. 204.
127. Ibid., p. 205.
128. For a full exposition of the *D.U.M*'s political and cultural affiliations see W.E. Houghton (ed.), *The Wellesley Index to Victorian Periodicals, 1824–1900*, vol. IV (Toronto, 1987), pp. 193–210.
129. For a discussion of the arrival of the Jesuits see Murray (1919), pp. 1–8. See also Chapter 4 below for an examination of the Irish Church in Argentina.
130. Juan Carlos Korol and Hilda Sábato, *Cómo fue la inmigración irlandesa en la Argentina* (Buenos Aires, 1981), p. 42.
131. Kathleen Nevin, *You'll Never Go Back* (Maynooth, 1937), p. 10.
132. Ibid., p. 11.
133. Laura Izarra, 'The Irish Diaspora in Argentina' in *British Association for Irish Studies*, bulletin 32 (October 2002), pp. 5–9.
134. Edmundo Murray, *Devenir irlandés* (Buenos Aires, 2004), p. 81
135. Letter from John James Murphy to Martin Murphy, 20 March 1864, quoted in ibid., p. 94
136. Murray (2004), p. 81
137. Ibid., p. 155.
138. Letter from John James Murphy to Martin Murphy, 26 January 1864, quoted in ibid., p. 93.
139. Letter from John James Murphy to Martin Murphy, c. 1864, quoted in ibid., p. 89.
140. Ibid.
141. See Fitzpatrick (1980), p. 134.
142. This is discussed fully in Chapter 3 below.
143. Letter from John James Murphy to Martin Murphy, 25 March 1864, quoted in Murray (2004), p. 94. For Irish land acquisition see Chapter 3 below.
144. Letter from John James Murphy to Martin Murphy, 20 March 1864, quoted in ibid., p. 95.
145. Letter from John James Murphy to Martin Murphy, 26 January, 1864, quoted in ibid., p. 92.
146. See Bulfin(1900).
147. See Chapter 6 below for a full exposition on William Bulfin.
148. See Fitzpatrick (1994), esp. discussion on 'Home', pp. 620–7.
149. Murray (2004), p. 51.
150. Ibid., p. 52.

CHAPTER TWO

European immigration and the development of Argentina, 1820–1920

This chapter examines European immigration under three key head-
ings and observes census material from 1855, 1869, 1895 and 1914.
The first section examines the political and economic landmarks in
Argentina from independence in 1816 to the end of World War I.
Immigrant arrival from 1840 to 1870 was characterised by a fledgling
but expanding economy, and an evolving but volatile political structure. In contrast, the post-1870s represented an epoch of substantive
economic growth, political stability and labour acquisition. In 1853,
the Constitution advocated state unity and espoused liberal policies
with regard to foreign capital investment and immigration strategy.
In spite of internal resistance, its articles were to form the basis of the
modern Argentine state. The ensuing labour acquisition and capital
investment – in particular the advent of the railway network –
brought about a series of social and economic changes that altered
both the nature of settlement and the structure of domestic productivity. By the early 1920s, not only had the Argentine economy been
transformed, but the profile of immigrant labour had diversified to
reflect the increasing urbanisation of society.

Section two presents a numerical account of European immigration decade by decade. Each European group experienced diverse
modes of settlement and underwent a varied process of assimilation, particularly with regard to return migration, gender and marital status, and occupation. These three aspects are, therefore, examined comparatively in relation to the 'Inglés' ethnic group and the
wider European immigrant population in order to establish points
of difference.

The final section assesses the Irish as a separate ethnic group and
compares their mode of settlement with that already established for
the generic 'Inglés' classification. As with section two, areas relating to
return migration, gender and occupation are examined. In addition,

religious denomination is assessed to establish the changing demographics of Irish immigration as the century progressed. In order to
isolate Irish immigrants from the catch-all *'Inglés'* group, the seminal work of Eduardo Coghlan has been used. By extracting surnames and nationality where stated, he identified Irish immigrants
from census returns in 1855, 1869 and 1895. Furthermore, Coghlan
examined ships' passenger records and newspaper lists, which published names of arriving Irish immigrants. Two sets of data thus
emerged. The first provided a relatively accurate snapshot of the
settled Irish community at the time of each census, regarding both
native born and subsequent generations. The second presented a
demographic profile of arriving immigrants. Analysis drawn from
these records is based on the available sample, which may not be
representative of the total group.

POLITICAL AND ECONOMIC FOUNDATIONS OF POST-INDEPENDENCE ARGENTINA

Nineteenth-century economic development in Argentina was
largely dependent upon trading opportunities with Europe and
North America.[1] Economic and political conditions prior to 1870
facilitated extensive foreign investment, with Britain in particular
capitalising on the commercial liberty afforded to investors in postrevolutionary Argentina.[2] In 1822, 50.9 per cent of imports into
Buenos Aires originated from Britain, compared with 12.1 per cent
from North America and 7.3 per cent from France.[3] Similarly, by
1830, approximately one hundred British commercial houses existed in Buenos Aires, compared to seven US and five French.[4]
Between 1826 and 1834 no other foreign group dominated the commercial sector as did the British, and early British residents went on
to form the nucleus of a premier foreign class.[5] Although successive
British governments adhered to a political non-intervention policy,
its extensive economic interests and capital investment guaranteed
that Argentina, at least in economic terms, would be subject to
British hegemony.[6]

Of all British pre World War I investment in Latin America, 40
per cent was directed to Argentina.[7] London's House of Baring was
the first foreign investment bank to raise money for Argentina, in
1824, and the principal house promoting Argentine securities in the
1880s.[8] However, the economic crisis of 1889–91, instigated largely
through the potential crash of Barings, prompted minimal official

response in Britain. Lack of interest in Argentine domestic affairs underlined Britain's non-interventionist approach, the principal attraction of Anglo-Argentine economic relations being the negligible political cost entailed.[9] By 1917, British investment far exceeded that of either Argentine or any other group, totalling £275 million.[10] The emergence of a free trading market after independence had created greater economic reliance on Britain than had previously applied to Spain.[11]

Political and social stability was vital for economic expansion in Argentina. The defeat of Juan Manuel de Rosas in 1852 did not, as liberals such as Domingo Faustino Sarmiento[12] had hoped, herald societal reform; nor did it address the political division between Buenos Aires and the rest of the nation.[13] Strongly influenced by the liberal intellectual Juan Bautista Alberdi, the constitution, approved on 1 May 1853, advocated balanced governance between central and provincial powers and espoused the benefits of a structured immigration, education and modernisation programme.[14] Based to a large degree on the constitution of the United States, it advocated a federal republic with power divided between the executive, the legislature and the judiciary. The legislature consisted of a senate, to which each provincial governing body elected two members, and a chamber of deputies elected by public vote.[15] The exercise of civil liberty, as stated in the constitution and practised through the Supreme Court of Justice and the Federal Court, were important prerequisites for guaranteeing the free movement of labour and capital.[16] Consecutive presidents, from Bartolomé Mitre to Juarez Celman, were committed to political and economic policies that induced rapid economic growth and expanded the agricultural sector.[17] Capital imports facilitated the development of railway and port infrastructure, and a progressive immigration policy ensured labour acquisition.[18]

However, the fragmented provincial structure of Argentina and the fractious relationship between the Buenos Aires ruling elite and regional *caudillos*[19] ensured an acrimonious response to the constitution's provisions. In the decade following, Buenos Aires remained a politically and economically independent state, whilst the rest of the country federalised under the governance of General Justo José de Urquiza.[20] Urquiza's open armed approach to foreign labour and capital investment was as much a reaction to the power struggle with Buenos Aires as it was a consequence of progressive policy making. Nevertheless, he espoused the principles of free navigation

along the tributaries of the Río de la Plata and signed mercantile
agreements with England, France and Brazil.[21] In spite of increased
trade with the provinces, the commercial strength of Buenos Aires
continued to dominate the economic landscape, instigating further
conflict between the rival states. In the early 1860s, and after more
than a year of political tension and military exchange, Buenos Aires
forces triumphed over Urquiza at the battle of Pavón, forcing him to
withdraw from the confederacy and consigning the future of
Argentina to the ruling Buenos Aires elite.[22] In 1862 the liberal
leader, Bartolomé Mitre, was pronounced first President of a combined federal Argentina with Buenos Aires as its centre, heralding
the cumbersome and problematic birth of the modern Argentine
state.[23]

Internal conflict continued to plague the federation, with regular
provincial insurrections threatening societal and economic stability.[24]
Bitter domestic political disputes between the Buenos Aires based
Nationalists and the Autonomist Party[25] created a series of institutional crises.[26] In the 1880 presidential election, opinion was irrecon-
cilably split between supporters of Governor Tejedor of Buenos
Aires, strongly supported by powerful economic interests in the
province, and General Julio A. Roca. At the heart of Roca's campaign was the premise that only a strong, cohesive central government could facilitate political and economic stability. A groundswell
of cross-political support, growing since the 1870s, was harnessed
amongst leaders of the provinces and the Buenos Aires elite.[27]
Roca's ultimate victory was secured against a series of violent con-
frontations between opposing camps and a death toll of 3,000.[28]
Nevertheless, his mandate finally established Buenos Aires as the
national capital and heralded a decline in the power of provincial
leaders, whilst concomitantly empowering the National Executive.[29]
The ensuing decade of the 1880s was, therefore, politically stable,
the first such occurrence since Independence, and helped underpin
economic growth at 5 per cent per annum.[30]

The relative stability of the 1880s was to be interrupted in the
early 1890s by a deep economic recession, which affected investment, labour and capital. External debt had increased by 200 per
cent to 300 million pesos between 1885 and 1892, and government
expenditure had risen from 26.9 million pesos in 1880 to 95 million
in 1890.[31] Crucially, the country's principal creditor, Baring Brothers
of London, declared that it would no longer postpone loan repay-
ments.[32] Barings faced bankruptcy as a result of underwriting the

port works in Buenos Aires in return for government bonds to the value of $25 million.[33] Failure to sell them to the investing public, coupled with a loss of confidence in the government's ability to pay, had led to foreclosure. By 1890, the crisis was at its peak as the economy continued to underperform: imports exceeded exports, prices rose faster than wages, government revenue was insufficient to pay creditors, and the peso was devalued.[34] As a result, immigration fell off sharply and infrastructure development all but ceased until the turn of the century.[35]

The first quarter of the twentieth century has been referred to as the golden age of the Argentine economy, characterised by increased population, real income, production and capital stock.[36] European immigration, railway network, urban centres and foreign capital facilitated a growth in manufacturing.[37] Whilst agriculture and ranching fell from 38 per cent of gross domestic product in 1900 to 30.8 per cent in 1925, mining, manufacturing and construction underwent an increase from 12.9 per cent to 16.5 per cent.[38] Commerce, transport and finance all equally registered increases.[39] In spite of the growing importance of manufacturing, the government was slow to promote capital investment in it. In 1917 only £16 million of the £275 million British funds invested in Argentina were in industry,[40] though this greatly exceeded other foreign industrial investment, which totalled £3 million.[41] Nevertheless, by the time of the crop failure in 1913, manufacturing was contributing 14 per cent of Argentina's gross national product.[42]

Factories were family owned, usually established and funded by immigrants' private means. Large scale processing industries such as meatpacking and textile plants, flour mills, electrical plants and sugar refineries surfaced.[43] In addition, a limitless number of small artisanal industries were relied upon to satisfy local consumer demand. In spite of this growing domestic productivity, the quintupling of imports in the early 1900s demonstrated the country's dependency on European consumer goods.[44] This reliance did not continue indefinitely. The effects of the 1913 agricultural collapse were deepened by the exogenous circumstances of World War I. Exports decreased and the flow of foreign capital into Argentina reduced substantially.[45] Europe could no longer be depended upon for consumer goods, and United States merchandise increasingly filled the void left by Britain.[46] US controlled enterprises emerged in the meat trade, transport and manufacturing sectors, supplanting British interests.[47] However, the war years had stimulated domestic production and by 1918 imports of food, hardware, paper, metals, clothing and coal had decreased by at least 50 per cent.[48] By 1929 Argentina was ranked as having one of the highest standards of living in the world.[49]

ARRIVAL OF EUROPEAN IMMIGRANTS

Spanish colonial rulers of the Americas restricted foreign settlement unless directly authorised by the Spanish Crown. Following Argentine Independence these restrictions were quickly abolished, and as early as 1822 Bernadino Rivadavia[50] espoused the importance of immigration to the fulfilment of labour requirements and to the development of the Argentine race.[51] In 1825 the first tentative steps to establish a European colony were taken in conjunction with the British government, and 250 Scottish men, women and children arrived from Edinburgh.[52] In addition to their passage, these rural immigrants received a subsistence of £23 pounds sterling.[53] The Argentine authorities had intended the settlement to be frontier based, but the importance of access to the Buenos Aires market dictated a location just south of the city at Montegrande. Although initially successful, the colony did not survive the economic and political turmoil of the late 1820s and the constant devaluation of the peso. By the end of the decade the community had dispersed.[54] In spite of its ultimate failure, Montegrande proved to be one of the more successful attempts at colonisation as few of these survived long term.[55] An official report in 1872 commented that, of the 29 English-speaking colonies, all had either dissolved or were in the process of doing so.[56] A Welsh colony, established in 1863 in Patagonia following an agreement between the Argentine government and the Welsh emigration society, proved an exception.[57]

Juan Manuel de Rosas did not share Rivadavia's vision of immigrant agricultural colonies. His absolutist regime abolished the immigration commission and allocated public lands for grazing instead of farming.[58] This myopic approach did not prevail after Rosas, and attracting European labour to the fledgling nineteenth-century economy became a conscious policy of consecutive Argentine governments from the late 1850s.[59] A series of aggressive campaigns were conducted across Europe and by the mid-1880s a network of immigration offices had been established in Paris, London, Berlin and Brussels. Incentives for travel were subsidies of

passage and the promise of land on arrival.[60] Building on a founda-
tion of Indian natives, Spanish settlers and black slaves, Argentina's
society began to grow through major influxes of immigration,
which became an important factor in demographic and social
development in the later nineteenth century.[61] In the 1895 census,
immigrants accounted for just over one quarter of the total population.[62] By 1914 this proportion had increased to three tenths (a frac-
tion estimated to be twice as large as that in the United States in
1910, when it reached its peak).[63] With their offspring, the foreign
born were then 58 per cent of all people in Argentina. This was
globally unprecedented even in this age of immigration.
Immigrants provided the necessary manpower to expand the
Argentine economy, with more than 40 per cent of the foreign born
employed as agricultural labour in the early decades of the twentieth century. They also accounted for 60 per cent of the urban prole-
tariat.[64] The Second National Census of 1895 recorded total
European immigration from 1857 to 1897 (see Table 2).

TABLE 2: IMMIGRANTS ENTERING BY NATIVITY GROUP, 1857–97

Decade	Italian	Spanish	French	'Inglés'	Austrian	German	Swiss	Belgian	Total
1850s	9,006	2,440	720	359	226	178	219	68	13,216
1860s	93,802	20,169	6,360	3,603	819	1,212	1,562	519	128,046
1870s	156,746	44,802	32,938	9,265	3,469	3,522	6,203	628	257,573
1880s	475,179	148,394	78,914	15,692	16,479	12,958	11,659	15,096	774,371
1890s	319,244	86,377	35,622	3,582	7,138	7,693	4,271	2,366	466,293
Total	1,053,977	302,182	154,554	32,501	28,131	25,563	23,914	18,677	1,639,499

Source: Compiled from data in *Segundo censo nacional, 1895*, tomo I, pp. 643–647.

Several difficulties arise when examining statistical data for
immigrants arriving in Argentina. The most immediate is ascertaining the criterion used to record immigrant nationality. The First
National Census in 1869 defined nationality as the country to which
the individual belonged.[65] Although such opaque exposition invites
ambiguity, it is likely that nativity rather than citizenship functioned as the criterion. The third census in 1914 was more definite
in its use of language, clearly soliciting the 'country of birth'.[66]
However, immigrants of 'Anglo-Celtic' ethnicity were returned in
all census material under the generic classification of '*Inglés*'. This
aberration thus further complicates the definition as a linguistic element is introduced. Donald Akenson encountered a similar obscurity in his study of the Irish in South Africa. He noted that the term
'English' referred to 'English-speaker' and not to ethnic origin.[67]

Any generic classification of 'British' for those hailing from the British Isles was, he argued, 'horrifically misleading'.[68]

Although presenting a similar complexity, Argentina differs in one crucial aspect. As with South Africa, the official category of '*Inglés*' did not take into account the ethnic distinctions associated with constitutional divisions within the United Kingdom. The classification appeared, therefore, to apply to those born outside of Argentina who spoke English.[69] However, since official Argentine data separately recorded the category of '*Americanos*', it is clear that North America was differentiated in spite of a common language. Similarly, the inclusion of a separate category for Swiss immigrants instead of incorporation within the linguistic amalgam of French or German would imply that nativity and not language functioned as the prime determinant. In the absence of an Irish, Scottish or Welsh group, the classification '*Inglés*' would thus indicate those born within the British Isles and not, as a direct translation of the term would imply, those born in England.

The clarity of this definition becomes increasingly problematic, however, when second and third generation immigrants are incorporated. Here, '*Inglés*' may refer to Argentine nativity, but British Isles ethnicity. This is of particular relevance in Chapter 5 below where official data on immigrant aberrancy did not solicit birthplace. Each recorded category of offence was thus listed under the ethnic group declared by the offender or assumed by the official, which may not be an accurate representation of nativity. For the current purpose, however, all following data will adhere to the Spanish classification of '*Inglés*' into which English, Irish, Scottish and Welsh immigration is subsumed.

As Table 2 demonstrates, in the decades prior to the 1890s all European groups registered an increase, but it was markedly so for Spanish and Italian immigrants. Recorded '*Inglés*' immigration was substantially smaller than many of its European counterparts, particularly that from Spain and Italy. Indeed, post 1870s the Italians had not only emerged as the dominant foreignborn group, but also formed a significant minority of the total population. The performance of the Argentine economy had a direct impact on the level and timing of immigration.[70] Thus numbers for each group expressed in Table 2 declined significantly in the period 1890–97, decreasing by 32 per cent for the Italians and 77 per cent for the '*Inglés*'. All other nationalities registered between a 40 and 60 per cent decline.[71] This reduction coincided with the economic crisis of 1890–2, which resulted in 58,000 Italians leaving Argentina in 1891, with only 16,000 entering.[72] Equally, the number of Spanish settling in the same period registered a net deficit for the first time since statistics had been recorded.[73] These statistics demonstrate two key points: first, that immigration was market sensitive; and second, that a well-informed communication network operated between immigrant populations in Argentina and the homelands.

Roberto Cortés Conde has argued that prior to 1870 government immigration and colonisation policy had 'met with scant success'.[74] Statistics in Table 2 appear to confirm this thesis. The 1880s saw the largest growth in European immigration in the nineteenth century, representing an increase across all groups on the previous decade. The years 1890–1920 brought a period of continued growth, with immigration totalling 3,617,000.[75] Official data recorded a sustained increase in the foreign born percentage of the total population after 1870. In 1869, for example, 12.1 per cent of the total population were foreign born, increasing to 25.4 per cent in 1895 and 29.9 per cent in 1914.[76] In the twenty-six year interval between the first and second censuses the foreign born percentage more than doubled, largely as a result of the growth in Italian and Spanish transients.[77] Both groups substantially increased numerically in the closing decades of the nineteenth century, peaking in the early decades of the twentieth.[78] However, in referring to the relative 'insignificance' of immigration in the earlier decades, Cortés Conde seemingly overlooked individual groups whose early arrival, although small numerically, was anything but insignificant culturally and economically.[79] Furthermore, his analysis appears to have neglected the 1855 census of Buenos Aires City and Province. Table 3 demonstrates the percentage of total population accounted for by the five principal European groups.

TABLE 3: POPULATION OF BUENOS AIRES CITY AND PROVINCE, 1855

Nativity group	No.	% of total population
Spanish	5,792	6.34
French	6,489	7.10
'Inglés'	2,048	2.24
Italian	10,279	11.25
German	655	0.72

Source: Compiled from *Registro estadístico del Estado de Buenos Aires, 1855*.

In a population of 91,395, these five groups collectively corresponded to more than one quarter of the total.[80] The Spanish representation at this juncture was lower than might be expected. In the decades immediately following Independence, Spanish settlement in Argentina was abruptly interrupted, with one in six Spanish residents of Buenos Aires electing to return to Spain.[81] Britain and Germany initially filled the void, followed closely by France.[82] Spanish immigration recovered substantially by the late 1850s, accounting for pre-eminent levels with Italian in the 1914 census.[83] In the early decades of the nineteenth century the Spanish group was characterised by its Basque contingent, the majority of these immigrants leaving from French ports.[84] What distinguished the

TABLE 4: 1869 AND 1895 CENSUSES

First National Census 1869:			Second National Census 1895:		
Nativity group	No.	%	Nativity group	No.	%
Argentine	1,531,360	88.09	Argentine	2,950,384	74.60
North American	1,095	0.06	North American	1,381	0.03
American	42,568	2.45	American	116,674	2.95
Spanish	34,080	1.96	Spanish	198,685	5.02
French	32,383	1.86	French	94,098	2.38
'Inglés'	10,709	0.62	'Inglés'	21,788	0.55
Italian	71,442	4.11	Italian	492,636	12.46
German	4,997	0.29	German	17,143	0.43
Swiss	5,860	0.34	Swiss	14,789	0.37
Portuguese	1,966	0.11	Portuguese	2,269	0.06
Austrian	834	0.05	Austrian	12,803	0.32
African	1,172	0.07	Russian	15,047	0.38
Other Europeans	4,886	0.28	Other Europeans	11,724	0.30
			Other nationalities	1,930	0.05
			Without specification	3,560	0.09
Total	1,738,466	100%	Total	3,954,911	100%

Source: Compiled from data in *Primer censo nacional, 1869*, pp. 636–7 and *Segundo censo nacional, 1895*, vol. I, table VIIa.

Basques in particular was the fluidity demonstrated in transferring skills between urban and rural sectors.[85] Basque immigration, however, did not continue indefinitely and by the mid-nineteenth century levels had significantly declined.[86] By the close of the century Galicia and Catalonia were the regional origins of the vast majority of Spanish immigrants.[87]

The reliability of the data presented in Table 3 is somewhat compromised due to the omission of several *partidos* (districts) in the 1855 compilation of census data.[88] It is difficult to estimate whether a more accurate recording would have increased or decreased the percentage of total population accounted for by each ethnic group.[89] Nevertheless, using the flawed 1855 records a comparative assessment of the 1869 and 1895 population figures in Table 4 can be made.

By 1869, all five European groups examined in 1855 had decreased as a percentage of total population. In 1895, only the Italians exceeded the 1855 figure, increasing to 12.46 per cent. These calculations do not account for the possibility of second and third generation Europeans being classified as Argentines in the 1869 and 1895 censuses, thus reducing ethnic representation. It remains the case, however, that an Italian increase of only 1.21 per cent of total population between 1855 and 1895 underlines the importance – not only in the case of the Italians, but also for the other four main European groups – of early European immigration in the 1855 figures for total population figures. As a proportion of total European nativity, the '*Inglés*' represented 6.4 per cent and 2.5 per cent respectively in 1869 and 1895.[90] This percentage is dramatically overshadowed when viewed against Italian and Spanish representation. The proportion of Italian immigrants, already substantial in 1869 and accounting for 42.7 per cent of total European population, further increased to 56.8 per cent by 1895. Spanish immigrant levels, although significant, were less than the Italian, increasing from 20.3 per cent to 22.9 per cent over the same period. As with '*Inglés*', both French and German representation had decreased, falling to 10.8 per cent and 1.9 per cent respectively by 1895. What is clear from these statistics is that between 1869 and 1895 the '*Inglés*' group had not only decreased as a proportion of total European population, but within the five principal groups it alone had decreased as a percentage of total population. Furthermore, European settlement in Argentina at the close of the nineteenth century was increasingly and significantly Italian dominated.

Italians, Argentina's largest immigrant stream, provide a comparative benchmark for many aspects of Irish immigration there, from periodisation of flows (and their consequences), rural settlement, the shift away from it later, to the emphasis on the cities after 1900/1902 or so. The extraordinarily rapid social mobility of the Italians in cities (by comparison with those of the United States, where the Irish enjoyed similar patterns) may even suggest that as 'urban pioneers' the two peoples behaved competitively and even exclusively. Despite their relatively late arrival, the Italians formed a substantial and influential minority of the total population, accounting for 12 per cent by 1914.[91] During the mid-1870s and throughout the 1880s, Argentina was the primary immigration zone for Italians. Although at the turn of the century North America emerged as the preferred destination, between 1876 and 1900 a total of 802,608 Italian immigrants arrived in Argentina, representing over 40 per cent of total Italian emigration. In contrast, 24 per cent opted for the United States in the same period.[92] Northern and central Italians were drawn to Argentina, but also, from 1888 to 1902, to Brazil's coffee plantations, to replace freed salves, whilst the poorer southern Italians chose North America, and Brazil after 1902.[93] Herbert Klein's 1983 study estimated that, between 1876 and 1930, southern Italians accounted for 80 per cent of Italian immigration to North America but only 47 per cent to Argentina.[94] Landownership was the principal attraction in Argentina, with immigrants moving into grain farming (cereal) and cattle production. Farmers and farm labourers accounted for more than two thirds of total immigration, compared with only one third of that to North America. Klein argued that differing labour markets were responsible for the distinct migration flows: availability of land and industrial expansion in Argentina attracted the northern Italian, who, Klein stated, was not only the most economically prepared for migration, but also the most literate.[95]

By 1914, exactly a quarter of Italians in Argentina over the age of twenty owned land or other property, not too far below the third of native born Argentines who did so, although amongst the country's rural dwellers the contrast was greater: amongst non-ranchers, one fifth of rural adult property owners were Italian and just under three fifths were native Argentines; although only 6 per cent of *estancieros* were Italian born, against 78 per cent Argentine born.[96] Similarly, Italians had diversified into commercial and industrial properties.[97] By 1908 it was estimated that Italians owned 38 per cent of all commercial establishments in the city of Buenos Aires, whilst representing only 22 per cent of the city's population.[98] Tulio Halperín-Donghi has challenged this thesis of rapid Italian capital accumulation, arguing that in the province of Santa Fe the proportion of Italian farmers cultivating their own land was 20 per cent, compared to the average of other foreign groups of 28 per cent and a figure for natives of 48 per cent.[99] He went on to acknowledge, however, that the native figure almost certainly included descendants of much earlier Italian immigrants who were now classified as Argentine.[100] The ability, therefore, of early immigrants to take advantage of a fledgling but prosperous economy laid the foundations of economic stability for future generations born in Argentina that was impracticable for later arriving immigrants. Nonetheless, the commercial fluidity of land transactions would also support the thesis that landownership was not impeded solely by late arrival, but also by the lack of available long term credit at manageable interest rates. Both the advent and spread of the rail network facilitated land acquisition before the late 1890s, but thereafter boosted land values so much that it became very difficult, even if the tenants (*arrendatorios*) could retain most of their harvest's value, and even diversify their activities.[101]

Of all European groups Italian immigrants in particular appear to have been attracted to Argentina for the benefits of short term economic gain, rather than aiming at permanent residency.[102] Sánchez Alonso calculated that, between 1871 and 1924, only 46.3 per cent of arriving Italian immigrants settled in Argentina compared to 60 per cent of Spanish.[103] Although many southern Italians did remain, seasonal migration became a facet of Italian settlement in the closing decades of the nineteenth century.[104] Sir Hugh MacDonnell, *chargé d'affaires*, wrote in 1872 that at least one third of all Italian immigrants arriving since 1862 had returned to Italy.[105] He contrasted this with British immigrants, who, he stated, had made Argentina their 'definite home'.[106] The sincerity of this comment must be measured against the likely propaganda that accompanied it. At a time when the British government actively encouraged emigration, it is plausible that an over-inflated appraisal was given of the success of British settlement in Argentina. MacDonnell went on to disparage Italian and Basque immigrants for their lack of social ambition, identifying their preference 'for amassing and hoarding money'.[107] In contrast, he approvingly evaluated the 'Anglo-Saxon', who 'with prosperity seeks to couple enlightenment'.[108] In so stating, MacDonnell implied an element of ethnic virtue in the very process of remaining, as opposed to accumulating wealth and returning.

Immigration to Argentina in the nineteenth century was male dominated. Fernando Devoto has calculated from the 1895 census that the mean gender ratio across all immigrants was 177 men for every 100 women.[109] This varied, of course, from group to group as well as over time. The changing levels within each of the five principal European groups is demonstrated in Table 5, which examines the male-to-female ratio recorded over the first three national censuses.

TABLE 5: PERCENTAGE RATIO OF MALES TO FEMALES BY NATIVITY GROUP

Nativity group	Census year		
	1869	1895	1914
Italian	268	179	172
Spanish	361	190	162
French	219	148	124
'Inglés'	246	185	217
German	263	178	182
Arithmetic mean of above groups	271	176	171

Source: Compiled from data in *Primer, Segundo y Tercer censo nacional, 1869, 1895, 1914.*

Table 5 suggests a general decline in the male-to-female ratio between 1869 and 1895, indicating a universal increase in female immigration over the same period. The Spanish, in particular, although accounting for the highest male-to-female percentage ratio across the first and second censuses, recorded a 47.4 per cent reduction in this ratio in 1895. This is consistent with the thesis that in the latter half of the century Spanish women were encouraged to emigrate to Argentina, as language compatibility allowed for an immediate transfer of skills into domestic sectors such as sewing, ironing and laundry.[110] It is likely that the decline registered in the *'Inglés'* male-to-female ratio in 1895 was a result of the adverse press reports that circulated in the closing decades of the century, which gave rise in official quarters to questioning as to whether Argentina was a suitable and economically viable destination for 'British' subjects.[111] Indeed, a family letter from Mullingar (in Westmeath) to

Buenos Aires in 1888 reported that there had been 'terrible reports about that country lately'.[112]

By 1914, both German and *'Inglés'* male-to-female ratios had risen, whilst the Italian group remained reasonably stable. Whereas the German increase was marginal, the *'Inglés'* was relatively substantial at 15 per cent; as a group the latter now represented the highest male proportion. Although suggesting a level of consistency with other nineteenth-century immigrant destinations where recorded male numbers were higher than female, Argentina is distinguished by the degree of male preponderance.[113] This is illustrated by gender data for immigrants arriving in the United States between 1831 and 1924, which consistently demonstrated greater proportions of males than females.[114] However, whereas in the United States the maximum did not exceed 69.8 per cent, in Argentina the male proportion from 1857 to 1920 lay between 70 and 80 per cent.[115] Average female immigration for the same period was 27.14 per cent of the total.[116] This huge gender discrepancy in levels of immigration is indicative of a high rate of return migration. Males often returned to settle and usually marry, or to secure brides to bring back to the new country. They were the more mobile migratory sex and constituted a higher proportion of 'birds of passage' immigrants.[117] The preponderant Italian and Spanish immigration to Argentina, much of which was temporary, showed a considerable excess of males.[118] However, as Table 5 demonstrates, in relation to the five principal European groups, the male-to-female *'Inglés'* ratio was significantly higher than the arithmetic mean calculated for two of the censuses.

This representation is typically consistent with high levels of outward movement. Between 1857 and 1924, distribution data of immigrant and emigrant passengers by sea to and from Argentina recorded 'British' outward movement thence as 70.4 per cent.[119] This was substantially higher than either the French or German estimate calculated as 53.0 and 48.9 per cent respectively; or the Italian and Spanish levels of 49.6 and 42.5 per cent.[120] Sir Hugh MacDonnell's thesis thus seems difficult to substantiate since the reported repatriation rate for 'British' immigrants, at least for the period 1857 to 1924, exceeded that of any other foreign group. None of the percentages detailed above allow for temporary departure due to commercial interests or leisure travel, which may equally have been male dominated. Although it could be argued that this practice was more prevalent amongst affluent 'British' residents, it is unlikely that this alone would fully account for the exaggerated activity.[121]

An examination of the substream of marital status amongst male immigrants, however, provides an additional insight. Argentina attracted predominantly single immigrants, with unmarried persons accounting for 66.48 per cent of total immigration between 1857 and 1920.[122] The 1914 census recorded numbers of single and married persons within each ethnic group per 1,000 inhabitants. Statistics demonstrated that across the same five European groups the '*Inglés*' had the highest number of single persons over the age of fifteen, calculated as 420.6.[123] Of this figure 83.8 per cent were male, a proportion higher than in any of the four remaining groups. Likewise for married persons, the '*Inglés*' group registered the lowest European level, calculated at 495.4 per 1,000 inhabitants. It would appear, therefore, that there was an excess of single male '*Inglés*' immigrants. This would plausibly substantiate high estimates of outward migration from Argentina within the group, in spite of MacDonnell's contradictory and somewhat tendentious anecdotal commentary.

TABLE 6: OCCUPATIONS OF IMMIGRANTS ARRIVING 1876–97 BY NATIVITY GROUP

Occupation:	Italian %	Spanish %	French %	'*Inglés*' %	German %
Farmer	66.76	41.33	53.02	27.28	50.01
Mason	1.57	3.25	1.57	3.42	1.17
Artisan	2.75	3.51	7.64	5.26	4.60
Artist	1.21	2.18	2.20	3.90	2.23
Tenant farmer	3.67	8.04	6.19	6.67	8.04
Merchant	1.07	1.48	3.21	7.68	5.13
Gardener	0.32	0.44	0.66	0.35	0.47
Labourer	11.08	15.98	7.19	7.08	6.97
Various	2.65	8.35	7.82	19.61	10.84
Without profession	8.92	15.44	10.50	18.75	10.54
Total	100%	100%	100%	100%	100%
No.	845,217	247,727	122,770	22,488	22,062

Source: Compiled from data in *Segundo censo nacional, 1895*, vol. I, table V, p. 651.

The 1895 census enumerated the occupations of immigrants at the point of their arrival in Argentina, via seaports, for the period 1876–97. Although data appear to relate to occupations practised in the homelands, it is reasonable to assume that returns may, on occasion, have been amended to reflect intended modes of employment within Argentina. Table 6 calculates the percentage of immigrants by stated occupation within each ethnic group.

The Italians, French and Germans were substantially represented in the rural sector, with more than half of each group returning themselves as 'farmer'. If Klein correctly identifies most labourers as rural, this sector also dominated the movement of Spanish newcomers.[124] The '*Inglés*' group had the lowest rural representation, reflecting the urban nature of immigrants' skill base. Within the categories of 'mason', 'artisan', 'artist' and 'merchant' the '*Inglés*' demonstrated higher proportions than all other groups, with the exception of the French in the category of 'artisan'. In both 'various' and 'without profession' the '*Inglés*' recorded significantly higher levels than each of their European counterparts. Both categories are difficult to quantify and census data provides no indication of whether occupations were of an urban or rural, employed or self-employed nature. The urban profession of shopkeeper, for example, absent as a category in its own right, may have been subsumed within 'various'.

As Table 6 demonstrates, the Germans had the second highest statistical representation in the merchant class, which formed the nucleus of the German economic oligarchy in Buenos Aires. Although, compared to the group's rural representation, merchant numbers were few, their influence within the community grew steadily.[125] By the mid-1860s, thirty-four German import-export houses were established in the city, rising to forty-three by 1873. Indeed, the three most prestigious German houses of the later nineteenth century had all been established between 1840 and 1864.[126] Success in this sector led the editor of the German community publication, the *Kunz Yearbook and Address Calendar of the German Colony in Buenos Aires*, to write in 1884 that 'in commerce, the German trading firms are on top. [...] One may well say that the leadership which the English once exercised in this area is today in the hands of the Germans on La Plata.'[127]

The success of the group's merchant class can, in part, explain the substantial number of arriving German 'farmers'. Klaus Stegman was a German merchant who imported the first high grade German sheep stock in 1830.[128] An 'English' firm had initially employed Stegman before he progressed to be a partner in his own enterprise. This was not uncommon in an Anglo dominated commercial sector, and in 1831 it was reported that the majority of German traders were employed in commercial rooms established by 'English' merchants from 1811.[129] Newly arrived German immigrants would frequently advertise their services in the English-speaking newspaper, *The Standard*, 'desirous of getting employment in a commercial house'.[130]

Unusually, and like the '*Inglés*', in 1914 the German born accounted for twice the (very low) proportions of rural property and ranch owners than there were in the overall population.[131] Stegman's diversification into sheep farming and acquisition of an *estancia* was testament to a desire amongst the German merchant class to integrate into the landed oligarchy of Argentine society. Landownership was the economic base of the upper classes in Argentina.[132] The elite was disdainful of engaging in commerce, allowing European immigrants to avail themselves of the gap in the market.[133] So German landownership was, in the main, a by-product of wealth accumulated in the commercial sector, and not a prime source of income.[134] Owning an *estancia* would elevate a merchant's social standing.[135] Consequently, it is probable that many of the 50.01 per cent of German immigrants declaring the occupation 'farmer' in Table 6 were stimulated by German diversification into landownership, with the majority operating as farm manager or labourer, and not owner.

Sánchez Alonso, in her study of Spanish immigrants, stated that in 1913 immigrants from Spain and Italy were heavily represented as farmers and labourers. Certainly, in relation to data enumerated in Table 6, the categories 'farmer', 'tenant farmer' and 'labourer' accounted for 65 per cent of all arriving Spanish immigrant occupations between 1876 and 1897. By Alonso's calculation, Spanish immigrants would seem to have demonstrated a high degree of occupational consistency between the homeland and Argentina. Examining other professions, she concluded that the Spanish appeared to be less qualified than the Italians or indeed other immigrants.[136] Nonetheless, the criteria used by Alonso to establish levels of professionalism are unclear. If the nature of employment was the sole criterion, then the cumulative total of 'labourer' and 'without profession' for arriving immigrants presented in Table 6 could verify this thesis, as it accounted for 31 per cent of total Spanish occupations. The comparable figure for Italian immigrants was 20 per cent.

However, in the category of 'without profession', the '*Inglés*' level exceeded those of the Spanish and all other groups. Without a clear explanation of what this category included it is difficult to come to any firm conclusion with regard to comparative levels of professionalism, at least for arriving immigrants. Be that as it may, other historians have agreed with Alonso's basic tenet, concluding that one third of Spanish immigrants remained in Buenos Aires employed in menial jobs.[137] Of those who settled in rural areas, the majority became unskilled labourers. This has been contrasted with the Italian artisan class, which reportedly expanded at the turn of the century, with one in four Italian immigrants in Buenos Aires becoming part of a growing urban workforce.[138] Furthermore, it has been argued that as early as 1886 the Italians were recognised for their skill in, and monopoly of, 'trades [such] as masonry and stone-cutting, house painting, plastering, saddle making, food handling and baking'.[139]

It should be noted finally, however, that in assessing the assimilation patterns of nineteenth-century immigrants a historiographical divide emerges between those commentators who emphasise the class struggle divide between the *estancieros* and the unpropertied, and those who argue that both rural society and urban economies and services (especially after 1900) were significant. In these terms, Argentina's social history is modified to reflect a more integrated social ladder where multiple identities emerged, not in simple polarised terms, but in complex and varied forms.

SEPARATING IRISH IMMIGRANTS FROM '*INGLÉS*'

Ascertaining the number of Irish who emigrated to Argentina is frustratingly but necessarily inconclusive. Contemporary commentators and later scholars have arrived at a variety of conflicting estimates. Edward Mulhall, editor and founder of *The Standard* newspaper, calculated that between 1861 and 1891 a total of 40,200 'British' arrived in Argentina.[140] He attributed the community's expansion to the 1825 trade agreement with England, the growth in sheep farming from 1835 and the fall of Rosas in 1852.[141] He went on to estimate that aggregate properties, which he argued belonged chiefly to Irish and Scottish sheep farmers, amounted in value to several million pounds sterling.[142] The Archbishop of Buenos Aires offered a further estimate of immigrant numbers when he reported in 1879 that 28,000 Irish were living in Argentina.[143]

Thomas Murray questioned whether this calculation represented the Irishborn population or the Irish community as a whole. He argued that it more accurately depicted first generation Irish, calculating that the combined Irish born and Irish-Argentine community was 110,000 at the time of his writing in 1917.[144] Monsignor Ussher was somewhat contradictory in his calculations. Writing in 1953 he estimated that, at the close of the nineteenth century, 20,000 Irish immigrants had settled in Argentina.[145] Two years earlier, however, he stated that the community had grown from 3,500 in 1844 to 25,000 (in ten chaplaincies only) by c. 1870.[146] When accounting for Irish born and Irish-Argentine he estimated a total community of 34,000 in 1880, increasing to 75,000 by 1900.[147] The more recent scholarly study of Juan Korol and Hilda Sábato incorporated estimates for in and out-migration as well as for mortality, to arrive at a total of 10,672.[148] This figure was, however, calculated for Buenos Aires Province only.

Patrick McKenna's 1994 study stated that, of the 40,200 'British' immigrants calculated by Mulhall to have arrived between 1898 and 1891, two thirds were Irish.[149] By adhering to contemporary estimates of the Irish born community pre 1861 as 10,000, McKenna estimated that the Irish born population in 1891 was 36,800.[150] He further argued that this did not account for mortality or out-migration, finally arriving at a figure of 40,000–45,000.[151] This is, as McKenna has conceded, highly speculative due to a combination of poor official documentation and the classification of *'Inglés'* for all immigrants of 'Anglo-Celtic' ethnicity. McKenna's figure is also far in excess of Korol and Sábato's calculation. Eduardo Coghlan's 1982 study, *El aporte de los irlandeses a la formación de la nación argentina*, is, therefore, the only substantial analysis of the Irish community in isolation from the catch-all *'Inglés'* classification.[152] In it Coghlan examined the 1855 census of Buenos Aires City and Province, as well as the first two national censuses of 1869 and 1895. Table 7 records his findings for those born in Ireland and those born in Argentina, and expresses the Irish born population as a percentage of the total community.

Coghlan established Irish ethnicity using three criteria. In the first instance he extracted returns where individuals had declared themselves Irish. Secondly, where *'Inglés'* had been recorded he proceeded by examining surnames, taking account of those with an

TABLE 7: ESTIMATED IRISH-ARGENTINE POPULATION AT EACH CENSUS

Census	Born in Ireland	Born in Argentina	Total	Irish born %
1855	516	188	704	73.3
1869	5,246	3,377	8,623	60.84
1895	5,407	13,210	18,617	29.04

Source: Compiled from data in Coghlan (1982), pp. 18–20.

obvious Irish origin. Finally, in cases of ambiguity where surnames could feasibly be of an English, Scottish or Irish ethnic pool, Coghlan referred to religion, identifying those declaring a Catholic denomination.[153] As he readily admitted, methodological difficulties arise when adopting this rather imprecise approach, but Coghlan argued that the margin of error was relatively insignificant and that any minor discrepancy in calculation did not affect his general conclusions.

There are, however, further quantitative and qualitative difficulties to consider. As already stated in relation to Table 3 above, the 1855 census returns were an inaccurate record of population statistics as not all *partidos* were returned. Coghlan thus recalculated this figure – using his own criteria for identifying Irish immigrants – by examining passenger arrival records for the port of Buenos Aires. He concluded that, although only 516 Irish residents of Buenos Aires City and Province were returned in the census, the actual figure more likely lay between 2,500 and 3,000, with the inclusion of the second and third generations increasing the total population to between 4,000 and 5,000.[154] This calculation amounts to a remarkable increase of around 500 per cent when compared with the official 1855 returns. Coghlan acknowledged that the revised estimate was itself dependent upon a somewhat inaccurate source, as port data were either inadequately recorded or subsequently lost.[155] Therefore, although the 1855 census undoubtedly under-represented the Irish community, Coghlan's calculations, based equally on an imprecise and deficient source, cannot be fully quantified.

Census information for 1869 and 1895 was, happily, more complete and Coghlan's transcription provides a plausible estimate of the Irish population. In it he separated Irish born immigrants from second and third generation Irish-Argentines. He demonstrated that, in the twenty-six year interval between 1869 and 1895, the Irish born community increased by only 2.91 per cent. The total foreign born immigrant population in Argentina for the same period increased by 80 per cent.[156] Irish immigration had, therefore, all but ceased at a time when the foreign born population as a whole was increasing. This is underlined by the falling representation of Irish born within the collective Irish-Argentine community. As Table 7 demonstrates, by 1895 second and third generation Irish accounted for over 70 per cent of the total community. Equally, as a percentage of the total *'Inglés'* immigrant population expressed in Table 4, the Irish accounted for approximately half in 1869 and around one quarter in 1895.[157] This would further indicate that Irish numbers had peaked in the intervening period. Inevitably, Coghlan's calculation is open to question given the poor quality of the original census returns and the subjectivity of his views on what did and did not constitute an Irish surname. The rigorous approach he adopted was, however, more likely to have resulted in an under-estimation of total Irish population than the opposite.

In addition to census returns, Coghlan examined a combination of passenger lists from 1822 to 1862, and an arrivals list published by *The Standard* newspaper between 1863 and 1880. Once again there are limitations to the data compiled as many records for the years prior to 1850 were lost or destroyed.[158] In 2003, Edmundo Murray transcribed Coghlan's work into a database to which he added the records of the Centro de Estudios Migratorios Latinoamericanos, (CEMLA).[159] Sources for CEMLA were (i) ship manifests, 1882–7, transcribed by immigration officers, (ii) passenger lists, 1888–1922, and (iii) standard immigration forms, 1923–9.[160] The result is a combined database of Coghlan and CEMLA, which details 7,159 Irish born immigrants arriving in Argentina between 1822 and 1929.[161] There is, however, a period of 28 months between when Coghlan's work finishes and CEMLA's begins; and records for some years, particularly during the 1880s, are either missing or contain limited information. Thus, although the combined database covers the period 1822–1929, it is not representative of total immigration for the period.[162] Nevertheless, when comparing the number of Irish born immigrants with the level of *'Inglés'* immigration between 1857 and 1897, expressed in Table 2 above, the Irish component forms a small part of total *'Inglés'* immigrant entry, varied time periods notwithstanding. All the following tables record data computed from the Coghlan/CEMLA database and relate only to Irish born immigrants arriving in Argentina. Findings cannot be applied to the collective Irish community, which incorporated the second and third generations.

Irish immigrants to Argentina came predominantly by way of ports outside Ireland, in particular via Liverpool, London and New York.[163] At the very least this demonstrates, as Donald Akenson has remarked, that their travel involved a multistaged journey.[164] What is not clear, however, in cases where ports were recorded in Europe or the United States is whether the journey had originated there or whether it was the final port of call prior to arrival in Argentina. The possibility of their having arrived in Buenos Aires direct from Marseilles, Boulogne or New York adds an interesting dimension of step migration. This is perhaps less likely in the case of European ports as advertisements in contemporary English-speaking Argentine newspapers advertised passage from Liverpool via Europe to the River Plate.[165] In the case of New York, it would seem plausible that immigrants arrived in Argentina having first made the decision to emigrate to North America. Indeed, a contemporary commentator observed that many arriving in Buenos Aires in the 1820s came via New York having attained United States citizenship.[166] But between the 1840s and 1880s it is likely that these cases were few. The nature of chain migration to Argentina from three specific counties, discussed in Chapter 1 above, would indicate a well-informed and conscious decision making process. Nevertheless, the database recorded six cases where immigrants described themselves as something other than Irish or '*Inglés*', indicating either ethnic affiliation or a protracted period of residence elsewhere. Significantly, as Table 8 demonstrates, five of these six

TABLE 8: ARRIVING IRISH IMMIGRANTS RECORDING 'FOREIGN' *NACIONALIDAD*

Surname	Christian name	Date of arrival	Port of embarkation	Class of travel	Born	Nacionalidad	Denomination	Occupation
Shanahan	José Joaquin	1824	Liverpool			Canada		
Lucas	John	1924	Santos	1st	Londonderry	US	Non-Catholic	Merchant
O'Higgins	Patrick	1925	New York	1st	Dublin	US	Non-Catholic	Merchant
Shea	John	1926	Santos	3rd		Russian		Master167
Vendrel	Antonia	1928	Boulogne		Cavan	Spanish		
Teall	Estelle	1928	New York	1st	Waterford	US	Non-Catholic	Housewife

Source: Compiled from the combined database of Coghlan (1982) and CEMLA (2003).

immigrants arrived in the 1920s during a period when traditional chain migration from the three key sending counties had declined.

The column detailing each individual's declared 'nationality' has been labelled in Spanish in order to reflect precisely the information requested from immigrants. Once again ambiguity surrounds its definition, but in the case of those four who clearly stated an Irish birthplace it would appear that citizenship functioned as the criterion. This explanation is less satisfactory in relation to the broader database and (if a strict citizenship criterion was employed) accounts insufficiently for immigrants declaring themselves Irish prior to the emergence of the Irish Free State in 1922.[167] Changes in recorded identity will be addressed below, but for the present purpose it is sufficient to note that, in the cases detailed, stated *nacionalidad* was most likely a reflection of acquired citizenship. All six cases in Table 8 are individually fascinating. Both Teall and O'Higgins departed from New York and their declaration of US *nacionalidad* could plausibly imply step migration. Lucas, who also described himself as a US citizen, departed from the port of Santos in Brazil, most likely *en route* from New York. These same three, two of which were merchants, entered 'non-Catholic' as their religion and travelled first class, attesting to the superior economic means of later arriving immigrants. Shanahan's case also implies step migration via Canada. It is possible that Antonia Vendrel, recording Cavan as her birthplace, was born of a Spanish father and an Irish mother, although this is by no means certain.

John Shea's case is particularly intriguing. Emmet O'Connor's study of Irish and Soviet communism discusses socialist and labour networks, which connected movements in Ireland and Russia during the early decades of the twentieth century.[168] This included Moscow inviting 'promising young communists' to train at the International Lenin School.[169] Although this was not until 1927, the year after Shea had arrived in Buenos Aires, his declaration of Russian *nacionalidad* provokes the beguiling possibility that he had initially moved to Russia as a consequence of political ideology. Furthermore, as the only passenger in the sample to register a third class mode of travel, his economic means were clearly less substantial.

Table 9 details a decade-by-decade account of Irish immigrants arriving in Argentina between the 1820s and the 1920s and records their stated *nacionalidad*.

Although all immigrants were required to declare their *nacional-*

TABLE 9: ESTIMATED NUMBER OF 'IRISH' IMMIGRANTS REACHING
ARGENTINA, 1821–1930, BY DECLARED *NACIONALIDAD*

Decade	*'Inglés'*	Irish	Other	Unlisted	Total
1820s	5	27	1	10	43
1830s	68	81	-	14	163
1840s	782	309	-	40	1,131
1850s	358	9	-	159	526
1860s	14	13	-	1,824	1,851
1870s	3	-	-	406	409
1880s	1,772	80	-	6	1,858
1890s	-	98	-	-	98
1900s	-	120	-	-	120
1910s	2	135	-	-	137
1920s	92	723	4	4	823
Total	3,096	1,595	5	2,463	7,159

Source: Compiled from the combined database of Coghlan (1982) and CEMLA (2003).

idad, approximately one third failed to do so. Of the total 7,159 recorded, 22.3 per cent stated Irish and 43.2 per cent *'Inglés'*. Of those declaring Irish, more than half were recorded before the 1920s, casting doubt on the citizenship criterion. However, the extent to which Irish or *'Inglés'* *nacionalidad* was stated by the individual immigrant or assumed by the returning official is unclear. Of the 1,776 Irish passengers arriving in 1889, for example, on the vessel *The City of Dresden* discussed below, all were recorded as *'Inglés'*. Similarly, of the fifteen passengers arriving in 1890 on the *Leibritz* from Southampton, all were recorded as Irish. This pattern was repeated on several ships. There were, however, cases where immigrants on the same vessel declared opposing identities, such as the six passengers arriving in 1924 on the *Highland Piper*: four were recorded as Irish and two as *'Inglés'*, both of whom were born in Ireland and were non-Catholic. It may well be, of course, that an *'Inglés'* or Irish nationality reflected little more than the political reality of the day or, indeed, a cultural pride in the tradition of Yeats, Hyde etc. But the extent of inconsistencies recorded would indicate that rather imprecise criteria applied, which were frequently prone to both immigrant subjectivity and official assumption.

Taking the official census returns' figures for arriving *'Inglés'* immigrants in Table 2 above, the Irish component, when calculated across the same broad period of 1850s to 1890s, accounts for just 14.59 per cent. This figure is inexact, of course, not only because years do not precisely correspond but also because the Irish data-base is somewhat inexact and incomplete. Nevertheless, in examin-ing the Irish sample, the total number of Irish born immigrants increased greatly in the 1840s, declined in the 1850s and peaked in the 1860s.[170] Equally, *'Inglés'* records in Table 2 are incomplete, with decades either absent (1840s) or containing incomplete data (1850s). What is significant in relation to the 1860s, however, is that, whilst Irish immigration had peaked, *'Inglés'* immigration continued to increase until the 1880s.

The marked increase in numbers of arriving Irish in the 1880s shown in Table 9 is representative of the state-sponsored artificial immigration known as 'The *Dresden* Affair', which did not follow the pattern of chain migration previously established.[171] In the late 1880s, two Irishmen, J. O'Meara and John S. Dillon,[172] were engaged as agents by the Argentine government to recruit Irish emigrants for passage on *The City of Dresden*. Would-be emigrants were recruited from 'cities and large towns' and consisted chiefly of the 'humbler classes', who were fed a string of false promises by the two agents.[173] With little or no official assistance on arrival in Buenos Aires, and with no familial ties to fall back on, the immigrants were left to sur-vive in a manner 'more fitting wild beasts than Christians'.[174] On a social level the exercise was a disaster, and in terms of empirical evi-dence the débâcle distorted figures for the entire decade. Of the 1,858 Irish immigrants recorded as arriving in the 1880s, only 82 were passengers on vessels other than *The City of Dresden*.[175] Murray suggests that the horrors of the scandal all but ended Irish immigra-tion to Argentina.[176] In terms of state-sponsored Irish settlement this may be so. However, when *'Dresden'* immigrants are subtracted from the immigrant total for the decade, numbers arriving had already significantly reduced, signalling a decline in Irish immigra-tion from the 1870s.

McKenna has claimed that, of the total Irish immigrants arriving in Argentina, broadly one in every two re-emigrated within a few years.[177] By his admission this calculation is based largely upon anecdotal evidence and McKenna provides no official documentary

support to substantiate his estimate. Nevertheless, if this approxi-
mation is for the moment accepted, it is significantly lower than
estimates of '*Inglés*' re-emigration rates, previously stated as 70.4 per
cent for the period 1857 to 1924.[178] Devoto has argued that the urban
centres of Argentina attracted young immigrant men with high
expectations of return migration.[179] As Tables 5 and 6 enumerate,
male dominated '*Inglés*' immigration was well represented within
urban occupations, and high estimates of outward movement
would seem consistent with Devoto's thesis. In relation to Irish levels, Gould's study of return migration from the United States calculated that the Irish repatriant ratio was one to six, the lowest of all
groups examined.[180] Similarly, Fitzpatrick concluded that Irish expatriates were more likely to return home as visitors than on a permanent basis.[181] Despite McKenna's unsubstantiated thesis, and assuming a level of consistency between Argentina and other models, it
would seem plausible that Irish re-emigration rates from Argentina
would have been lower than '*Inglés*', and that the rural nature of
Irish settlement may have curtailed Irish re-emigration in a way
that urban '*Inglés*' settlement did not. In the absence of official documentary evidence, however, this thesis cannot be satisfactorily
confirmed.

Coghlan's examination of records for Irish immigrants arriving
at the port of Buenos Aires between 1822 and 1880 demonstrates, as
with the '*Inglés*' group, an excess of males. However, not only is
available data incomplete, but also immigrant details are somewhat
polluted by the fact that, of the 5,306 records, 1,285 were not gender
specific.[182] Of the remaining 4,021 records, 67.02 per cent were men
and 32.98 per cent women. This corresponds to a ratio of 203 males
for every 100 females. Using this calculation to establish a comparison with '*Inglés*' data is problematic as ratios changed substantially
over time and port records do not correspond precisely with the
periods for '*Inglés*' computations. For a more direct comparison,
Coghlan's estimation of Irish born immigrants in census material
must be employed. In the 1869 census, the Irish male-to-female
ratio using Coghlan's criteria computed as 182 men for every 100
women. By the second census in 1895 this proportion had
decreased to 141.[183] Both estimates were substantially lower than
Devoto's calculation of 265 Irish men for every 100 women. Devoto
cited the 1869 census as his source of computation, but in the
absence of Irish specific data it would seem difficult to substantiate.[184] Coghlan's analysis, although not without its limitations,

provides a more accurate basis of calculation. Most significantly, a comparative assessment of these estimates with corresponding data in Table 5 indicates a significantly lower proportion of males among Irish immigrants than in the '*Inglés*' or other European groups.

This is consistent with all other Irish migrant streams, which recorded approximately equal ratios of male to female immigrants, with higher proportions of females than any of their European counterparts.[185] Of total emigrants from Ireland between 1856 and 1880, for example, 54.72 per cent were male and 45.32 per cent female.[186] Although the differing time periods preclude a direct comparison with gender ratios among Irish emigrants to Argentina, broadly speaking before 1880 – employing Coghlan's criteria for 'Irish' – the female proportion of the latter group was around 12 percentage points lower than that for total emigrants from Ireland. Seemingly, therefore, even within a national migratory group where a balanced gender ratio prevailed, Argentina attracted more Irish males. Notwithstanding a reduced female representation, the proportion of females among Irish immigrants to Argentina was still remarkably higher than among the generic '*Inglés*' classification.

Irish immigrants' religious denominations demonstrate a number of demographic irregularities. Table 10 assesses the religious persuasions of immigrants arriving post 1880, as documented by CEMLA for the period 1882–1929. The structure of CEMLA records was such that information relating to religion was recorded within a general comments section, which also detailed occupation. At no point did the classification 'Catholic' appear; only 'non-Catholic' was recorded. In instances where religion was not stated, it is reasonable to assume that a Catholic denomination was implied. It is plausible, however, that not all arriving non-Catholic immigrants declared their religious denomination. Whilst these cases were probably few, the following computations may represent an under-estimation of arriving non-Catholic Irish. Furthermore, the incomplete nature of available records limits the results in Table 10 to those listed in the CEMLA database, which are not representative of total immigration for the period.

The relatively low percentage of non-Catholics recorded in the 1880s significantly increases to 30.48 per cent when assessed as a proportion of the 82 passengers arriving by alternative means on *The City of Dresden*. Of the 22,488 '*Inglés*' immigrants to arrive

TABLE 10: RELIGIOUS DENOMINATIONS OF 'IRISH' IMMIGRANTS, 1880–1929

Decade	Total immigrants	No. of non-Catholics	% of total
1880s	1,857	286	15.40
1890s	97	43	44.33
1900s	119	59	49.58
1910s	136	57	41.91
1920s	822	432	52.55

Source: Compiled from data in the CEMLA database (2003).

between 1876 and 1897, only 16.98 per cent registered as Catholic.[187] Falling Irish immigrant numbers and an increase in Irish non-Catholic immigration would certainly have contributed to this low representation. Between 1880 and 1900, for example, approximately 50 per cent of Irish immigrants were non-Catholic.[188] In establishing the point at which Irish immigration had peaked, these statistics would indicate that chain migration from the traditional Catholic sending areas had declined substantially by the 1870s, and that Irish immigration thereafter was largely of a non-Catholic persuasion.[189]

Significantly, there was a substantial shift in declared *nacionalidad* between pre-1870s Catholic immigrants and post-1870s non-Catholic arrivals. The non-Catholics in Table 10 predominantly recorded themselves as Irish not '*Inglés*'. In the 1920s, although 52.55 per cent of 'Irish' immigrants stated their religion as something other than Catholic, 87.85 per cent declared themselves Irish.[190] The rationale behind these chosen identities is not easily explained, but certain points are clear. Within Anglophone pre-1880s Argentine society there were immediate social and economic advantages in maintaining an overt '*Inglés*' identity. Indeed, the most efficient networks of communication, which served to integrate the newly arrived immigrants into the English-speaking community, effectively demanded this. In the years after 1880 the situation changed significantly. As nationalist sentiment intensified in Ireland, so an embryonic consciousness of an Irish-Argentine identity began to emerge in Argentina. Irish nationalism developed in a detached and at times conflicting form out of the collective '*Inglés*' community. The sources and consequences of this cultural process will be discussed in Chapter 6 below. For the present it is sufficient to note that this largely, but not wholly, accounts for the marked change in declared identity discernible in post-1880 immigrant returns.

Table 11 assesses the occupations stated by arriving Irish immigrants between 1880 and 1929. The data computed is somewhat limited in so far as, of the 3,036 immigrants recorded, less than one third gave their employment type. Also, in each decade a substantial number recorded the broad classification of 'employee', making it unclear whether occupations were rural or urban. Thus, the categories detailed have been extracted from the database in order to broadly compare, as far as data will allow, levels of rural and urban settlement.

The agricultural categories of 'landowner', 'farmer'[191] and 'unskilled' labour show a general decline in representation. In the 'unskilled' category, in which 'farm labourer', 'labourer' and 'railway worker' were subsumed, 'farm labourer' was most heavily represented and its falling percentage reflects, in part, the extent of rural decline. 'Railway worker' appeared in the 1920s only and most likely accounted for the slight 'Unskilled' increase on the previous decade as industrial labour arrived. McKenna has argued that Irish immigrants arriving between 1846 and 1865 had accumulated disproportionate levels of wealth and capital.[192] Property inheritance rather than acquisition, he stated, became the means of landownership after 1881.[193] The difficulty in acquiring land post 1880s could have contributed to rural decline and McKenna's thesis may have some validity. However, since the percentages enumerated in Table 11 detail the occupational status of arriving immigrants, the profession of 'landowner' would have referred to the homeland not Argentina. As with Table 6, it is likely that some immigrants adjusted their declared occupations and stated desired or intended professions, so it is not possible to either substantiate or refute McKenna's assertion through recorded statistics.[194] The decline in

TABLE 11: RECORDED OCCUPATIONS OF ARRIVING 'IRISH' IMMIGRANTS,
1890s–1920s

Decade	No.	Landowner %	Farmer %	Unskilled %	Merchant %	Professional %	Artisan %
1890s	56	-	26.79	7.14	10.71	12.50	12.50
1900s	58	6.90	12.07	5.17	17.24	15.52	12.06
1910s	98	9.18	10.20	4.08	14.29	16.33	7.14
1920s	67	15.07	5.22	4.32	15.80	18.48	5.51

Source: Compiled from the CEMLA database (2003).

farm labouring was not replaced by an increase in urban labour, which might be expected as a result of expanding manufacturing industry at the turn of the century. Instead, agricultural decline was matched by a rise in the commercial sector and reflected the change in immigrant profile that occurred post 1880s.

In this regard, the combined representation of the 'merchant' and 'professional' categories increased from 23 per cent in the 1890s to 34 per cent in the 1920s.[195] This sample, although small in number, suggests that non-Catholic Irish immigrants arriving at the turn of the century were not unskilled rural or urban labour, but were part of a growing upwardly mobile class of professionals and merchants that operated within an increasingly diversified Argentine economy. A number of factors might be considered in accounting for this: deteriorating opportunities in Ireland and increasing opportunities in Argentina certainly figured. Equally, cultural factors such as religious identity, considered in Chapter 4 below, were notable; but once again it is sufficient here to acknowledge the structural changes in the character of Irish immigration in the closing years of the nineteenth century.

In contrast to the details of arriving immigrants, Table 12 records the declared occupations of Irish immigrants, using Coghlan's criteria, in both the first and second censuses.

TABLE 12: RECORDED OCCUPATIONS OF ARRIVING IRISH IMMIGRANTS, 1869 AND 1895

	1869	%	1895	%
Farm hand	743	26.9	119	4.4
Shepherd	660	23.9	247	9.1
Landowner	426	15.5	670	24.7
Servant	236	8.6	210	7.7
Poster*	214	7.8	151	5.6
Cattle dealer	139	5.0	26	1.0
Teacher	67	2.4	79	2.9
Labourer	56	2.0	611	22.5
Merchant	53	1.9	95	3.5
Breeder	50	1.8	257	9.5
Employee	46	1.7	148	5.5
Cook	41	1.5	86	3.2
Share-cropper	26	0.9	15	0.6
Other	299	10.8	624	23.0
Total	2,757	100%	2,714	100%

Source: Extracted from Coghlan (1982).[196]

* the shepherd in charge of tending a flock

There is an immediate and striking difference between the occupational categories listed here and in Table 6. Whereas Table 6
records occupational categories of arriving *'Inglés'* immigrants,
which referred, in the main, to employment in their native home,
Table 12 represents census returns from Irish immigrants settled in
Argentina. The differing modes of employment are reflective of the
nature of the Argentine economy. Categories such as 'breeder', 'cattle dealer', 'shepherd' and 'landowner' are heavily represented,
indicating skill transferability and immigrant adaptability. Irish representation in sheep farming is not fully reflected in Table 12: in
1869 the category of 'shepherd' represented less than one quarter of
all occupations. By 1895 this proportion had substantially reduced
to 9.1 per cent.

In 1869, however, neither cattle ranching nor crop growing were
as widely practised as sheep farming. Irish immigrants involved in
either sector would most likely have reported themselves within
the respective 'cattle dealer' or 'share cropper' category. The
remaining rural categories of 'farm hand' and 'breeder' would thus
most probably refer to employment in sheep farming. Similarly, at
the time of the 1869 census it is likely that the majority of those in
the 'landowner' category were involved in sheep farming. This thesis is by no means foolproof, as a proportion of 'farm hands' could
well have been employed on cattle ranches owned by Irish
'landowners'. Nonetheless, given the dominance of sheep farming
in Argentina's economy pre 1870, it is probable that such cases were
few. Of the 68.1 per cent of total Irish occupations accounted for by
'farm hand', 'shepherd', 'landowner' and 'breeder' in 1869, it is feasible that the lion's share related to employment within the sheep
farming sector.

By 1895 the evaluation becomes more complex. The significant
decrease in 'shepherd' and 'farm hand' from the 1869 census was
largely, although not wholly, matched by a corresponding increase
in 'landowner'. This could be indicative of two things. First, that
early Irish immigrants went into the sheep farming industry on
arrival in Argentina and benefited from the system of flock shar-
ing.[197] Second, that the subsequent level of social and economic
advancement attained as 'farm hands' and 'shepherds' elevated
their position to 'landowner'. This would not fully account for the
substantial reduction in both categories in 1895. At the close of the
century the Argentine export market was no longer solely dependent upon the sheep sector, and diversification into cattle breeding

and crop production had changed the rural landscape. Although 'cattle dealer' registered a reduction, it is likely that the significant increase in the category of 'breeder' included cattle as well as sheep farmers. Considering the historical representation in sheepfarming, however, this proportion was probably still quite insubstantial. Indeed, CEMLA occupation data included only twelve individuals arriving between 1890 and 1929 that were recorded as 'cattle hand' or 'cattle dealer'.[198] Nevertheless, their very presence would indicate stimulated activity within the sector and, furthermore, CEMLA data would not reflect immigrants who had diversified into cattle after arrival. This is demonstrated by an advertisement in *The Southern Cross*, which announced one farmer's intention of selling 'two flocks of fine mestizo sheep, the owner wishing to put cattle in their place'.[199]

The four 'sheepfarming' categories previously identified for 1869 ('farm hand', 'shepherd', 'landowner' and 'breeder') had collectively decreased from 68.1 to 47.7 per cent of total occupations by 1895. Although still a substantial proportion, the decrease signals a considerable decline in Irish rural activity. Significantly, the categories of 'merchant' and 'employee', although relatively small in number, both registered increases of approximately 50 per cent between these dates, indicating growth in the urban sector. Unfortunately, this thesis cannot be tested for the category of 'labourer' as urban versus rural data was not recorded. But this occupation's disproportionate rise in 1895 is most likely explained by the influx of unskilled immigrants via the *'Dresden'* imbroglio of 1889.[200] A further consideration, however, may well have been the construction of the railway network. In the United States, by 1900 as many as 100,000 Irish born and second generation Irish were working on the rail systems. With the extensive development of the British railroad network in Argentina, it is feasible that Irish labour was recruited, thus accounting for some of the 22 per cent recorded as 'labourer' in 1895. But perhaps even more significantly, the general reduction in Irish rural employment toward the close of the century may reflect the increasing urbanisation of Argentina, and Buenos Aires Province in particular. In many US rural areas (Minnesota, Wisconsin, Iowa, upstate New York) Irish offspring headed disproportionately to the cities. In Argentina, Irish communities had settled largely in areas that were most heavily urbanising then and later.[201] This may, to some extent, contribute to their partial 'disappearance' in the twentieth century as the urban melting pot replaced their more traditional rural existence.

On arrival in Argentina, the Irish as an ethnic group were transplanted into a homogeneous *'Inglés'* classification that distorted demographic and statistical data for all immigrants of an 'Anglo-Celtic' origin. Although Irish-specific data provided a limited and somewhat disjointed record of immigration, its analysis demonstrates significant areas of differentiation from the catch-all *'Inglés'* group. Most noteworthy was the rural nature of Irish settlement. The *'Ingleses'* predominated in the urban centre of Buenos Aires, operating commercially as merchants and artisans. In contrast, Irish immigration pre 1880s was rural, with more than two thirds of the recorded population engaged in pastoral employment. Whether this geographical and occupational dichotomy was instrumental in rates of re-emigration is difficult to quantify. The *'Inglés'* immigrant profile of male, single and urban based is consistent with the high rates of re-emigration established by Willcox for the period 1857–1924. In contrast, the Irish registered a higher proportion of female immigrants and were predominantly rural based. Both factors may have significantly contributed to the group's apparent propensity to remain. The unsubstantiated nature of corresponding Irish statistics precludes final analysis, however, at least in terms of empirical data.

Post 1880s, Irish immigration demonstrated an acute departure from previous certainties. The rural proportion recorded in 1869, predominant in sheep farming, had substantially decreased by 1895. This was reflective not only of the development of a mixed farming economy, but also of an increasingly urbanised Argentine society. Whereas Argentina had once required mass European labour of a largely unskilled nature, its changing economic structure in the early twentieth century demanded a more skilled, professional workforce. Nevertheless, mass Italian immigration, largely rural, which took place from 1870, demonstrates the continued importance of the rural sector to the Argentine economy, despite industrial and technological advances elsewhere. Although it is likely that the political and economic progress of an evolving Argentine state affected the nature of Irish immigration, it is also probable that the demographic flow was governed by an already established pattern of chain migration. As the traditional pampas sheep industry declined, so too did the traditional Irish immigration. Thus, demographic profiles at the turn of the century registered changes in profession and religion as urban, professional, non-Catholic immigration increased.

Although the combination of a shared language, collective identity and cultural familiarity had tended to create a seamless ethnic group, the Irish remained 'outside' the social and commercial '*Inglés*' inner sanctum. Whereas 'British' interests flourished in the mercantile and financial centres of Buenos Aires, the traditional 'separateness' of Irish immigrants necessarily entailed the adoption of an alternative commercial route. The lingering sense of Irish immigrants' 'otherness' thus manifested itself in the pursuit of a hitherto largely untried rural existence within the Argentine economy. Their distinctive pastoral background pre 1880s facilitated this transition, in turn providing a sense of security and familiarity. The native Irish farming experience, however, had ill prepared immigrants for the isolation and desolation of the Argentine *campo*, thus further compounding the gulf between their settlement and that of the urban '*Ingleses*. Their at times uneasy position within, and relationship to, the '*Inglés*' group was largely the result of their country existence. As such, nineteenth-century Argentine rural society and the role of the Irish within it were fundamental to the community's economic progression and social development.

NOTES

1. H.S. Ferns, *Argentina* (London, 1969), p. 95.
2. Tulio Halperín-Donghi, 'La integración de los inmigrantes italianos en Argentina: Un comentario' in Fernando J. Devoto and Gianfranco Rosoli, (eds), *La inmigración italiana en la Argentina* (Buenos Aires, 1988), pp. 87–93.
3. National Archives, Kew, Foreign Office Papers: 6/4, 30 July 1824.
4. See John Paul Bailey, *The British Community in Argentina* (unpublished PhD thesis, University of Surrey, 1976), p. 245. Bailey goes on to acknowledge the conflicting numbers reported in different sources, with estimates varying from sixty-four to thirty-eight British houses.
5. Devoto, Fernando J. *Historia de la inmigración en la Argentina* (Buenos Aires, 2003), p. 209.
6. Eduardo Galeano, *Las venas abiertas de América Latina* (rev. ed., Madrid, 2003), p. 258.
7. Jonathan C. Brown, *A Socio-Economic History of Argentina, 1776–1860* (Cambridge, 1979), p. 228.
8. Galeano (2003), p. 257.
9. Ferns (1969), p. 128.
10. Bailey (1976), p. 521.
11. Susan Midgen Socolow, 'Economic Activities of the Porteño Merchants: The Viceregal Period' in *The Hispanic American Historical Review*, vol. 55, no. 1 (1975), pp. 1–24
12. Elected President, 1868–74.
13. For a discussion on the political structure of the Argentine state see John Lynch, Roberto Cortés Conde, Ezequiel Gallo, David Rock, Juan Carlos Torre and Liliana de Riz, *Historia de la Argentina* (Barcelona, 2001). See also Juan Carlos Garavaglia, *Poder, conflicto y relaciones sociales: El río de la Plata, XVIII-XIX* (Rosario, 1999).
14. Lynch et al. (2001), p. 91.

15. John Lynch, 'The River Plate Republics from Independence to the Paraguayan War' in Leslie Bethell (ed.), *The Cambridge History of Latin America*, vol. III (Cambridge, 1985), pp. 615–675.
16. Roberto Cortés Conde, 'The Growth of the Argentine Economy, c.1870–1914' in LeslieBethell (ed.), *The Cambridge History of Latin America*, vol. V (Cambridge, 1986), pp. 327–357.
17. Bartolomé Mitre, 1862–8; Domingo Faustino Sarmiento, 1868–74; Nicolás Avellaneda, 1874–80; Julio Roca, 1880–6; and Juarez Celman, 1886–90.
18. Roberto Cortés Conde, 'Migración, cambio agrícola y políticas de protección: El caso de Argentina' in Hebe Clementi (ed.), *Inmigración española en la Argentina* (Buenos Aires, 1991), pp. 17–32.
19. Provincial leaders
20. Tulio Halperín-Donghi, *Historia contemporánea de América Latina* (5th ed., Madrid, 2004), pp. 242–4.
21. Ibid.
22. José Maria Rosa, *Historia Argentina: El regimen 1878–1895*, vol. VIII (Buenos Aires, 1969), p. 124.
23. President Rivadavia had attempted to proclaim Buenos Aires the capital of the republic in 1826 but it was not passed into law. See Rodolfo C. Taboada, (ed.), *1000 fechas que hicieron historia en la Argentina* (Buenos Aires, 2001).
24. Ezequiel Gallo, 'Argentina: Society and Politics, 1880–1916' in Leslie Bethell (ed.), *The Cambridge History of Latin America*, vol. V (Cambridge, 1986), pp. 359–91.
25. Led by Dr Adolfo Alsina.
26. Lynch et al. (2001), p. 89.
27. Halperín-Donghi (2004), p. 328.
28. María Sáenz Quesada, *La Argentina: Historia del pais y de su gente* (Buenos Aires, 2001), p. 386.
29. Lynch et al. (2001), p. 92.
30. Cortés Conde (1986), p. 355.
31. Ibid., p. 346.
32. Sáenz Quesada (2001), p. 412.
33. Ferns (1969), p. 103.
34. Ibid.
35. Devoto (2003), pp. 261–72.
36. Lynch et al. (2001), p. 115.
37. See Guido Di Tella and Manuel Zymelman, *Las etapas del desarrollo económico argentino* (Buenos Aires, 1967).
38. Ferns (1973), p. 88.
39. Ibid.
40. Bailey (1976), pp. 521–2.
41. Ibid.
42. James R. Scobie, *Argentina: A City and a Nation* (2nd ed., New York, 1971) p. 178.
43. Ibid.
44. See Galeano (2003), pp. 255–70.
45. See Alejandro E. Bunge, *La desocupación en la Argentina: Actual crisis del trabajo* (Buenos Aires, 1917).
46. Galeano (2003), pp. 271–8.
47. Bailey (1976), p. 522.
48. Scobie (1971), p. 179.
49. Lynch et al. (2001), pp. 158–62.
50. President, 1822–6.
51. Alberto Kleiner, *Inmigración inglesa en la Argentina: El informe* (Buenos Aires, 1983), p. 2.
52. Ibid., p. 4.
53. Ibid.
54. Many of these original Scottish settlers returned to the city and entered into commercial business; others became small *estancia* owners.
55. D.C.M. Platt, 'British Agricultural Colonization in Latin America' in *Interamerican Economic Affairs*, vol. XVIII, no. 3 (1961), pp. 23–42.
56. National Library of Ireland [hereafter NLI], Parliamentary Papers: (1872, 35, vol. LXX), p. 19.

57. Bailey (1976), p. 193.
58. Scobie (1971), p. 98.
59. See introduction of Lilia Ana Bertoni, *Patriotas, cosmopolitas y nacionalistas: La construcción de la nacionalidad Argentina a fines del siglo XIX* (Buenos Aires, 2001).
60. Ibid., pp. 19–20.
61. Domingo Faustino Sarmiento, *Facundo: Civilización y barbarie* (2nd ed., Madrid, 1993), p. 63
62. *Segundo senso de la República Argentina, 1895* [hereafter, *Segundo censo nacional, 1895*].
63. Alejandro E. Bunge and Carlos Garcia Mata, 'Argentina' in Walter F. Willcox (ed.), *International Migrations*, vol. II (New York, 1931), pp. 143–160. See also Torcuato S. Di Tella, *Historia social de la Argentina contemporánea* (Buenos Aires, 1998), p. 50.
64. Carl Solberg, *Immigration and Nationalism: Argentina and Chile, 1890–1914* (Austin and London, 1970), p. 44.
65. The verb *pertenecer* is used.
66. *Tercero censo de la República Argentina, 1914* [hereafter *Tercer censo nacional, 1914*), vol. 1, see 'Ficha Personal'.
67. D.H. Akenson, *The Irish in South Africa* (Grahamstown, 1991), p. 14 .
68. Ibid.
69. For a more detailed account of linguistic and national identities see Chapter 6 below.
70. Blanca Sánchez Alonso, *La inmigración española en Argentina, siglos XIX y XX* (Barcelona, 1992), p. 76.
71. Computed from *Segundo censo nacional, 1895*.
72. Bunge and Garcia Mata (1931), p. 154.
73. Alejandro Enrique Fernández, 'Los españoles de Buenos Aires y sus asociaciones en la época de inmigración masiva' in Hebe Clementi (ed.), *Inmigración española en la Argentina* (Buenos Aires, 1991), pp. 59–83.
74. Cortés Conde (1986), pp. 327–57.
75. Computed from Bunge and Garcia Mata (1931) , p. 155.
76. Ibid., p. 335. Other sources give 30 per cent: Gino Germani, *Política y sociedad en una época de transición* (Buenos Aires, 1965), p. 175.
77. For a discussion of Italian migration to Argentina see Herbert S. Klein, 'The Integration of Italian Immigrants into the United States and Argentina: A Comparative Analysis' in *The American Historical Review*, vol. 88, no. 2 (1983), pp. 306–29;Fernando J. Devoto and Gianfranco Rosoli (1988). For a discussion of Spanish migration see Sanchez Alonso (1992); Maria Liliana Da Orden, 'Liderazgo étnico y redes sociales: Una aproximación a la participación política de los españoles en la Argentina, 1880–1912' in Alejandro E. Fernandez and José C. Moya (eds), *La inmigración española en la Argentina* (Buenos Aires, 1999); José C. Moya, *Cousins and Strangers: Spanish Immigrants in Buenos Aires, 1850–1930* (Berkeley and London, 1998).
78. Sanchez Alonso (1992), p. 79.
79. For a discussion on links between Irish prosperity and early settlement see Patrick McKenna, *Nineteenth Century Irish Emigration to, and Settlement in, Argentina* (unpublished MA thesis, 1994, St Patrick's College, Maynooth), pp. 257–81. For analysis of the impact of early European immigration see Fernando J. Devoto (2003), pp. 246–89.
80. Calculated from *Registro estadistico del Estado de Buenos Aires, 1855*.
81. Devoto (2003), p. 208.
82. Idem.
83. Fernández (1991), p. 67.
84. José Hugo Rodino, *Inmigración española en la Argentina: Adapción e identidad* (Buenos Aires, 1999), p. 9.
85. Devoto (2003), p. 224.
86. Moya (1998), p. 32.
87. Rodino (1999), p. 10.
88. Eduardo Coghlan, *El aporte de los irlandeses a la formación de la nación Argentina* (Buenos Aires, 1982), p. 18.
89. Coghlan substantially revised upwards levels of total Irish population from what he extracted from the 1855 census, using his criteria of 'Irish'. To arrive at this revised estimate Coghlan assessed records of arriving immigrants at the port of Buenos Aires. The methodology employed in his calculations is discussed in this chapter's last section, 'Separating Irish immigrants from "Inglés"'.

90. Computed from *Primer y segundo censo nacional, 1869* and *1895*.
91. Herbert S. Klein. 'The Integration of Italian Immigrants into the United States and Argentina: A Comparative Analysis' in *The American Historical Review*, vol. 88, no. 2 (1983), pp. 306–329, esp. p. 318. He also provides comparative data on the Irish and Italians in the two countries: Table 12, p. 328.
92. Calculated from ibid., Table 1, p. 308, and what follows, pp. 309–310.
93. Ibid., Table 2, p. 309. For a commentary, Samuel L. Baily, 'Italian Immigrants in Buenos Aires and New York City, 1870–1914: A Comparative Analysis of Adjustment' in Samuel L. Baily and Eduardo José Míguez (eds), *Mass Migration to Modern Latin America* (Wilmington, 2003), pp. 69–80.
94. Klein (1983), p. 311.
95. Ibid., p. 315, with data provided in Tables 4 and 5, pp. 312, 313, and discussed pp. 311–314.
96. Ibid., Table 9, p. 322, cumulative comparative datafrom *Tercer censo nacional de la República Argentina, 1914* [hereafter *Tercer censo nacional, 1914*], vols 2, pp. 395–396; 3, pp. 295ff.; 4, p. 68; 5, p. 837; and 6, p. 679.
97. Baily (2003), p.77.
98. Klein (1983), p. 321.
99. Halperín-Donghi (1988), p. 88.
100. Ibid.
101. Carlos F. Díaz Alejandro, *Essays on the Economic History of the Argentine Republic* (New Haven and London, 1970), p. 40. Díaz Alejandro goes on to argue that, after several years of hard work, late arrivals were able to purchase smallholdings. For maps of the spreading rail grid, in 1866, 1882, 1896 and 1914, see Walter Nugent, *Crossings: The Great Trans Atlantic Migrations, 1870–1914* (Bloomington, 1992), p. 115. See Chapter 3 below for a discussion on land acquisition.
102. Nicolás Sánchez-Albornoz, 'The Population of Latin America, 1850–1930' in Leslie Bethell (ed.), *The Cambridge History of Latin America*, vol. IV (Cambridge, 1985), pp. 121–52.
103. Sánchez Alonso (1992), p. 81.
104. Solberg (1970), p. 37. The nature of Italian seasonal migration will be discussed more fully in Chapter 3 below.
105. 'Remarks on the River Plate Republics as a Field for British Emigration', NLI, Parliamentary Papers (1872, 35, vol. LXX), p. 30.
106. Ibid.
107. Ibid.
108. Ibid.
109. Devoto (2003), p. 265.
110. Sanchez Alonso (1992), p. 104.
111. The failed 'Dresden Affair' in particular was widely reported and is discussed at length in this chapter's last section, 'Separating Irish immigrants from "Inglés"'.
112. Letter from James McCormick to Rose and Thomas Rattigan, 11 March 1888: by kind permission of the Rattigan family, Buenos Aires.
113. See Devoto (2003), p. 219–221.
114. Willcox (1929), vol. I, p. 211.
115. Ibid.
116. Computed from Bunge and Garcia Mata (1931), p. 156. Married immigrants accounted for 31.83 per cent and widowers for 1.70 per cent.
117. For a discussion on this see Willcox (1931) vol. II, pp. 89–91. See also Devoto (2003), p. 234.
118. Willcox (1929), vol. I, p. 211
119. Calculated from Willcox (1929), vol. I, pp. 543–546, Table V. The term 'British' has been used in this instance for consistency with Willcox's presentation of data.
120. Ibid.
121. Bailey (1976), pp. 177–180.
122. Computed from Bunge and Garcia Mata (1931), p. 156. Married immigrants accounted for 31.83 per cent and Widowers for 1.70 per cent.
123. *Tercer censo nacional, 1914*, vol. I, p. 192.
124. Klein (1983), p. 314

125. Ronald C. Newton, *German Buenos Aires, 1900–1933: Social Change and Cultural Crisis* (Austin and London, 1977), p. 8.
126. Ibid., p. 7.
127. Ibid., p. 4.
128. Ibid., p. 6.
129. Ibid., p. 5.
130. *The Standard,* 2 February 1870, p. 2.
131. Klein, (1983), p. 322.
132. Solberg (1970), p. 5.
133. Bailey (1976), p. 184.
134. Ingrid Wiedman, 'La Colonización Alemaña y Alemaño' in Ingrid Wiedman et al. (eds), *La Colonización Alemaña en Misiones* (Posados, 2001), pp. 13–32.
135. Newton (1977), p. 8..
136. Sanchez Alonso (1992), p. 103.
137. See Solberg (1970), p. 39. See also Moya's observations (1998), pp. 211–225.
138. Solberg (1970), p. 37.
139. Quoted in Newton (1977), p. 19
140. M. G. and E.T. Mulhall, *Handbook of the River Plate* (Buenos Aires, 1869), p. 6.
141. Ibid.
142. Michael G. Mulhall, *The English in South America* (Buenos Aires, 1878) p. 335.
143. Murray (1919), p. 401.
144. Ibid., p. 502 .
145. Monsignor Santiago and M. Ussher, *Los capellanes irlandeses en la colectividad hiberno-argentina durante el siglo XIX* (Buenos Aires, 1953), pp. 22–23.
146. Monsignor Santiago and M. Ussher, *A Biography of Anthony Dominic Fahy, O.P., Irish Missionary in Argentina, 1805–1871* (Buenos Aires, 1951), p. 169.
147. Santiago and Ussher (1953), p. 27.
148. Juan Carlos Korol and Hilda Sábato, *Cómo fue la inmigración irlandesa en Argentina* (Buenos Aires, 1981), pp. 189–195. This figure was based on the premise that Eduardo Coghlan's thesis was accurate.
149. McKenna (1994), p. 183.
150. For a discussion on pre-1861 estimates see Murray (1919) and Mulhall (1883).
151. McKenna (1994), pp. 182–183.
152. Coghlan(1982).
153. Coghlan (1982), p. 18.
154. Ibid., p. 19.
155. See ibid., pp. 16 and 18.
156. Eduardo Coghlan, 'Origines y evolución de la colectividad hiberno-argentina' in *The Southern Cross, Centenario Edición* (Buenos Aires, 1975), pp. 29–31.
157. See Coghlan (1982), p. 19, and Table 4 above.
158. Coghlan (1982), p. 7.
159. Centre for Latin American Migration Studies [hereafter CEMLA] .
160. Records are contained in the files of the Dirección General de Inmigración, Buenos Aires, Argentina.
161. The contents of this database are from Eduardo Coghlan (1982) and CEMLA (2003). Transcription: Edmundo Murray, Irish Argentine Historical Society, 2003. All rights reserved. [Records for the year 1929 finish in March.]
162. Coghlan's data finishes in February 1880, and CEMLA's begins in June 1882.
163. Coghlan (1982) and CEMLA (2003).
164. Akenson (1991), p. 55.
165. See as an example the *Buenos Aires Herald,* 6 February 1878, p. 5.
166. Murray (1919), p. 64.
167. It is unclear exactly what Shea's occupation was as it was recorded only as 'Master' but this could have meant 'Master of a ship'.
168. See Emmet O'Connor, *Reds and The Green: Ireland, Russia and the Communist Internationals, 1919–43* (Dublin, 2004).
169. Ibid., p. 3.
170. Although the 1880s' figure was slightly higher, this was artificially stimulated by 'The Dresden Affair'.

171. See Murray (1919), pp. 440–449, and *Buenos Aires Herald* ,17 March 1899, p. 3.
172. Brother of Canon Dillon, founder of *The Southern Cross* newspaper, 1875
173. Murray (1919), p. 440.
174. *The Southern Cross*, 4 April 1890, p. 2.
175. Computed from Coghlan (1982) and CEMLA (2003).
176. Murray (1919), pp. 440–449.
177. McKenna (1994), pp. 205, 342.
178. Willcox (1931), vol. I, Table V, pp. 543–546.
179. Devoto (2003), p. 234.
180. J.D. Gould, 'European Inter-Continental Emigration: The Road Home: Return Migration from the U.S.A.' in *Journal of European Economic History*, vol. IX, no. 1 (1980), pp. 55–60.
181. David Fitzpatrick, 'The Irish in Britain, 1871–1921' in W.E. Vaughan (ed.), *A New History of Ireland: Ireland under the Union, I, 1801–70*, vol. V (Oxford, 1989), pp. 606–652, esp. p. 634.
182. Coghlan (1982).
183. Computed from Coghlan (1975), pp. 29–31.
184. Devoto (2003), p. 218.
185. See Cormac Ó Grada, 'Across the Briny Ocean: Some Thoughts on Irish Emigration to America, 1800–1850' in T.M. Devine and David Dickson (eds), *Ireland and Scotland, 1600–1850* (Edinburgh, 1979), pp. 118–130; D. Fitzpatrick, *Irish Emigration 1801–1921* (Dublin, 1984).
186. Computed from Walter F. Willcox (ed.), *International Migrations*, vol. 1 (New York, 1929), pp. 303–306.
187. *Segundo censo nacional, 1895*.
188. This mean calculation is based on the 1880s figure of 30.48 per cent , which excludes the 'Dresden' immigrants. See Table 17 below.
189. Westmeath, Longford and Wexford accounted for 73.43 per cent of total immigration to Argentina. See McKenna (1994), p. 175.
190. Computed from Coghlan (1982) and CEMLA (2003).
191. Category includes those declaring occupation as 'cattle hand' or 'cattle dealer'.
192. McKenna (1994), p. 249.
193. Ibid.
194. Korol and Sábato's analysis of Irish owned land across twenty *partidos* in Buenos Aires Province would, however, broadly support McKenna's assertion. See Chapter 3 below for a discussion in this regard.
195. Professional category includes teacher, lawyer, accountant, engineer, physician, vet, dentist.
196. I am grateful to Edmundo Murray for both compiling these figures and allowing me access to them.
197. See Chapter 3 below for a detailed analysis of the practice.
198. See Table 19 below for a breakdown of occupations.
199. *The Southern Cross*, 7 January 1881, p. 8.
200. See Murray (1919), p. 440.
201. Of the top fifteen cities in Argentina, seven are in the pampean region.

CHAPTER THREE

Getting on: the Irish in Argentine rural society

Argentina, from its northern boundary with Bolivia and Paraguay to its southernmost point of Tierra del Fuego, stretches over two thousand miles.[1] Four distinct geographical areas support diverse terrain and climate conditions.[2] To the south, Patagonia covers approximately one quarter of the nation's territory. The extreme polar conditions of this region's southern tip hindered human settlement in the nineteenth century, but the short grasslands of its plateaux afforded good grazing and supported sheep farming.[3] The Andean region to the west continues its natural mountainous border with Chile northward into Bolivia. Although sheep roamed the highlands, settlement concentrated on the irrigated lands of the valleys on its eastern edge. Agricultural produce supported a predominantly local demand as the region's geographical isolation impeded trade with the growing Buenos Aires market.[4] The northern lowlands is the third major geographical zone. This area supports diverse eco-systems, from the rainforests and swamps of Corrientes in the northeast to the grassy plains of Entre Ríos. The climate ranges from subtropical to temperate, with sufficient rainfall to support agriculture and pastoral farming.[5] All three zones enclose the final and most promising region of nineteenth-century Argentina: the pampas.

Situated along the fertile coastal zone, the pampas incorporate the Buenos Aires Province, southern Santa Fe, southeastern Córdoba and eastern La Pampa.[6] Although comprising less than one fifth of the country's terrain, its well-irrigated, flat, grassy plains supported two thirds of the population, and formed the nucleus of economic growth in the nineteenth century.[7] Proximity to ports and financial centres in the city of Buenos Aires facilitated rural expansion and attracted extensive capital, labour and foreign investment. Land values increased accordingly, accumulating wealth and status for landowners. This rapidly evolving commercial and social phenomenon, however, was a facet of post-Independence Argentina and re-presented an acute departure from colonial societal structures.

Before Independence, the Spanish colonial elite was predominantly a merchant class whose commercial interests were urban based.[8] Surplus capital was diversified into either shipping, retail sales or manufacturing but rarely into land. As a commercial venture, land and livestock yielded poor returns but, even more significantly, the *estanciero* occupied a subordinate social status in Spanish colonial society.[9] This served as a sufficient deterrent to rural investment for the financial and social elite. Post Independence, with the trading restrictions of the Spanish Crown fully eradicated, Argentina's markets were exposed to foreign interests.[10] The arriving competition commercially usurped native merchant families, who sought alternative financial ventures. Thus, the rapidly expanding rural sector drew, for the first time, extensive capital investment.[11] This incursion into land and livestock not only transferred the economic power of the colonial Spanish elite but also, in turn, socially elevated the landowner class. By the close of the nineteenth century, political and intellectual life was dominated by wealthy landowners of distinguished Castilian ancestry.[12]

Rural development and economic expansion cannot, of course, be attributed to the activity of a small number of powerful investors. On the contrary, their commercial diversification opportunistically capitalised on, rather than contributed to, growing social, economic and political change in post-Independence Argentina. However, the legacy of an elite ruling colonial class, which underpinned the social and economic development of the formative nineteenth century republic, fostered – certainly in Buenos Aires Province – what one might almost term feudalistic overtones.[13] The prevalence of vast areas of land comprising only a limited number of estates was one of the most contentious aspects of rural Argentine society. Oligarchical structures and absentee landlordism ran contrary to the usual principles of rural development, which advocated smallholdings farmed by owner-occupiers.[14] Why this latter arrangement was not the case in Argentina will be discussed at length below, but the origins are to be found in the legacy of colonial rule and contemporary attitudes toward land.

Since the arrival of Spain in the sixteenth century the pampas grasslands had fostered wild cattle and free roaming horses.[15] Considered unsuitable for settlement by colonial powers, the region was instead exploited for its hides. Prior to 1750, hunting expeditions for feral cattle provided virtually the only hides for export.[16] Gauchos herded cattle without fences or boundaries and *estancias* developed across vast extensions of land that carried little economic value.[17] The Spanish Crown frequently awarded expansive areas of the pampas to colonists or military leaders, but the economy and social structure of Spanish society did not favour its full exploitation and settlement as a region, so the pampas remained virtually uninhabited.[18] Although heralding rural revolution, Independence in 1816 did little to address the structure of landownership.[19] The desirability of large holdings remained embedded in the Argentine psyche, with land itself functioning as an economic commodity from which to extract maximum short term return.[20] Smallholdings had little viability in coarse grass regions, or others with backward technology and poor transportation, and offered no defence against Indian assault. *Estancias* of hundreds or even thousands of square miles were established in areas that remained largely unpopulated and given over to sheep farming or cattle ranching.[21]

Bernardino Rivadavia's liberal unitarian administration in the 1820s was the first to make attempts at land reform, the precursors to later efforts by presidents Domingo Sarmiento and Nicolás Avellaneda. Rivadavia stressed the importance of populating rural society as a prerequisite to attaining economic expansion and social stability. Recognising the need to attract foreign labour and to facilitate broader access to land, Rivadavia introduced the Law of Emphyteusis.[22] Under its provisions, landownership remained in the hands of the state but large areas were distributed to natives and immigrants on the condition that an annual rent was paid.[23] Broadly, areas allotted varied between 150 and 300 km, with rent calculated at 8 per cent of land value.[24] In spite of its egalitarian intentions, the law fell victim to extensive abuse and manipulation. Speculators and prominent families attained areas of up to one million acres, in the process securing their economic and social ascendancy for posterity.[25] While the law undoubtedly increased available land within the frontier, the chief beneficiaries were not those intended.

Exploitation of the Law of Emphyteusis was further compounded during the regime of General Rosas. In contrast to his predecessor's liberal ideology, the federalist Rosas advocated provincial structures and championed the interests of the landed elite. His policies systematically nullified the effects of the law, frequently reallocating land that had been rented under its provisions.[26] In 1832, Rosas decreed that all tenants were to settle outstanding rents within three months. Unitarian supporters unable to abide by the diktat lost their holdings, while federalists were aided with grants. In addition, federalists who were economically solvent were permitted to buy their land on exceptionally easy terms.[27] In 1826, for example, the government granted a plot of one and a half leagues in Mercedes to Don Juan Bautista Rodriguez under the Law of Emphyteusis.[28] Over the next six years the tenancy of the land was transferred three times, finally being sold under Rosas' regime in 1832 to the then tenant, Tomás Aspreelu. Thirteen years later in 1845, the same plot of land was sold to an Irishman, Patrick Flemming.[29] Although records do not state the price paid by either Flemming or Aspreelu, the fact that the latter was allowed to purchase it in 1832 would indicate that he was a federalist supporter.

Rosas, like other post-Independence leaders, continued the Spanish colonial practice of awarding land to loyal military and political supporters in recognition of their services.[30] By 1840, over 20 million acres of Buenos Aires Province was in the possession of 293 people.[31] Rosas reallocated huge areas to soldiers, all but reversing Rivadavia's attempts at land reform.[32] By Rosas' fall in 1852, the hegemony of the landed oligarchy was established. Jonathan Brown has argued that the economic reality of large holdings was a prerequisite to pastoral expansion and that this, rather than any conscious preferential policy by government toward chosen individuals, was the dominant factor in creating such vast *estancias* in post-Independence Argentina.[33] Certainly, the tradition of awarding land was observed by leaders before and after Rosas, and cannot be solely attributed to the pro-*estanciero* policies of his regime. Equally, political instability and economic recession deterred many small investors from entering the land market in the early years of the republic.[34] However, the frequency and scale of appropriated land passing to private individuals; the wide scale sale of land at below market rates to political supporters; and the sustained obstruction by the landed elite to any real reform, challenges Brown's reading.

Roberto Cortés Conde, in his economic appraisal of Argentina from 1870 to 1914, recognised that, although extraordinary growth was achieved post 1870, the expansion of the sheep farming industry in the early to mid-nineteenth century contributed to the nation's export trade and economic prosperity.[35] Emerging in the 1820s, the export of unwashed wool became of major importance to the economy. By 1837 it represented 10.8 per cent of total exports, rising to 12.5 per cent in 1848 and reaching a peak of 33.7 per cent by 1859.[36] Despite the expansion of available land to accommodate the growing number of sheep, Cortés Conde argued that the pre-1870s' predominantly pastoral economy had vast regions of under-utilised land beyond the frontier line. The population was then relatively sparse, transport and railway networks inadequate, port facilities insufficient and capital scarce.[37]

A combination of factors was, therefore, responsible for the economic upturn post 1870s. The final offensive against the native Indian population, led by General Julio A. Roca in 1879–80, crucially secured territorial expansion on which the success of an agricultural economy was based.[38] Land opened up along the frontier, heralding the extension of the railroad network and facilitating growth in the agricultural sector. Livestock increased, with heads of cattle more than doubling from 13 million in 1875 to 31 million in 1913, and the number of sheep rising by 30 per cent to 80 million in the same period.[39] Not until the 1890s did crop farming become dominant, in particular the production of wheat, which emerged as a principal export of the Argentine economy. Economic success was dependent upon the concomitant expansion of the railway system and the resultant ease in goods transportation from outlying areas of the province.[40] Between 1870 and 1880 the laying of railway tracks doubled, further increasing to 9,254 km by 1890.[41] By the early twentieth century Argentina possessed the tenth largest railway network in the world, the greater part of which was British owned.[42] Arable land under wheat production simultaneously increased from 73,000 ha in 1872 to 4,903,000 ha in 1904.[43] Chief export markets were Brazil, Germany and Great Britain.[44]

Following the unprecedented growth in immigrant population post 1870s, President Avellaneda drafted what he considered to be the first comprehensive land law.[45] Land was to be divided into areas of 100,000 acres and further subdivided into plots of 250 acres. The first 100 lots in any given area were to be awarded free of charge to immigrants, with the remainder sold to individuals at a maximum of four lots per person.[46] Once again, loopholes designed to facilitate private colonising companies were exploited, and much of the land disappeared into the hands of developers and large landholders.[47]

The effective expansion of the national terrain following Roca's successful Indian campaign led to a swift turnover of public land to private ownership as a means of increasing government income.[48] Controversially, many landowners who benefited most from the transaction abandoned expansive rural interests to reside in the city. They passively retained holdings and patiently awaited optimum

returns. Such endurance was rewarded over time as the government removed the Indian threat; the British provided access and
transportation; the Irish built up their pastoral stock; and the
Italians harvested their crops.[49] In addition, land and stock values
soared further, impeding the small investor.[50]

The ills of absentee landlordism perhaps appear less stark when
viewed against commercial considerations. Although much of the
day-to-day running of the large *estancia* was left to the resident
manager or foreman, profitable business affairs required a regular
city presence. Ranchers, merchants and factory owners dealt directly
to facilitate exports and delivery of livestock. Thus, the economic
viability of the *estancia* depended upon strong commercial networks.[51] Many of the larger *estancia* owners had diversified their
interests in order to maximise profits, operating as merchants and
warehouse proprietors in the city.[52] Notwithstanding these business
considerations, there were undoubted social advantages for the
elite landowner and his family in residing in the sophisticated
ambiance of Buenos Aires City rather than the rural backwater of
the *campo*.[53] Furthermore, to suggest that all landowners were
absent for such commercially pragmatic reasons would be an over-
statement. Many were content to profit from the labours of their
tenants in the short term, whilst in the long term they could realise
the capital growth of their investment.[54]

In 1862 the United States Congress passed the Homestead Act, building on parallel legislation running back to the Land Ordinance of 1785
and Harrison's Act of 1800, distributing the national domain.
Following Independence in 1776, the US government ceased the practice of awarding free land grants to settlers. As the value of land
increased and rising numbers of immigrant farmers headed west, lob-
byists argued that Congress should award land to settlers as recompense for the harsh conditions of the wilderness. But it was not until
the 1830s that any concerted drive toward establishing land legislation
occurred as Eastern labourers and reformers in the more general
sense joined western farmers in pressing for a homestead act. But it
was not without its opponents. Bills introduced in 1846 and 1852
failed, largely as a result of opposition from Eastern employers and
landowners, who feared either an exodus of low paid labour to farm
in the West, or were threatened by the devaluation of land. In addition, Southern slaveholders viewed such legislation as antislavery
and so equally opposed it.

Nevertheless, following the secession of the South in 1861 the Homestead Act was passed. The new legislation was designed to tackle the contentious disposition of public lands now opening up on the more western prairies and the high plains by facilitating landownership for the growing immigrant community.[55] In turn, it was hoped that owner-occupiers would populate the vast areas of deserted terrain. Under its provisions, all applicant citizens or immigrants who could demonstrate a genuine intention of farming and some capacity for it were granted 160 acres for the insignificant cost of title registration. This revolutionary redistribution of public wealth into private ownership consolidated and extended a nation of small landowners – which was not matched in Argentina. Yet railroads and land companies did corner vast amounts of US public land under special provisions or by various loopholes.

While the US legislation was generally admired and acknowledged to have fashioned a prosperous and democratic society, implementing comparable land reform in Argentina was widely opposed.[56] Large *estancia* owners did not regard the settlement of small owners as overtly beneficial to their personal interests, viewing agriculture as secondary and subsidiary to pastoral farming.[57] A combination of political corruption, large landowner lobbying and borrowing difficulties for small investors ensured that the primary beneficiaries of future Argentine land legislation would be the already landed elite.[58] When in 1884 a version of the 'Homestead Act' was finally approved, it decreed that land was to be allocated in holdings of 1,500 acres in the marginal areas of the Patagonian south, here paralleling the timber land and 'dry lands' provisions of the US acts of 1877 and 1888. Not only was land here of lowgrade farming and pasture quality, but the size of holdings allocated was insufficient to support sheep or cattle grazing.[59]

As a consequence of sustained land appropriation, by the close of the century central government was no longer an owner of land in the agricultural zone. Any assistance that may previously have been offered to immigrants was now beyond the reach of the national authorities.[60] Official government land policy and legislation had repeatedly failed to assist the small farmer, who was, to a large extent, excluded from any 'first entry' ownership of this component of the country's basic wealth.[61] Later operations of the land market were another matter. As a contemporary report commented, the land market itself was extremely fluid and open to competition, in spite of financial difficulties facing would-be lesser owners:

> The Argentine landowner has no feudatory traditions to live up to, neither
> is he troubled with questions of entail, primogeniture, and other inheri-
> tances of a classic past; he regards his property from a business standpoint.[62]

While it may be true that superficial barriers to entry were of an
economic rather than a hereditary nature, the dominance of a small
number of landowners whose social position depended upon their
landed status, precluded accession to many small investors for reasons other than financial. The cachet attributed to large scale
landownership within the broader domain of Argentine political
and social circles augmented the obvious and immediate economic
advantages. Relinquishing such an asset was an unattractive proposition, both economically and socially. European labour was viewed
essentially in terms of manpower – of a subordinate social class –
whose function was to manage the interests of the landholder.[63]
Thus, the prospect of a landowning European farming population
threatened some Argentine concerns. At the close of the century,
this conflict of interest would instigate a heated national debate in
relation to the societal position and contribution of foreigners,
which will be discussed in Chapter 6 below. In many regions, a
socially mobile immigrant community was neither desired nor facilitated by the native landowning elite.[64] Consequently, the small
farmer was doubly disadvantaged in his attempts to secure a
foothold in much of what was an already zealously monopolised
pampean zone.[65]

The thesis that landownership lay beyond the grasp of the vast
majority employed as peon, share-cropper, tenant farmer or tiller of
land, is overly simplistic, however.[66] Tenancy terms became extremely fluid and competitive as the century progressed, leading in many
cases to accumulated wealth by both tenant and landowner.[67]
Furthermore, commodity production by tenants or *arrendatorios*
(although not by share-croppers or *medieros*) yielded a higher return
than that by owners because incentives, scale and intensity were all
usually greater.[68] Far from hindering land purchase, in many cases
tenancy facilitated its eventual realisation as capital was amassed
and transferred into ownership.[69] Immigrants arriving in the closing
decades of the nineteenth century were fully cognisant of the land
tenure system and the potential exclusion from ownership it
fostered. One might expect the Irish, especially those of midland
background, to accept such terms of contract, given their traditions.
That few perhaps did so may indicate that attitudes were changing
amongst them, in Argentina for reasons of social ambition, in

Ireland due to increasing estrangement from landlords by the 1880s, and in both from the drive to secure less dependent status and incomes. Instead of acting as a deterrent to settlement this system at times complemented the immigrants' long term goals. Many Europeans approached their rural labours in Argentina as a means of financial accumulation rather than a putting down of roots. Post 1890s, for example, cheap steerage passage between Argentina and Italy facilitated seasonal migration of Italian labour to take advantage of dual harvests.[70] Many chose to work the land only as a means either to move to the city or to return to Europe.[71] This short term financially-motivated strategy created a series of social issues and conflicts between native and immigrant communities, which, again, will be addressed in Chapter 6. Nonetheless, in relation to land, tenancy agreements facilitated the movement of labour between markets in a way that ownership prohibited.

If the land system did not entirely disadvantage the immigrant tenant farmer, therefore, and equally provided financial benefits for the landowner, any detrimental effects of sustained short term plundering were felt in the fabric of rural society itself.[72] Transient settlement and the maximisation of returns led to extensive soil abuse: overcultivation, low yields, increasingly short tenancy agreements and sparse rural population created an exploited rural environment.[73] Social and cultural associations were rare amongst later arrivals, many of whom had no permanent dwellings.[74] The tenancy system thus fostered a disparate, nomadic environment in which a vibrant rural community could not flourish.[75] Nevertheless, critics of its structure acknowledge that, although deficient in just and practicable social provision, it supported an effective and competitive export market, which underpinned economic performance in the nineteenth-century republic.[76]

By the late 1870s, the rapid expansion of agriculture, and in particular wheat production, altered the rural landscape.[77] Argentina, an importer of wheat since colonial times, was now not only satisfying domestic consumer demand but also providing a surplus for exports.[78] The development of the sector was closely related to the arrival of the railway and the subsequent colonisation of Santa Fe Province. The completion of track between Rosario and Cordoba in 1870 opened up agricultural land in the province, which had previously been isolated from the urban centre of Buenos Aires.[79] As in the United States, huge areas of land on either side of the track were auctioned off to railway companies as an enticement for further rail expansion.[80]

Land was awarded to the Central Argentine Land Company, a subsidiary of an English contractor, which in turn created colonies of
Italian and Swiss immigrants by either renting or selling portions of
the land.[81] Private companies and individual landowners quickly
emulated the success of the Central Argentine Land Company's
colonisation foray. Since poor grazing had restricted the growth of
sheep farming and cattle ranching in the province, landowners
increasingly encouraged immigrants to buy or rent plots for wheat
production.[82] Many subdivisions returned three to four times their
value and colonists were able to capitalise on the growing demand.
In addition, transportation costs had eased substantially as the railroad facilitated movement of produce to the port of Buenos Aires.[83]

Unlike in Santa Fe Province, where the principle of colonisation
had, to a large extent, successfully taken root, in Buenos Aires
Province the agriculturalist continued to be viewed in purely labour
terms.[84] By the 1880s, land value was estimated as four times that of
Santa Fe and *porteños* (inhabitants of Buenos Aires Province) were
less willing to subdivide their property, at least at prices newly
arrived immigrants could afford.[85] The three factors that had facilitated immigrants acquiring land in Santa Fe – defeat of the Indian,
arrival of the railroad and the emergence of a mixed economy –
had, in equal measure, excluded them from obtaining a foothold in
the increasingly valued land of the littoral. Here, the immigrant was
consigned to life as a tenant farmer, whose agricultural exploits provided diversified income for the pastoral landowner.[86]

Labour was used to open up new land and plant new crops, crucially breaking up the soil and replacing the coarse pampas grass
with necessary forage for livestock. Alfalfa in particular was produced as cattle fodder. *Estancieros,* reluctant to embark on the costly
planting of the crop, were happy to lease land on a three year term
to agricultural labour on the understanding that it would be left
sown with alfalfa.[87] But since wheat was usually tenants' crop of
choice to ready the land for alfalfa, they too benefited from this
arrangement. Between 1890 and 1915, the area under crop
increased from 400,000 to 6.7 million ha.[88] Such rapid expansion
facilitated further growth in cattle ranching and, by 1925, meat
exports, including beef, accounted for 24 per cent of the value of
commodity exports in gold pesos, and 34 per cent when hides and
skins, with lesser diary products, were added.[89] In contrast, wool,
which in 1875 had accounted for approximately half of all exports,
had now fallen to 18 per cent.[90] The stranglehold on land by a rela-

tively small number of owners in Buenos Aires Province resulted in increased tenancy.[91] Although providing a living for himself and his family, the tenant farmer had little economic, social or geographical consistency.[92]

In other areas, notably the drier western pampas, permanent or periodic concentration upon wheat made better economic sense. In spite of the potentially more attractive conditions in Santa Fe, numbers of actual farmers working their own land were low in both provinces. Statistics recorded at the turn of the century stated that, of the 11,500 wheat farms in Santa Fe and 8,000 in Buenos Aires, only 39 per cent were owned by the cultivator, with share-croppers or tenant farmers working the rest.[93] These figures were to further decline over the first decade of the twentieth century as steadily increasing land prices entrenched the tenant farming system.[94] In his appraisal of the 1914 census, Díaz Alejandro identified differentials between the nationality of stockowners and lessees of agricultural holdings. He concluded that sheep and cattle were predominantly managed by Argentine ranchers; cereal and linseed farming was mainly immigrant based. And immigrant participation in the agriculture sector was above the average representation in the total labour force.[95] This would certainly be in keeping with the thesis that immigrants, excluded from landownership or with holdings insufficient in size to support livestock, diversified into the agricultural sector. In the rich pampean zone, *estancias* of more than 10,000 ha, of which there were 584, covered nearly one fifth of the total region.[96]

The 1914 census recorded that the largest holdings were predominantly given over to livestock, with smaller concerns producing cereal and linseed.[97] When examined across the pampean provinces the pattern was repeated. The proportion of holdings in excess of 1,250 ha devoted to livestock was consistently higher than that given to agriculture, accounting for 56 and 2.6 per cent respectively.[98] Further examination of the proportion of stockowners who were also the landowner revealed that 44 per cent were owner-operators, whilst in the lucrative pampean zone this had fallen to 33 per cent. Of the total Argentine stockholders, 61 per cent owned their holding, falling to 47 per cent in the pampean zone; compared with 32 per cent of foreign born stockholders, 27 per cent in pampean provinces.[99] This analysis demonstrates not only that immigrants were disadvantaged in acquiring land, but also that in the pampean zone, where large estates dominated, absenteeism was more common among Argentine landowners than elsewhere. Also, the high percentage of estates managed by the foreign born, probably on short term tenancy agreements, reinforced the weakness of rural society. By the early twentieth century, many of the large estates were broken up and sold, not to farming tenants, but to investors and speculators.[100]

Irish migration to Argentina distinguished itself from other European migration because of its dominant position in the agrarian sector.[101] In contrast to *'Inglés'* immigrants, who became urbanised, contemporary commentators reported that it was the Irish who capitalised on the expanding sheep farming industry.[102] Table 12 in the previous chapter supports this thesis, particularly with regard to the 1869 census, where 66 per cent of recorded Irish occupations were accounted for by 'farm hand', 'shepherd' or 'landowner'.[103] Nevertheless, their position as controlling partner within the sheep farming sector is challenged by contemporary reports of Scottish and Basque representation. Following the collapse of the Montegrande colony, some Scottish immigrants did move south to establish rural colonies in Quilmes, San Vicente and Chascomús, although they were just as likely to diversify into cattle ranching, with many earning the title 'cattle baron'.[104] The majority of these colonists moved into the city, where they interspersed with the resident urban 'British' community.[105] Indeed, Murray's description of English and Scottish immigrants as almost 'wholly engaged in commerce' is largely substantiated by official *'Inglés'* data, which recorded the urban nature of arriving immigrants.[106] Conversely, it was reported that 'the number of Irish residents in the city hardly [reached] 200 persons'.[107] This contemporary observation, although not providing conclusive evidence of Irish sheep farming as such, is significant in that it reinforces the extent of Irish rural settlement. If accurate, Irish immigration to Argentina, unlike other nineteenth-century destinations, was uncharacteristically and overwhelmingly 'tilted' to a rural existence.

In relation to sheep farming, the assorted occupational representation of Scottish immigrants, not only between urban and rural but also within the rural sector itself, diminishes the Scottish position. Moreover, where Scottish sheep farming was prevalent, such as in the isolated southern regions of Patagonia,[108] the distance from the Buenos Aires market impeded their ability to compete with Irish *estancias*, the majority of which were advantageously situated on

the rich pasture land of Buenos Aires Province. Although, as transportation networks improved, meat and wool were exported from
Patagonia, in the decades prior to the 1880s much of the produce
satisfied a local market.[109] Similarly, Basque sheep farming has been
likened in notoriety to that of the Irish.[110] As with the Scottish, however, diversification into urban sectors diluted Basque concentration
within rural industries. In addition, since the embargo on Spanish
immigration in the immediate aftermath of the revolution had
restricted Basque settlement, early domination of the sheep farming
sector belonged to the Irish.[111] From this stronghold, both in terms
of land, stock and capital accumulation, the Irish became unassail-
able. Although both Scottish and Basque groups were clearly represented, principal governance was Irish.

By the 1840s, the sheep farming industry underpinned the
nation's export market.[112] In 1875, Argentina had 13 million cattle
(against 35 million in the United States) but 57 million sheep
(against 37 million). By 1895 it had 22 million cattle and, by 1920, 27
million, whereas its sheep numbers had peaked and then declined,
from 74 million in 1895 to 45 million in 1920. The United States had
more than double Argentina's cattle numbers in both 1895 and 1920,
but considerably fewer sheep in both years, and its livestock populations were indeed relatively *much* less when comparative acreages
are considered. In Australia, there were just over 100 million sheep
in 1895, also the peak (until 1926), and 26 million cattle the same
year; like Argentina, Australia too, from the depression of the 1890s,
multiplied what was a counter speciality. In short, all three countries were competitively driven by international markets.[113]
Although one of the chief beneficiaries of the sheep industry's
expansion, the Irish farmer was rarely in a position to acquire land
on arrival; ownership was often the result of many years' labour.[114]
Michael Hanley was described in 1853 as a 'prosperous [Irish] man;
possessor of a splendid sheep farm with a good house, surrounded
by plantations'.[115] However, his holding was acquired only after fifteen years of enduring the harsh and nomadic working conditions
of a shepherd on the Argentine *campo*.[116] It was the promise of future
prosperity, no matter how distant, that encouraged arriving Irish
immigrants to invest what little financial means they had in obtaining an entry level stake in the sheep farming sector.[117] Even holders
of extensive land did not become so overnight, and many began by
managing the *estancias* of others or, on rare occasions, by working
within the commercial centres of Buenos Aires.

Peter Sheridan from County Cavan, for example, had arrived in Argentina in 1817.[118] The commercial success of his mercantile ventures in the city had permitted diversification of capital into land.[119] In the mid-1820s, Sheridan bought 100 Merino sheep imported by the government.[120] Through cross-breeding he greatly improved the quality of the Argentine stock, and at the time of his death in 1844 Sheridan owned a flock in excess of 40,000, as well as sixteen *puestos* or small farms.[121] Sheep farming success was augmented by a thriving import-export enterprise, which Sheridan conducted with his brother, as well as operating a *saladera*, or beef salting and curing plant, in the city.[122]

Not all Irish immigrants were landowners on the scale of Sheridan, and in this regard the Irish experience in Argentina has been greatly exaggerated: the majority were employed as labour on the *estancias* of others. Such was their growing reputation within the sheep farming sector, however, that employment was not found exclusively with Irish landowners. Many Argentine land and stockholders preferred the Irish shepherd to his native counterpart.[123] It was a preference that did not go unnoticed by native labour. In 1852, a petition to the House of Representatives stated the injustice of landholders' bias towards 'European shepherds' and their predilection for 'strangers over native fellow countrymen'. In particular, the Irish were identified as being 'yesterday in rags and tatters, today property owners'.[124] Although an exaggeration, this anecdotal impression reflects the image of the Irish within the sector. Certainly, for Irish immigrants the path to landownership was to be found largely, although not exclusively, in sheep farming.[125] As Table 12 in the previous chapter demonstrated, 15.5 per cent of Irish immigrants in 1869 describe themselves as 'landowner', increasing to 24.7 per cent by 1895.[126]

Attempts at establishing a foothold within the sector were made, in the first instance, as a wage labourer. The hired party was given responsibility for a flock of sheep – up to 2,000 heads – in return for receiving either a monthly salary, or part thereof, coupled with subsistence.[127] Between 1820 and 1840, the exceptional growth in the sheep farming industry ensured that labourers received handsome recompense for their toil, in turn accumulating significant capital.[128] As a sector, however, it was highly susceptible to natural disasters such as drought or disease. Contemporary commentators reported overnight losses of up to 'one million sheep' following the cholera outbreak of 1869, during which time the price of wool plummeted to 'half its former price so that a large number of our poor country-men [were] reduced to poverty'.[129]

Nevertheless, the dominance of the large estate, and the prosperity it potentially afforded, continued to foster a rootless and itinerant labour force.[130] The added dimension of seasonal labour further entrenched this phenomenon as a stream of temporary workers, initially from Uruguay and Paraguay, but also from Italy toward the close of the century, destabilised the rural landscape.[131] Despite occasional Italian colonies, notably around Santa Fe and in Entre Rios, the social vigour and combined economic force infused by the group co-operative, so effective for European farmers in the Canadian prairies, did not take root amongst the disparate workforce of Argentina.[132] Success or failure was arrived at individually, with little attempt to harness the economic potential that a collective agrarian movement could imbue. Irish immigrants did benefit from an information network, instigated largely through the Church, which assisted in establishing rural contacts.[133] However, this did not extend to functioning as an economic *tour de force*, and it remained incumbent upon the individual to establish terms for his labour and his yield. Once these were agreed, the shepherd would then tend his flock in complete isolation across the pampas, often going weeks or even months without human contact.[134]

The preferred mode of operation for Irish immigrants was a form of share-cropping applied to herding. This type of contractual agreement was embarked upon either directly or after a period employed as a wage labourer. In effect, 'share-cropping' resembled the terms of the *mediero* or true share-cropper, who received seed, implements, land, often a cabin, and even subsistence to get started, and in return halved his harvest with his patron or landlord. Known as *mediería* or 'halves', this form of sheep farming was usually negotiated over a three or five year period.[135] In the closing decades of the century, as land values increased, share-cropping terms progressively favoured the landowner, reducing the shepherd's share to *tercería* or *cuartería*.[136] Edward Quinn from Westmeath, for example, in 1870 migrated to Argentina, where he commenced work as a *peon* in San Pedro on the *estancia* of John Harrington. After two years he entered into a *tercería* agreement for a three year period with Michael Doherty. At the end of the term, and presumably with an increased amount of capital, Quinn negotiated a new contract, of *mediería*, with Señor Achaval.[137]

Quinn's case substantiates Korol and Sábato's assertion that capital accumulation for immigrants arriving in later decades was more difficult, as terms were more competitively negotiated on the part of the landowner. It had taken him five years of hard toil to negotiate a contract of *mediería*, previously available to immigrants on arrival. Furthermore, although Quinn's initial foothold within the sector was secured through Irish networks, his contract reflected prevailing market conditions; his employment not subject to preferential terms as a consequence of his ethnicity. In this regard, Irish landowners functioned on a strictly commercial basis. In a letter written in 1900 by Laurence Gahan, an Irish *estanciero* from Navarro who had inherited his holding, he chastised other Irish *estancieros* for their unjust treatment of the labouring classes employed on Irish owned estates:

> The treatment the unfortunate *peon* or *puestero* gets at the hands of most of our *estancieros*, is, to say the least, cruel and not in keeping with the way their fathers treated their men, lots of which through hard, but better paid work, in their turn, became masters and owners of the same places in which, now, the descendants pay at the lowest wages their poor *peons* will live for.[138]

Gahan went on to state that, were it not for the luxury of inheritance, the current owners would themselves be *'puesteros* as their fathers and grandfathers were'. His own father, Thomas Gahan, had arrived in Argentina in the 1840s and had fully availed himself of the advantages early immigrants enjoyed in acquiring land at affordable prices. On his death in 1890, aged 80, he was described as an 'owner of most extensive property', who was a 'noble type of that generation of Irishmen' and regarded by 'those who lived and worked on his *estancia* as always kind and generous – a man to whom rich and poor safely confided their best interests'.[139] Some ten years later, his son concluded his letter with the stark summation that 'money saved from wages from the poor cannot bring much luck.'[140]

It is perhaps significant, therefore, that in negotiating the more favourable contract terms of *mediería* Quinn operated outside his own community, indicating the limitations of Irish networks and the marketability of Irish shepherds. Alternative and more complex negotiations could take place where the potential shepherd had sufficient means to invest a small amount of capital to cover overhead costs.[141] Such terms would often include the provision of a portion of the flock itself. Here, the share-cropper in effect became a minority partner in the enterprise.[142] Although facilitating more rapid progression, this was open only to those with sufficient resources to take advantage of it, often only achieved after many years of working on less attractive terms.

In spite of its drawbacks, the sheep farming system enabled those without land to make a substantial living and in some cases led to eventual landownership. Korol and Sábato's 1981 study of Irish sheep farming examined twenty *partidos* where Irish immigrants had bought land. They calculated that on average 17.34 per cent of land in each *partido* belonged to Irish families, rising to 25 per cent in certain districts.[143] Between 1860 and 1875 Irish land purchase was conducted largely through private sale; however, immigrants who had bought prior to this had, in general, arrived before 1840 and purchased land from the state.[144] Many such owners had accumulated handsome fortunes through state-sponsored transactions. In spite of legislative attempts to restrict further acquisition, it would seem that several prominent Irish landholders continued to purchase state land well into the 1870s and 1880s.

Eduardo Casey was one such landowner: he purchased 300,000 ha of state owned land in the *partido* of Tres Arroyos in 1881.[145] Casey made a down payment of 600,000 pesos, which was to be followed by a further eight payments of 675,000 pesos over forty-two months. Similarly, albeit on a smaller scale, George Keen bought one square league of public land in the *partido* of Juarez in 1879, paying 60,000 pesos.[146] Both Casey and Keen were already part of the landowning class and their transactions, like so many others of this nature, were conducted in the period following Avellaneda's attempted land reform. Their successful purchase of state owned land not only demonstrates the ease with which those wishing to take advantage of its loopholes circumvented the law, but also that Irish landholders, like the natives, were fully *au fait* with exploitative land acquisition measures.

Increased land values dictated that the Irish community went west of Buenos Aires to areas such as Lobos, Navarro, Mercedes and Arrecifes in search of affordable holdings.[147] Land in Arrecifes, situated in the rich pampean zone, suited pastoral farming and it is estimated that 60 per cent of Irish owned estates in the area were in excess of 1,000 ha.[148] Patrick Ham and Edward Cavanagh, for example, both owned *estancias* in Arrecifes of more than 5,000 ha.[149] Ham was the son of Peter Ham, who was born in Ireland in 1813 and had emigrated to Argentina in 1842.[150] On his death, a newspaper tribute estimated an amassed fortune of 'eighteen million, currency'.[151] His son Patrick was born in Buenos Aires in 1852 and was one of eight children. He inherited much of his wealth, including a *graseria* (plant where animals such as horses were rendered into grease).[152] The Ham family owned substantial holdings in several *partidos* as well as operating successful commercial enterprises in the city of Buenos Aires, advertising their services as wool and produce brokers.[153]

Like the Ham family, affluent Irish migrants accumulated land in a variety of *partidos* and, in so doing, elevated themselves socially within Argentine society. Peter Casey had arrived in Argentina from Westmeath c. 1830 and entered the sheep farming business. His success was rapid and he was reportedly the first *estanciero* to pay one million pesos for a league of land.[154] His son Eduardo was born in Buenos Aires in 1847 and followed in his father's footsteps. In addition to his rural investments, in 1882 Eduardo became a founder member and vice president of the illustrious Jockey Club.[155] The president of the club was the future vice president of the republic, Carlos Pelligrini.[156] Casey had successfully risen to the highest echelons of society, but many of those who did not soar to such celebrated positions were still owners of extensive landed interests. In the 1901 *Plano Catastral*, names consistently appeared across various *partidos*. The Duggan family had holdings in Colón, San Antonio de Areco, Chacabuco and Salto; the Gahans in Lobos and Navarro; the Cavanaghs in General Lopez and Arrecifes; and the Hams in Salto, Las Heras and Lincoln.[157] In many cases more than one plot of land was owned in a *partido*, or a second in close proximity in an adjoining *partido*. This would indicate a desire, where possible, to consolidate holdings given the huge expanse of the Argentine landscape and the distances entailed in travelling between regions. Amongst the elite classes, land was bought and sold readily, often as a means of releasing capital. In 1885, Francisco Molina sold an area of 632 ha to Julian Mullen.[158] The Irishman's plot was surrounded on all sides by Molina land, indicating a partial sale. In 1873, Adelina Zapiola sold approximately 762 ha of the Zapiola holding to Michael Wade, effectively halving the plot.[159] Similarly, the MacDonagh estate of 1,300 acres was divided in the 'testimony of land division' between three children but, in addition, a plot of 250 ha was allocated for sale.[160] This deliberate reservation of a small, but not insignificant, portion of the estate for public sale is evidence that, as with the native landholder, Irish estates were in the market of realising the value of land for sale.

The discrepancy between land records that verify Irish land purchase, and landholders' names appearing in the 1901 *Plano Catastral*, underlines the buying and selling of holdings. In 1883

Laurence Quinn purchased 674 ha in Arrecifes, but his name did not appear on the 1901 *Plano Catastral*.[161] The erratic nature of land documentation in Argentina does not permit further investigation into the sale of this plot. Increasing land values, however, did not attract short term speculation and, once acquired, land was retained and expanded where possible. Sale of a complete holding was more likely to represent a geographical relocation than an end of ownership. It is likely, therefore, that Quinn sold in Arrecifes only to buy elsewhere, perhaps expanding his holding in another *partido*. Korol and Sábato's examination of official land data concluded that, in 1890, twenty holdings in Arrecifes were Irish owned.[162] This calculation is inconsistent with the 1901 *Plano Catastral*, which recorded a total of seventy-eight holdings, thirteen of which were Irish owned.[163] Even allowing for discrepancies in data between the two sources, the reduced number of Irish owned holdings would suggest that, as in North America, once departed from the homeland Irish immigrants in Argentina followed the practices of native society in relation to land transactions. Land was thus accumulated as capital, to be bought and sold as relevant commercial interests dictated; its purchase was not a static investment.

In spite of the difficulty later immigrants faced in affording land purchase, issues of primogeniture did not overly encumber the commercially mobile market. In describing it as 'mobile', however, a potentially misleading delineation is implied. The majority of landholders did not sell land outright and move off; they retained it. Large landowners in the main consolidated their holdings by further acquisition, often by selling concerns in one *partido* and purchasing in the next; or by releasing sections of the estate for sale, not its entirety. The resulting market mobility is best seen, therefore, as a symptom of property accumulation rather than as a readily available investment opportunity. The MacDonagh estate, in selling a small portion, is representative of a landed class that retained its investment. Similarly, a rectangular portion of Patrick Ham's estate in Las Heras was sold to the Garrahan family.[164] In 1868, Casey sold 783 ha of his land in Arrecifes to Amalia Francisco and a further 763 ha was sold to Victoria Zapiola in 1876. As discussed above, Zapiola had previously sold land to the Irishman Wade. Both Casey and Zapiola had holdings elsewhere, with Casey in particular being the owner of extensive landed interests. Selling these relatively small plots was almost certainly an exercise in capital release, and would not have reduced the overall value of the estate.

Although land transactions were relatively fluid, therefore the nature of the market was such as to exclude the small investor. It functioned only for those who had sufficient capital to take advantage of it – namely the already landed *estancieros*. Across the twenty *partidos* examined by Korol and Sábato, for example, three hundred Irish families owned 610,415 ha.[165] Since for many Irish immigrants acquiring land remained permanently out of their financial reach, an exclusive market developed within the landed class, which was not driven by ethnic allegiance. Land transactions were open to all within the socio-economic class of landowner. While there are clear examples of Irish landholders selling estates or portions thereof to other Irish landowners, ethnicity was not a criterion of sale.[166] The frequency of land trading across ethnic divides, and the regularity of names appearing on the *Plano Catastral*, would indicate that an elite social group controlled the buying and selling of land, and that transactions were driven by economics rather than ethnicity.

Landownership in Argentina did not only function as an indicator of economic wealth, but carried the broader connotation of high social status. This influential and self-perpetuating sector jealousy protected its interests and, in the process, thwarted the aspirations of the labouring classes. Thomas Garrahan, a tenant farmer in the 1870s, recorded his dealings with the Ham family.[167] In 1875, poor business management had led Garrahan to owe a substantial amount of money to the Hams. He entered into an agreement whereby he would purchase sheep on their behalf for a payment of 3 pesos per head. He would not collect any monies, however, until his debt had been fully repaid. Garrahan delivered approximately 43,000 sheep to a variety of Ham holdings across Buenos Aires Province, incurring substantial expense in the process. At the end of the season, Ham refused to pay the agreed 3 pesos per sheep, instead offering 1 peso. Garrahan instigated a lawsuit, which was to last three years and from which he emerged empty handed.[168] It would seem, therefore, that the Irish did not behave as a distinct ethnic group in matters of commercial dealings. Some evidence thus suggests instead that, as amongst native landowners and their dependents, a clear social divide emerged between Irish *estancieros* and other owners, and the tenants, shepherds, agents and drovers they dealt with. These relationships were not necessarily subject to the rules of engagement afforded to fellow members of their own class.

The structure of the Argentine agrarian market in the nineteenth century was fundamentally based on the pre-eminence of the large *estancia*. Spanish colonial legacies and the failure of successive post-Independence administrations to implement reform consigned the rural landscape to its oligarchical fate. An expanding international export market, underpinned by sheep farming and cattle ranching, rapidly increased the value of land and, in turn, facilitated the expansion and entrenchment of the tenancy system. In the midst of this, the Irish were advantageously positioned to profit from the evolving economic revolution. Their dominance of a sector that lay at the heart of the republic's transformation facilitated rapid economic progression. Furthermore, their own acquisition of land fortuitously coincided with the social phenomenon of its increasing desirability in the eyes of an elite Argentine class.

In this way, a sizeable proportion of the Irish community joined the ranks of the privileged landholders. For the labouring classes, however, access to land ownership became increasingly difficult from the 1870s onwards, not only as a consequence of economic barriers but also because of the increasing reluctance of landowners to relinquish assets. Maintaining clear divides between the social strata was fundamental to the landholders' interests, as was the continuance of an inverted rural structure whereby the majority stake was owned and controlled by the few. Their marked and deliberate opposition to successive legislative attempts at reform compounded the small investors' plight. Although the agricultural expansion in Santa Fe Province did provide land opportunities for immigrant labour, land transactions within the rich pampean zone often amounted to little more than a redistribution of holdings between members of an exclusive landed club.

This behaviour ran counter to the moral and cultural pretensions of the Irish community in Argentina and elsewhere. And this contradiction highlights the Irish immigrants' peculiar connection with a central institution that everywhere sought to impose on them religious and moral conformity: the Catholic Church, to whose relationship with the Irish community this study now turns.

NOTES

1. James R. Scobie *Argentina: A City and a Nation* (2nd ed., New York, 1971), p. 13. This estimate is close to the proud description in the introductory section of Thomas Murray, *The Irish in Argentina* (New York, 1919).
2. George Pendle, *Argentina* (3rd ed., Oxford, 1963), pp. 1–10.
3. Scobie (1971), p. 13.

4. Domingo Faustino Sarmiento, *Facundo: Civilización y barbarie* (2nd ed., Madrid, 1993), p. 60
5. Ibid., p. 57.
6. Scobie (1971), p. 23.
7. Carlos F. Díaz Alejandro, *Essays on the Economic History of the Argentine Republic* (New Haven & London, 1970), p. 35.
8. Tulio Halperín-Donghi, *Historia contemporánea de America Latina*, (5th ed., Madrid, 2004), p. 40.
9. Susan Midgen Socolow, 'Economic Activities of the Porteño Merchants: The Viceregal Period' in *The Hispanic American Historical Review*, vol. 55, no. 1 (1975), pp. 1–24, esp. p. 16
10. Until the closing decades of the eighteenth century Buenos Aires had been forbidden by the Spanish Crown to enter directly into trading markets, in order to protect the ascendancy of Lima. See Socolow (1975), p. 1.
11. John Lynch, Roberto Cortés Conde, Ezequiel Gallo, David Rock, Juan Carlos Torre y Liliana de Riz, *Historia de la Argentina* (Barcelona, 2001), p. 9.
12. Carl Solberg, 'Immigration and Urban Social Problems in Argentina and Chile, 1890–1914' in *Hispanic American Historical Review*, vol. 49, no. 2 (1969), pp. 215–232, esp. p. 218.
13. Díaz Alejandro (1970), p. 150.
14. See Scobie (1975), ch. VIII.
15. The horse was not indigenous to the continent of Latin America but was introduced by the arrival of the *conquistadors*. See James R. Scobie, *Revolution on the Pampas: A Social History of Argentine Wheat* (Austin, 1967), p. 12.
16. Díaz Alejandro (1970), p. 148.
17. Scobie (1967), p. 12.
18. María Sáenz Quesada, *La Argentina: Historia del país y de su gente* (3rd ed., Buenos Aires, 2004), p. 82.
19. For a discussion of the various stages of Independence from its declaration in 1810 see Scobie (1971), p. 88.
20. Scobie (1967), p. 31.
21. Juan Carlos Korol and Hilda Sábato, *Cómo fue la inmigración irlandesa en Argentina* (Buenos Aires, 1981), pp. 69–70.
22. Lynch et al. (2001), p. 10.
23. Jonathan C. Brown, *A Socioeconomic History of Argentina, 1776–1860* (Cambridge, 1979), p. 149.
24. A.F. Zimmerman, 'The Land of Argentina: With Particular Reference to the Conquest of the Southern Pampas' in *The Hispanic American Historical Review*, vol. 25, no. 1 (1945), pp. 3–26, esp. p. 11.
25. Ibid.
26. See Arturo Enrique Sampay, *Las ideas políticas de Juan Manuel de Rosas* (Buenos Aires, 1970), p. 58.
27. Eduardo Galeano, *Las venas abiertas de America Latina* (Madrid, 2003), pp. 237–244.
28. Approximately 9,000 acres
29. *Dirección de geodesia catastro y mapa de la Provincia de Buenos Aires*: Mercedes, no. 39.
30. Andrés M. Carretero, *El pensamiento politico de Juan Manuel de Rosas* (Buenos Aires, 1970), p. 127.
31. John Lynch, 'The River Plate Republics from Independence to the Paraguayan War' in Leslie Bethell (ed.), *The Cambridge History of Latin America*, vol. III (Cambridge, 1985), pp. 615–676.
32. Lynch et al. (2001), p. 11.
33. Brown (1979), p. 150.
34. Lynch (1985), p. 618.
35. Roberto Cortés Conde, 'The Growth of the Argentine Economy, c. 1870–1914' in Leslie Bethell (ed.), *The Cambridge History of Latin America*, vol. V (Cambridge, 1986), pp. 327–357.
36. Brown (1979), p. 81.
37. Cortés Conde (1986), pp. 329–343.
38. See Ezequiel Gallo, *La pampa gringa* (Buenos Aires, 1983).
39. Computed from B.R. Mitchell, *International Historical Statistics: The Americas, 1750–1988* (2nd ed., New York, 1993), p. 245. Figures quoted are rounded to the nearest million.
40. Torcuato S. Di Tella, *Historia social de la Argentina contemporánea* (Buenos Aires, 1998), p. 22.
41. Cortés Conde (1986), p. 331. See the maps shown in Walter Nugent (1992), p. 115, cited p. 68, n. 101.

42. Lewis (1983), p. 5.
43. Mitchell (1993), p. 149.
44. Ibid., p. 470. For a discussion on German import-export figures pre 1914 see Ronald C. Newton, *German Buenos Aires, 1900–1933: Social Change and Cultural Crisis* (Austin & London, 1977), esp. ch. 1.
45. For a discussion in this regard see Alvaro Barros, *Indios, fronteras y seguridad interior, 1872–1876* (Buenos Aires, 1975).
46. Díaz Alejandro (1970), p. 121.
47. Di Tella (1998), p. 31.
48. The Indian campaign itself was partly funded by the sale of government bonds redeemable in land. See Díaz Alejandro (1970), p. 38.
49. Scobie (1967), p. 120.
50. Ibid.
51. Brown (1979), p. 148.
52. Ibid., p. 149.
53. Sarmiento (1993), p. 66.
54. Scobie (1967), p. 120.
55. Ibid., p. 116
56. Lynch, et al. (2001), p. 121.
57. Carl E. Solberg, 'Land Tenure and Land Settlement: Policy and Patterns in the Canadian Prairies and the Argentine Pampas, 1880–1930' in D.C.M. Platt and Guido Di Tella (eds), *Argentina, Australia and Canada: Studies in Comparative Development, 1870–1965* (London, 1985), pp. 53–75.
58. Díaz Alejandro (1970), p. 39.
59. Scobie (1967), p. 117.
60. Ibid., p. 118
61. Díaz Alejandro (1970), p. 39.
62. *The Argentine Year Book, 1915–1916* (Buenos Aires, 1916), p. 229.
63. Carl Solberg, 'Immigration and Urban Social Problems in Argentina and Chile, 1890–1914' in *Hispanic American Historical Review*, vol. 49, no. 2 (1969), pp. 215–232.
64. Ibid., p. 217.
65. Scobie (1967), p. 6.
66. For a more detailed account of this argument see Scobie (1967), esp. ch. III.
67. H.S. Ferns, *The Argentine Republic, 1516–1971* (New York, 1973), pp. 87–115.
68. Cortés Conde (1986), p. 333.
69. Roberto Cortés Conde, 'The Growth of the Argentine Economy, c. 1870–1914' in Leslie Bethell (ed.), *The Cambridge History of Latin America*, vol. V (Cambridge, 1986), pp. 327–357.
70. Solberg (1970), p. 37.
71. Ibid., p. 62.
72. Ferns (1973), p. 94.
73. Solberg (1985), p. 65.
74. Ferns (1973), p. 94.
75. Solberg (1985), p. 67.
76. Ibid.
77. See Chapter 2 above for a detailed discussion on agricultural development.
78. Díaz Alejandro (1970), p. 38.
79. See Colin M. Lewis, 'La consolidación de la frontera Argentina a fines de la década del setenta: Los indios, Roca y los ferrocarriles' in Gustavo Ferrari y Ezequiel Gallo (eds), *La Argentina del ochenta al centenario* (Buenos Aires, 1980).
80. Galeano (2003), p. 259.
81. Scobie (1967), p. 37.
82. Ibid.
83. Lynch et al. (2001), p. 66.
84. Scobie (1967), pp. 45–7.
85. Ibid., p.51
86. Fernando J. Devoto, *Historia de la inmigración en la Argentina* (Buenos Aires, 2003), pp. 262–270.
87. Scobie (1967), pp. 45–47.
88. Solberg (1985), p. 64.

89. Computed from Mitchell (1993), Table E3, p. 516, and C15, p. 275.
90. Ibid.
91. Ibid., p. 39.
92. Sáenz Quesada (2004), p. 395.
93. Ibid., p. 49.
94. Landownership declined to 26 per cent in Buenos Aires and 37 per cent in Santa Fe. See Scobie (1967), p. 50.
95. Díaz Alejandro (1970), p. 155.
96. Ibid., p. 150.
97. *Tercer censo nacional de la República Argentina, 1914*, vol. 5, p. 73.
98. Díaz Alejandro (1970), p. 154.
99. Ibid., p. 156.
100. Scobie (1967), p. 51.
101. See Korol and Sábato (1981).
102. Michael G. Mulhall, *The English in South America* (Buenos Aires, 1878), p. 335
103. See Chapter 2 above, p. 33.
104. Andrew Graham-Yooll, *The Forgotten Colony: A History of the English Speaking Communities in Argentina* (London, 1981), p. 166.
105. Ibid.
106. See Murray (1919), p. 56. For recorded '*Inglés*' occupations see Chapter 2 above, Table 6
107. Mulhall (1878), p. 432.
108. Lucía Gálves, *Historias de inmigración: Testimonias de passion, amor, y arraigo en Tierra Argentina, 1850–1950* (Buenos Aires, 2003), p. 109.
109. For a discussion on transportation development see Scobie (1971), p. 123–124.
110. Tulio Halperín-Donghi, 'La integración de los inmigrantes italianos en Argentina: Un comentario' in Fernando J. Devoto and Gianfranco Rosoli (eds), *La inmigración italiana en la Argentina* (Buenos Aires, 1988), pp. 87–93.
111. Mulhall (1878), p. 335.
112. Cortés Conde (1986), p. 328.
113. B.R. Mitchell, *International Historical Statistics: The Americas*, Table C10, p. 245; U.S. Bureau of the Census, *Historical Statistics of the United States, Colonial Times to 1970* (Washington, D.C., 1972), series K564, K568; Wray Vamplew, ed., *Australians: Historical Statistics* (Broadway, N.S.W., 1987), series AG 54, AG 63 and AG 72, pp. 78–79, 80, 81.
114. Monsignor James M. Ussher, *Father Fahy* (Buenos Aires, 1951), p. 51.
115. William MacCann, *Two Thousand Miles' Ride through the Argentine Provinces*, vol. I (London, 1853) p. 150.
116. Ussher (1951), p. 51.
117. Ibid., p. 49.
118. Mulhall (1878), p. 416.
119. Murray (1919), p. 186.
120. Korol and Sábato (1981), p. 19.
121. http//:www.irishargentine.org/biography.
122. Murray (1919), p. 55.
123. Murray (1919), p. 186.
124. Quoted in Murray (1919), p. 189.
125. The regions of Quilmes and Matanzas supported Irishmen in farming, although many were employed as hired workmen and did not progress to landownership. See Murray (1919), p. 199.
126. Compiled by Edmundo Murray from Coghlan, (1982).
127. See Korol and Sábato (1981), ch. V.
128. See Murray (1919), pp. 185–198.
129. All Hallows College: Fahey to Woodlock, 28 June 1869.
130.   Solberg (1969), p. 68.
131. Devoto (2003), p. 217.
132. Ibid., p. 58; for the *colonización privada* system see Nugent (1992), p. 117–118.
133. Dedier Norbeto Marquiegui, *Circularidad y permanencia: La inmigración irlandesa en Luján, Provincia de Buenos Aires, Rep. Argentina, 1830–1895* (unpublished article), p. 28.
134. For a discussion in this regard, please see William Bulfin, *Tales of the Pampas* (London, 1900).

135. See Korol and Sábato (1981), ch. V.
136. Translated as 'thirds' and 'fourths'. See ibid.
137. *The Southern Cross*, 8 February 1878, no pagination [hereafter, n.p.].
138. National Library of Ireland, William Bulfin Papers: Ms. 13,810/13.
139. Obituary of Thomas Gahan, *The Southern Cross*, 30 May 1890, p. 12.
140. Ibid.
141. See Korol and Sábato (1981), ch. V.
142. Ibid.
143. Ibid., p. 90. The results reflect the findings across *partidos* where Irish immigrants were concentrated and are not, therefore, representative of national averages.
144. See Korol and Sábato (1981), esp. ch. V.
145. Instituto de Dardo Rocha, Ciudad de la Plata: *Indice de Escribanos*, leg. 284, exp. 19184
146. Ibid., leg. 251, exp. 17426.
147. James R. Scobie, *Argentina: A City and a Nation* (2nd ed., New York, 1971), p. 84.
148. Computed from Korol and Sábato (1981), p. 96.
149. Korol and Sábato list only two *estancias* in this *partido* as having in excess of 5,000 ha, but do not attribute them to individual landholders. Names were identified, however, by cross-referencing this information with the *Plano Catastral*, 1901 .
150. Eduardo Coghlan, *Los irlandeses en la Argentina: Su actuación y descendencia* (Buenos Aires, 1987), p. 449.
151. *The Southern Cross*, cited in Coghlan (1987), p. 450.
152. Murray (1919), p. 55.
153. See as an example *The Buenos Aires Herald*, 6 February 1878 , p. 2.
154. http://www.irishargentine.org/biography.
155. Extensive speculation on the financial markets led Eduardo Casey to lose his vast fortune in the 1890 crisis. He died impoverished in a railway accident in 1906. See Roberto Landaburu, *Irlandeses: Eduardo Casey, vida y obra* (Venado Tuerto, 1995).
156. *Acta de la session de la instalacion de la Jockey Club, 1882.* By kind permission of the Jockey Club, Buenos Aires.
157. See Figure 3.
158. *Dirección de geodesia, catastro y mapa de la Provincia de Buenos Aires*: Capitan Sarmiento, no. 72, 1887.
159. Ibid., no. 31, 1871. The year stated on the registration of this document is obviously in error since the date of transaction is two years following it.
160. *Dirección de geodesia, catastro y mapa de la Provincia de Buenos Aires*: Bartolomé Mitre, no. 87, 1894.
161. Ibid., no. 69, 1883.
162. Korol and Sábato (1981), p. 93.
163. *Plano Catastral*, 1901. By kind permission of The Jockey Club, Buenos Aires.
164. *Plano Catastral*, 1901.
165. Korol and Sábato (1981), p. 90.
166. Scobie (1967), p. 6.
167. The memoirs of Tom Garrahan, 1864–1912. By kind permission of Dr Patrick J. Garrahan.
168. Ibid.

CHAPTER FOUR

Irish Catholicism
and Latin religiosity

The Hispanic conquest of Argentina did not entail the vehement religious subjugation witnessed in Mexico and Peru. Both of those territories, densely populated and rich in natural resources, were strategically positioned as centres of administrative rule.[1] The imperative of economic and political domination was accompanied by the religious uniformity of Hispanic decree, enforced through the systematic purging of indigenous belief systems.[2] In contrast, as one of the most isolated and unpopulated regions of the Spanish empire, the colonial Roman Catholic Church in Argentina faced little opposition to its spiritual hegemony. As a result, its institutional structures were relatively modest when compared with other colonial heartlands.[3] Only three dioceses were established at first, each covering an average 1 million km and administering to a scattered population of approximately half a million.[4] Following the *patronato real*, a sixteenth-century agreement between Rome and Spain, Rome relinquished ecclesiastical control both spiritually and administratively over territories under Spanish domain.[5] Church governance in the Americas was, therefore, administered from Madrid. The burgeoning demands of religious conquest throughout the New World necessarily meant that, in the relatively acquiescent Argentina, fortifying the Catholic Church was subordinate to more pressing imperial priorities elsewhere. Some two and a half centuries later, the legacy of institutional neglect was to prove costly in the political mêlée that raged between Church and state in the aftermath of the nineteenth-century revolution.

During the War of Independence, 1810–16, the objectives of the revolution were by no means universally agreed. The decades that followed victory were subject to fierce political and military turmoil.[6] Led by the Buenos Aires liberal elite, the *unitario* supporters were well versed in contemporary European philosophy and espoused an anticlerical ideology, which advocated the primacy of secular law and allegiance to the state.[7] In contrast, opposing *federalismo* conservative forces argued that the liberal agenda was anathema to provincial and rural structures.[8] They rebuked colonial centralist and temporal policies, which had systematically appointed peninsular personnel to key administrative and ecclesiastical positions, disadvantaging provincial leaders in the process. For *federalismos*, the revolution was to herald an end to centralist government and buttress regional autonomy and clerical decree.[9]

Far from representing a unified call for emancipation and independence, therefore, the revolution was, in part, a complex response to Spain's eradication of traditional doctrinal and scholastic philosophy.[10] In the opinion of one historian, Latin America had failed to respond to the intellectual challenges of the Enlightenment, with traditional Christian dogmas surviving to shape religious teaching as much by default as by design.[11] The anticlerical Bourbon reforms of the late eighteenth century, most notably under Carlos III, were both admired and reviled by liberal *unitarios*. With equal enthusiasm, the Spanish dynasty had scrupulously extended its regal authority whilst reducing the Church's theological influence and material wealth.[12] Whilst denigrating regal absolutism, *unitarios* celebrated the accompanying programme of social and ecclesiastical modernisation.[13] The dramatic expulsion of the Jesuits from Argentina in 1767 and the systematic erosion of Church privileges thereafter both inspired *unitarios* and alienated *federalismos*. Paradoxically, therefore, the combination of Spain's anticlerical and absolutist sovereignty incited a unification of arms against her by *unitario* and *federalismo* factions, whilst simultaneously exposing ideological divisions within their joint revolutionary force. Spanish rule thus emerged in a dichotomy, which formed the basis of opposing political principles in the independent state; with central-secular forces on one side, and provincial-clerical on the other.

After Independence, the short lived liberal administration of Bernardino Rivadavia, although largely utilitarian in its ideals and laws, nevertheless continued a version of central absolutism with far reaching implications for the Church. Tithes, which during the war years had been reduced, were now discontinued and Church land, property and income were sequestered by the state.[14] Furthermore, in the immediate aftermath of Independence, several bishops and other Church hierarchy fled to Spain, leaving diocesan sees vacant: Buenos Aires from 1812 to 1834, Córdoba from 1810 to 1831 and Salta from 1812 to 1860.[15] Clergy of a 'strong monarchical predilection', chiefly hierarchy, denounced the revolution, whilst paradoxically the names of many 'Catholic Churchmen' were found amongst local revolutionary leaders.[16] Rivadavia's sweeping reforms, though, were not so much anticlerical as pro-democratic.[17] His efforts to establish an antiregalistic concordat, however, misjudged the mood of the broader populace, which was unfamiliar and ill at ease with European philosophies such as those of the Enlightenment. The ensuing climate of anticlericalism exacerbated the gulf between a central secular state and the wider population.[18] Civil war followed the inevitable collapse of Rivadavia's administration, and the resultant social and political turmoil facilitated the emergence of Juan Manuel Ortiz de Rosas. His populist cry of 'federación o muerte' found immediate and potent resonance in a fractured state for which he promised the return of the rule of law – in the form of provincial *caudillos* – and the protection of the Church. [19]

Rosas, although indifferent to religion, recognised its capacity to advance his own absolutist diktat.[20] Despite his pro-ecclesiastical posturing he did little once in power to reinstate Church privileges, reducing its institutions to servile instruments of tyranny.[21] Early Church subordination to his regime, although earning initial concessions such as the return of the Jesuits, ultimately resulted in its censorship and impotency. Compromised and vulnerable, with an increasingly licentious and derided clergy, the Church had no alternative than to seek political sanctuary within the fold of its prime assailant. This uncomfortable alliance nurtured a spiritually sterile agency of religious values, inculcated by an autocratic political agenda.[22] Whilst the state experienced rapid growth in population, capital and economic investment, the Church withered, unable to provide basic sacraments to communicants. An Irish cleric commenting on Argentina's ecclesiastical institutions, stated that 'ecclesiastics [were] without a flock and churches without congregations – churches that are melancholy and silent memorials of a vanished faith'.[23]

Nevertheless, the ingrained nature of Catholicism within popular culture ultimately ensured its survival despite deficiencies in pastoral care and, in time, the Church carried out its own reforms. Independent modernisation of religious institutions and seminaries followed the elevation of Buenos Aires to an archdiocese in 1865.[24] Rejuvenated, the Church underwent a series of organisational and institutional expansions, which injected much needed confidence into its societal position.[25] In the closing decades of the nineteenth century it emerged from the confines of the sacristy to confront the new age of secularism.[26] The benefits of this revival were not fully realised, however, until the early decades of the twentieth century, when clerics of this generation joined conservative nationalist forces in re-establishing traditionalist ideology.[27]

In the interim, decades of institutional neglect continued to hamper Church attempts to combat the growing impetus of a modernising state that espoused the principles of secularism. Church and state clashes over primacy in education were accompanied by secular challenges to the legitimacy of the sacraments, manifested most acutely in the Civil Marriage Law of 1888, which decreed Church marriage discretionary and state marriage compulsory.[28] Additional anticlerical reforms included the abolition of Church cemeteries, parish registers and religious oaths.[29] The unbridled ecclesiastic opposition evoked by such radical change was to inflame emerging nationalistic sentiment, which increasingly opposed liberal anticlerical ideology.[30] The significance of this movement will be discussed in Chapter 6 below, but at this juncture it is sufficient to note that Church failure to prevent a secular onslaught signified increasing liberal control over the apparatus of state.[31]

The Constitution of 1853 guaranteed freedom of religious conscience and worship.[32] The prime architect of many of its articles, Juan Baustista Alberdi, recognised the importance of pluralism in populating an immigrant nation.[33] In arriving at a concordat that would satisfy opposing political factions, the Constitution declared that the state would support the Catholic faith without obligation to profess it.[34] Furthermore, in keeping with its regal past, the president of the republic had rights of patronage above Rome for the appointment of bishops, selected from a shortlist proposed by the Senate. While not officially recognised by the papacy, this process was tolerated and the president's choice summarily endorsed by the Vatican.[35] Catholicism was, therefore, the dominant religion of the state and, while immigration to Argentina was not subject to denominational prejudice, the magnitude of immigrants arriving from Catholic Europe was testament to its ascendancy. In this regard, Irish Catholic immigration contributed to the immediate homogeny, albeit superficial, of the native and immigrant Church. In spite of disparate devotional observances, with often distinctly different frequency of sacramental reception, the Catholic umbrella facilitated a cultural fusion between established and arriving ecclesiastical populations.

Although churchmen perhaps often exaggerated such differences to spur their own and others 'cares' to more self-conscious practice, indifferent observance was not unprecedented amongst many rural Irish too before the 1850s (if less in Wexford than in the midlands), and amongst Italian and Spanish newcomers thereafter.

Although predominant, Catholic immigrants were joined by a small, but not insignificant, Protestant Church. Its institutional establishment following Independence contributed to the state's evolving pluralist ideology, and directly affected relations between Catholic Irish and non-Catholic *'Inglés'*. The early granting of religious freedom to 'Englishmen' in 1825, extended to all faiths by 1853, facilitated religious liberty.[36] Indeed, the treaty of 'amity, commerce and navigation' signed in 1825 between the British *chargé d' affaires*, Sir Woodbine Parish, and the Argentine minister of finance and foreign affairs, Manuel José Garcia, stated:

> The subjects of his Britannic Majesty residing in the United Provinces of Rio de la Plata shall not be disturbed, persecuted or annoyed on account of their religion, but they shall have perfect liberty of conscience there in, and to celebrate divine service either within their own private houses, or in their own particular churches or chapels, which they shall be at liberty to build and maintain in convenient places, approved of by the Government of the said United Provinces.[37]

Accordingly, the first Protestant Church was founded under the guidance of Reverend William Brown, an evangelical minister ordained by the Presbyterian Church in Glasgow, who served the first colony of Scottish immigrants in Montegrande.[38] Brown spent a total of twenty-three years in Argentina, retiring to Scotland in 1849 where he was made Professor of Divinity at St Andrews University, a chair he held for the remaining eighteen years of his life.[39] Whatever political nuisance the emerging republic experienced in the early years of its birth, the creation of a Protestant Church so soon after the collapse of the Spanish Crown demonstrated a radical commitment to pluralism and an early awareness of the economic benefits a multireligious society could foster. Indeed, Alberdi and Rivadavia firmly extolled the benefits of importing a Protestant work ethic, which they viewed as superior to Catholic indolence.[40] The merging of Catholic Ireland into an *'Inglés'* community was thus, in part, facilitated by the state's commitment to economic advancement over traditional confessional division.

Historians broadly agree that arriving Europeans significantly influenced social and cultural change in Argentina. What is contested, however, is the extent to which European immigration contributed to the secularisation of Argentine society.[41] A polarised exposition of the debate situates natives as Catholic and immigrants – although predominantly Catholic – as anticlerical.[42] Traditional interpretation of Italian immigration would support this thesis by emphasising the predominance of republican philosophy in contemporary Italian-Argentine press and cultural institutions.[43] Indeed, in 1907 the Archbishop of Buenos Aires commented that Italian immigrants 'en America se pierde la fe'.[44] More recent studies have challenged this linear analysis, suggesting that there were two streams of Italian immigration. The first was urban, learned and anticlerical; the second was rural, uneducated, with conventional religious beliefs.[45] Thus, the community was more ambiguously divided between Catholic and anticlerical sympathies. Furthermore, Italian regionalism was even more crucial than was Irish amongst immigrants, and utterly different patterns and expectations of worship affected Italian dioceses. These tensions of religious subcultures, once transported to Argentina, must surely have been significant in creating internal conflict and misunderstanding within the community itself.

Fernando Devoto's microstudy of a *barrio* (district) in Buenos Aires endorses this complexity. La Boca, situated southeast of the city, underwent rapid population growth between 1855 and 1895, increasing from 1,534 residents to 30,842.[46] It was not only considered the most densely populated Italian district in urban Buenos Aires, but also one of the most anticlerical enclaves.[47] Nonetheless, Devoto argued that, in the decades prior to the 1870s, anticlerical sentiment in the La Boca was relatively insignificant. Only after the arrival of the prominent Italian Salesian order in 1875[48] did conflict manifest itself, largely as a result of overt religious involvement in education and local government.[49] The lack of conflict in earlier decades could, of course, reflect low levels of Italian immigration prior to 1870, as well as a politically subordinate and impotent Church. Notwithstanding these certainties, the thesis that Italian immigration was homogeneously anticlerical is difficult to support, given that the ideological wrangle of clerical versus secular would appear to have been as much an internal dispute as an external confrontation.

Despite the presence of anticlerical sentiment, however, Italian religious orders contributed greatly to the expansion of the Catholic Church in the closing decades of the nineteenth century. By 1906 there were twenty-three Italian parishes and eighty-three churches within the diocese of Buenos Aires.[50] Of all Catholic Europeans, the Italians caused the greatest concern to the native hierarchy by virtue of their number. Other arriving ethnic groups in contrast 'no ofrecen grandes dificultades por su número relativamente reducido'.[51] Italian immigrants accounted for 265,000 parishioners, compared with 122,000 Spanish and 30,000 French.[52] Whereas the Spanish were easily absorbed into Argentina's religious culture by virtue of language and race, the Italians remained separate, further exacerbating native ecclesiastical fears of foreign orders creating ethnic strongholds.[53] The 'revolutionary' nature of Italian ecclesiastics, described as offering 'neither useful nor edifying accessions to the clerical staff', prompted the 'Bishop' of Buenos Aires' insistence that 'good credentials' be presented by each cleric upon arrival.[54] However, the potential menace of Italian anticlericalism and Italians' increasing 'loss of faith' was sufficiently grave as to convince the native hierarchy that the Salesian order should be called upon to 'recatolizar' the Italian populace.[55] In so inviting them to establish a foothold in Argentina, a degree of ecclesiastical quality control over arriving clergy was also enforced. As the century drew to a close, the order had expanded to occupy eleven churches within the Buenos Aires diocese, administered by a total of forty-two priests.[56]

Whereas the size and potential dominance of the Italian Church had aroused native ecclesiastical concerns, the German community constituted a smaller but not insignificant minority.[57] Of the 22,062 German immigrants arriving in 1895, fewer than 44 per cent described themselves as Catholic.[58] The non-Catholic majority quickly established institutional structures, with the first German evangelical congregation founded in 1843 and the construction of its church commencing in 1851. In spite of this early incursion, the population was small enough to share a Protestant cemetery with the *'Inglés'* and North American communities.[59] German Catholics were absorbed into native institutional structures.[60] Not until 1911 did mixed families of German-Argentine antecedents form a substantial portion of the 'German' Catholic community, resulting in the establishment of St Bonifacius and the arrival of German priests.[61] It is argued that early accommodation of predominately non-Catholic immigrant groups such as Germans and *'Ingleses'* facilitated a relatively gradual disestablishment of Catholic institutions, thus avoiding unnecessary societal instability.[62] Although this may have been the end result, its actuality was as much a consequence of internal battles between clerical and secular forces impeding either side's ultimate dominance as it was a consciously designed political objective. Moreover, any relinquishing of Church power occurred in the first instance as a consequence of it being a historically weak colonial institution; and, secondly, as a result of compromised doctrinal legitimacy due to alignment with a politically and socially corrupt regime.

Of all arriving immigrants from Catholic Europe the Irish were, for the major part, and from the outset, the most determined to preserve the ideals of their religion, especially as they came from more religiously active counties at home.[63] Their judgements reflected this. The structure of the native Church was viewed as an organ of 'lifeless Catholicity, characteristic of Spanish America' and potentially damaging to the propagation of Irish Catholicism.[64] In the perhaps tendentious view of an Irish ecclesiastic, a dishevelled and embattled Argentine Church had limped through the decades following Independence, spawning a generation of 'young men that scarcely know how to read mass'.[65] Certainly in the diocese of Buenos Aires established in 1620,[66] the absence of suffragan bishoprics had led to institutional disarray and, by 1864, only thirty-five priests administered to a vast but stagnant diocese.[67] By the close of the century institutional structures had expanded and reorganised, however, to consist of an archbishop of Buenos Aires and seven provincial bishops seated in Córdoba, La Plata, Paraná, San Juan de Cuyo, Santa Fé, Salta and Tucumán.[68] All of these, except Salta, were suffragans to Buenos Aires. Each bishop was provided with a chapter, for which they nominated a number of canons, and ecclesiastical officials appointed by the government.[69] Obviously only then did the jurisdictional looseness that had promoted Irish autonomy finally give way to normal Church governance.

But, until then, the establishment of the Irish Roman Catholic Church was not dependent upon integration within native institutional structures. Although the Argentine hierarchy sanctioned the arrival of clerics who were officially recorded as operating within the diocese, once *in situ* their ministry was relatively autonomous.[70] Irish Catholicism was thus, in the main, separately administered from the native Church. From the 1820s, the dispersed nature of Irish *campo* settlement necessitated that designated 'mass houses', not parochial churches, served as places of worship.[71] Furthermore, the scale of the terrain meant that clerical visits were irregular and sacraments received sporadically.[72] The limitations of resources were such that each priest 'had to do the work of four'.[73] By 1870 a total of twelve secular clergy had arrived from All Hallows Seminary College in Dublin, each administering to a distinct region within Buenos Aires province where Irish immigrants predominated.[74] A series of quasi parishes was created, with boundaries fixed outwards from the city.[75] Each district became known as an 'Irish chaplaincy', the number and geographical limits of which changed according to the expansion of Irish settlement and the arrival of Irish priests.[76] The locations of the first Irish chapels were largely decided as wealthy Irish landowners donated land for the construction of churches.[77] This practice ensured the primacy of the chaplaincy as the cornerstone of Irish religious worship, further isolating the community from a 'maligned' native Church.[78] Be that as it may, by the close of the century the ill-defined chaplaincy construct became gradually obsolete within an expanding native institutional structure and a declining Irish ecclesiastical presence.

The propagation of the Irish faith in Argentina was qualitatively different from the Irish experience elsewhere. In other destinations, the relationship between the receiving country's native Catholic Church and the arriving Irish Catholic immigrants frequently caused subcultural clashes within a common doctrinal culture. In Scotland, for example, the Irish immigrant temperament was not compatible with natural Scottish reserve, and tensions were reported not only amongst communicants but also within Irish and Scottish clerical circles.[79] The predominance of Scottish priests administering to a largely Irish congregation incited vehement protests from Irish clerics, who were excluded from the determined Scottish nature of the Church.[80] Similarly in England, priests were distrustful of arriving Irish Catholics, whom they viewed as harbouring nationalist sympathies, and to whom they set about the 'necessary' task of re-education in the ways of English Catholicism.[81]

In North America, pre-Famine Irish Catholic immigrants adjusted rather better to a new 'republican Catholicism' than did the later arriving Famine and post-Famine masses. Estimated as accounting for nine-tenths of all Irish immigration to the United States between 1845 and 1855, the sheer number of Irish Catholics altered the shape of Irish-America.[82] But it was the emergence of a nativist political movement emphasising the importance of nationality, Protestant piety and anti-Irishism that both encouraged Irish Protestants to divorce themselves from their Catholic countrymen, and accelerated the emergence of a distinct Catholic Irish-American community.[83] Having secured hierarchical representation from the mid-1800s, therefore, the Irish Catholic Church in the United States actively promoted its own version of Irish separateness.[84]

The contrasting experience of the Irish in Argentina was, in no small part, the result of Catholicism being the official state religion. As the only Catholic country to attract substantial Irish numbers (if one excludes Quebec, not integrally part of Canada until 1867), immigrants uniquely formed part of the religious majority. Unlike native ecclesiastical responses elsewhere, arriving Irish immigrants did not threaten established Catholic institutional interests.   But that is not to say that cultural differences in modes of worship did not exist.   Churches in Argentina were traditionally without pews, and Argentine Catholic men demonstrated an entrenched reluctance to receive the sacraments or attend mass.[85] The relatively benign nature of such variance from Irish practice, however, did not incite religious acrimony. This may have been a result of native apathy towards religion within an increasingly secular state or, perhaps more significantly, a consequence of a lack of denominational prejudice or insistence on religious uniformity within Argentine society.

Whereas the Irish experience elsewhere had fervently entrenched confessional divisions, in Argentina the general atmosphere was more benign. That is not to say that sectarianism was absent or religious affiliation insignificant in shaping local communities; rather that, in comparison with other destinations of nineteenth-century immigration there was a more tolerant underlying *ambiance*.[86] Nevertheless, tensions were very real. Edward F. Every, writing in 1915 on the establishment of the Anglican Church, stated that an efficient and systematic institutional structure was required as a 'means of self-preservation'.[87] Every was acutely aware that small congregations and ever-shifting communities within the Anglican tradition created a lack of 'cohesion and sense of fellowship' that threatened its future development.[88]   And yet, despite such concerns, by the late nineteenth century the increasing number of clergy and followers of Protestantism in Argentina – which, of course, included Irish immigrants – was of mounting concern to a Catholic Church that equated such growth to secularism, an example of the ills of constitutional religious tolerance.[89]

But in relative terms the incidence of religious bigotry was limited. And its absence was to prove most significant in how the Irish community responded to, and was influenced by, native forces. For

Irish immigrants, their acceptance and adoption of an *'Inglés'* identity was not only a measure of social and economic advantage but was, in equal part, reflective of an easing of cultural tension within a liberal society where religious practice was not subject to sanction. An *'Inglés'* identity did not entail the cultural rejection of their inherent Catholicism, and economic and social progression under *'Inglés'* auspices was not incompatible with Irish religiosity. Although significant, religion was not the driving dynamic of Irish immigration.[90] In spite of the Church's formative role it was the economic potential of rich farmland that had encouraged Irish settlement.[91] The establishment of a distinct Irish Catholic separateness was seemingly subordinate to more pressing financial and social considerations.

This is perhaps most clearly demonstrated by the Irish Church itself. In a predominately Catholic Argentine state, generic reference to 'the Church' was taken to mean 'Catholic', with other religions individually and separately classified. An example of this is demonstrated in Every's 1915 study, where the term 'British Protestant Church' appeared in official records, which Every himself described as a 'foreign-sounding' title used in Argentina.[92] Thus it would appear that the term 'Iglesia Inglesa' referred to English-speaking Catholics. Since most non-Irish English-speakers within the *'Inglés'* group were non-Catholic, its application would appear appropriate to Irish Catholics.   However, this does not consider the religious and ethnic subtleties attached to *'Inglés'* when translated from the Spanish vernacular. Representation as the 'English Church' immediately compromised what was a distinct and integral element of Irish immigrant identity in the nineteenth century: Irish Catholicism.

By embracing the generic *'Inglés'* classification in matters of religiosity, it would appear that the accompanying social benefits were sufficiently attractive to transcend Old World loyalties and identities. The community perceived no contradiction between the term *'Inglés'* and Irish Catholicism. This was a wholly Argentine phenomenon: Irish religious sensibilities were neither threatened nor diluted by application of the generic term. The implicit association of social superiority inferred by *'Inglés'* did not jeopardise their religious identity. Neither did their Catholic religion jeopardise the social superiority of their *'Inglés'* identity. It would seem, therefore, that Irish religious, economic and social identities were uniquely facilitated, albeit to varying degrees of success, under the linguistic auspices of *'Inglés'*.

Of far greater threat to their Catholicity than the adoption of an *'Inglés'* identity was the lamentable condition of the native Church. Ecclesiastics were widely viewed as taking 'no interest' in Christian teaching and flagrantly abandoning their vow of celibacy.[93] Fears emerged that Irish children, left to the devices of a native institution considered a 'caricature of religion', would grow up 'without any religion whatever.'[94] Avoiding this apocalyptic vision was the kernel of acquiring Irish ministry for the community, and not, as was rather unconvincingly suggested by a contemporary commentator, the problem of linguistic barriers.[95] Although language functioned as a criterion of exclusion it was no less so for Italian, German and French immigrants. Unlike other European groups, however, Irish preoccupation with doctrinal dilution exceeded linguistic concerns. Indeed, even after acquiring the Spanish language the Irish community would 'go to none but Irish priests'.[96] Consequently, after the death in 1828 of Father Burke, the first official 'Irish chaplain', residents wrote to Archbishop Murray of Dublin to request a replacement.[97] Father Patrick Moran was duly sent, followed a year later by Reverend Patrick O'Gorman, due to Moran's untimely death.[98] Thus, from the late 1820s, the Irish community had an established Irish chaplain attending their spiritual needs.

The arrival of Father Anthony Dominic Fahey in 1844 marked a watershed.[99] Fahey, a Dominican from Loughrea, had studied in the San Clemente Priory in Rome and had previously served two years as a missionary in Kentucky and Ohio.[100] On arrival in Buenos Aires he was described as a 'somewhat severe man, scarcely ever jocose and never what we would call familiar.'[101] Fahey's commanding presence quickly established him as a community leader both spiritually and in the more general sense. His indomitable demeanour enforced a stringent social and moral code over the community, imparting an authoritarian style of religious instruction.[102] Fahey's journey to social and religious autocracy was facilitated by the 'deplorable' nature of the native Church and its lack of 'ecclesiastical discipline'.[103] He lost no opportunity in exposing, both to the local Irish community and to the Church hierarchy in Dublin, the threat of Protestantism 'poisoning the minds of the Irish children' as a result of weakened institutional Catholic structures.[104] Moreover, Fahey chastised other European orders for their inadequacy in confronting the perils of a secular society, undermining their ministry in the process. German and French Catholics were described as 'completely lost' for want of religious instruction from their own clergy, many of them 'falling off from their faith and [joining] the Protestant Church'.[105] Similarly, priests from 'Spain and Italy [were] little qualified to stem the torrent'.[106]

The failing, as Fahey described it, was twofold: not only were European clerics derelict in their religious duty, but the failsafe of native institutional structures was absent. The only alternative to lack of Catholic teaching, therefore, was conversion to Protestantism. Whether his choice of words was a deliberate falsification designed to instruct the laity in terms they could understand, or a rallying call to Dublin, Fahey's interpretation demonstrated the gap between popular Catholic culture and institutional decay. In so stark an appraisal, he tactically positioned himself, and the Irish Church, as representing one of the few bastions of ecclesiastical hope. Describing Argentina as 'mission' territory, he boldly declared that 'as it may become an Irishman, I am destined to do all in my power to save it'.[107] Fahey's use of language was almost evangelical as he steadfastly resolved to permeate the Argentine ecclesiastical landscape with Irish Catholicism, without which the 'torch of faith' would be extinguished.[108] On encountering a 'naturally docile' native population, he believed them 'well disposed' to receive 'serious religious instruction' from appropriate quarters.[109] If he were successful in his mission, Irish Catholicism, with him at its helm, would provide such a quarter and be at the vanguard of Catholic resurgence.

Executing such an ambitious plan, however, required an institutional strategy that would facilitate the expansion of Irish Catholicism. This was realised in the first instance through Fahey securing the training of six priests at All Hallows.[110] His zeal for the self-prescribed mission included the overseeing of seminarians' doctrinal discipline. All Hallows was fervently instructed on the 'stock' of men to be apportioned to him, stressing that the temptations presented by Argentina necessitated their being 'well governed and instructed in the principles of religion'.[111] Fahey's obsession with social and moral control within the Irish community was extended to clerics under his auspices, whose ministry he viewed as subordinate to his authority.[112] As such, the discipline of arriving ecclesiastics reflected directly upon Fahey. To discredit him, and by extension the Irish community, through licentious behaviour was wholly unacceptable; better in fact to 'leave the people without a priest than that our holy religion be disgraced'.[113] His concern was so acute that he implored All Hallows that, should any doubt arise

as to the spiritual and moral resolve of an individual, 'for goodness
sake, do not send them'.[114]

It was not only on the character of seminarians that Fahey wrote,
but also the importance of their acquiring 'a perfect knowledge of
the Spanish language'.[115] Although a seemingly sensible request,
such perfection would not have been required for administering to
the Irish community, as a working knowledge would have been sufficient to function initially in the environment. Furthermore, Fahey
persistently requested that documentation be sent confirming his
agreement with the college 'to deposit with the ecclesiastical
authorities here acknowledging the receipt of this money and stating that the College agrees to educate six ecclesiastics for this diocese and to have them ready in five years'.[116] The £300 forwarded for
the provision of training was acquired through the community
itself, and Fahey was under no financial obligation to Church
authorities in Buenos Aires to account for the transaction. Yet there
appeared urgency on his part to be in possession of formal confirmation that the process of training linguistically proficient Irish
priests had begun.

This was the first indication of Fahey's intent to politicise the
Irish mission in Argentina. In courting the Church hierarchy in
Buenos Aires, and in an attempt to increase the Irish mission's political significance, it was essential that Fahey demonstrated commitment to the development of the native Church.   By cultivating
Spanish-speaking priests, Fahey was extending the usefulness of
Irish ecclesiastics beyond the Irish community itself. Priests who
had successfully acquired the language prior to ordination would
be 'doubly useful' in their ministry.[117] Moreover, Fahey's astute
political antennae were such that he realised that only those with
'fluency in Spanish [would] achieve high ecclesiastical office.'[118] His
emphasis on linguistic proficiency revealed a pastoral ambition
both in relation to the Irish Church and to his own personal aspirations.

Fahey was in close contact with Bishop Escalada of Buenos Aires,
who himself had written to the Archbishop of Dublin confirming
that 'every provision and faculty [would be provided] to ordain the
young men educating in your college for this mission.'[119] It was
reported that Escalada was 'highly delighted' on hearing Irish
priests speaking Spanish, so much so that he contributed a 'present
of thirty pounds' to Fahey's training funds.[120] Having so advertised
the bilingualism of the mission, however, native expectations were

raised to levels that were not always met by the linguistic proficiency of Irish priests. The arrival of Father Carolin, some six years after initial negotiations with All Hallows had begun, was marred by the bishop's disappointment at his 'ignorance of the Spanish language.'[121] In so expressing his displeasure, the fragility of native patronage was exposed in the face of Irish clerical inability to satisfy native expectations. Fahey's unease at such an eventuality sharpened his own 'disappointment' and led to the rather desperate plea that All Hallows 'tell the young men to pound away at [Spanish] on their voyage', in a last ditch attempt to be of maximum value on arrival. The consequence of such blatant nurturing of ecclesiastical relations in Argentina had conflicting effects on Fahey's relations with Dublin, which will be discussed below, but, having secured the arrival of Irish priests from All Hallows, albeit with varying levels of success, he continued his expansionist bid by turning his attention to Irish religious educationalists.[122]

Fahey had stated that he 'was in great want of male and female schools' as all 'English speaking schools [were] Protestant'.[123] In order to facilitate the arrival of the Christian Brothers and the Sisters of Mercy, he expertly used the continued threat of Protestantism infiltrating the Irish community as leverage with Dublin.[124] In so doing, he achieved with equal dexterity continued financial support from the Irish community itself. As with priests already secured, the Irish community provided funding as a means to ensure Irish Catholic instruction. In 1856, having forwarded the sum of £100, seven Sisters of Mercy arrived in Argentina.[125] With Mother Evangelista Fitzpatrick as their Superior, the nuns travelled from St Catherine's, Baggot Street, Dublin, to their convent in Buenos Aires, which Fahey had previously secured.[126] Their arrival added much needed depth to the Irish mission and received native political endorsement when the sisters were awarded the deeds of a friary previously owned by the government, in exchange for educating native girls.[127] This represented a stamp of national approval for the Irish Sisters over other religious, and a personal coup for Fahey. Although the government had previously considered the 'Sisters of Charity from France', Sister Evangelista triumphantly proclaimed that 'as they had us on the spot they could not see why they should go out of their way for them'.[128]

Fahey's increasing alignment with political bodies in Argentina was, however, to prove detrimental in securing the arrival of the Christian Brothers. Repeated requests to Archbishop Murray to establish the religious educationalists went without acknowledgement, eliciting the veiled barb from Fahey that 'the letters must never have reached [you?] as I got no reply'.[129] Relations were further strained with the apparent failed remittance by Murray of funds supplied by Fahey for the Brothers' passage.[130] Frustrated by the impasse and believing that prospects for the Argentine mission would 'continue still the same in Dublin', Fahey came to the determination that lay schools were the only option.[131] Appraisal of his bleak correspondence with Murray suggests that Fahey's threats were more likely to have been posturing than expressing any real intent. His own preference for religious educationalists was based in large part on wanting to exact control over the educational syllabus, which he himself managed through the procurement of designated school books shipped to him via agents in Liverpool.[132] Relinquishing the task to lay parties would have undermined his personal primacy and that of the Irish Church.

The resistance encountered by Fahey in relation to the Christian Brothers was symptomatic, not causal, of underlying tensions with Dublin. Institutional strategies employed to establish the Irish Church in Argentina had necessarily entailed a level of politicisation on Fahey's part. Religious orders required a licence from the government prior to arrival in Buenos Aires before the diocesan bishop could grant authority.[133] Consequently, any expansion of the Irish Church was subject to both political and religious sanctions. Fahey astutely recognised that, for the Irish community to have an ecclesiastical voice, they must also have a political one. Without it, they would jeopardise their clerical and social influence. It was fortunate, therefore, that Fahey arrived in Buenos Aires during the presidency of Rosas. The cleric's exacting social code was compatible with the dictator's ethos in a way that was absent from his fellow ecclesiastics. His religious and social absolutism complemented the regime's diktat in so far as a strict code was used to control the masses and enforce societal conformity. In steadfastly asserting the rights of the Irish priest over the community, Fahey demonstrated, as did Rosas, the autocracy of his governance.

But it was the brutality of Rosas' regime that distinguished it and from which not even the Irish community escaped. In 1847, Camila O'Gorman, aged twenty, eloped with a Catholic priest, Fr. Uladislao Gutierrez. O'Gorman, third generation Irish, was from a wealthy and influential family, and had connections with Rosas' daughter, Manuelita.[134] When they were discovered, Rosas ordered their execution in front of a firing squad, in spite of Camila being pregnant.[135] But it is Fahey's role in the proceedings that remains somewhat ambiguous despite extensive literature. The couple's fate was first sealed by Father Michael Gannon, nephew-in-law of Admiral William Brown, who betrayed their whereabouts. Since O'Gorman and Gutierrez would have caused considerable embarrassment to the broader Irish community, it is likely that their exposure was Gannon's attempt to demonstrate loyalty to Rosas and publicly castigate the couple. And yet it is Fahey, not Gannon, that is alleged to have had a direct hand in the couple's tragic fate through his close relationship with Rosas.

As a priest of a relatively small ethnic group his mission had certainly, over time, evolved and expanded beyond what might have been expected, a process undoubtedly aided by his convivial relations with Rosas. Indeed, contemporary clerical descriptions of Fahey as 'tenia más facultades que el Arzobispo' would appear particularly poignant.[136] But, at the time of O'Gorman's execution, Fahey had been in Argentina for only three years. The elevated political standing enjoyed by the Irish Catholic Church through Fahey could not be, and was not, crafted and realised within three years of his arrival. Fahey would still have been a relative novice at the point of the couple's execution. Thus, whilst the active courting of Rosas' good opinion did not, perhaps, allow for any open display of criticism on Fahey's part, it is unlikely that he wielded any particular influence on the dictator's final judgement. Murray's 1919 account of events registered the horror of the Irish community, describing the act as 'inhuman and unpardonable.' Although Fahey went on to fashion an Irish community that was indeed the product of conservative forces both ecclesiastically and politically, there is little direct evidence in the public domain to suggest that he personally sought or sanctioned the execution.

But in spite of such dramatic events, Fahey's much-vaunted relationship with Rosas fostered allegiance within the Irish community to the *federalismo* leader. The dictator's stringent enforcement of a rigid social order contributed to his rather ironic reputation as 'a ruler highly serviceable to the cause of religion and good morals'.[137] The extent of Fahey's patronage, and the ecclesiastic and secular control he garnered as a result, was of mounting concern to Dublin. Through his political and clerical associations in Buenos Aires, Fahey increasingly operated outside Irish, and indeed Roman, ecclesiastical control. Murray's apparent reluctance to engage in correspondence with Fahey and to expand his institutional capability was symptomatic of Dublin severing the arterial supply to his perceived megalomania. Fahey himself demonstrated an awareness of the escalating difficulties with Murray by facetiously writing:

> I am very happy to learn that I was labouring under a mistake in thinking that your Grace had any doubts of my character. Something of the kind was mentioned to me on the eve of my departure from Dublin.[138]

If indeed Murray did have reservations about Fahey prior to his departure, they were surely exacerbated by the increasing gulf that had subsequently opened up between the two clerics. The extent of strained relations culminated in 1849 when an article appeared in the *Dublin Review* severely criticising the regime of Rosas and the methods used to ensure the continuance of his power. Quoting M. Chevalier de Saint Robert, a Frenchman who had extensive knowledge of Argentina, the article charged Rosas with:

> [Letting] loose, in the broad day, into the streets of Buenos Ayres, bands of assassins, who massacred the population [...] We do not believe that hypocrisy and audacity ever reached to such an extreme degree of shameless impudence [...] Europe was mislead as to the real character of [...] the man who has never ceased for eighteen years to be on the banks of La Plata, the element of sanguinary wars, of crimes, and of violence of every kind.[139]

For confirmation of this account the article further referred to a letter from General J. Thomond O'Brien, Consul General to Uruguay, to the Earl of Aberdeen in which he stated:

> 'I am aware of wretches being staked into the ground for forty-eight hours before their heads were sawed, not cut off; – of the lasso being flung over persons' necks, and then dragged by horse at full speed until life became extinct; – of spikes being driven into the mouths of human beings, and they, whilst living, thus nailed to trees.[140]

Appearing in an organ of ecclesiastical interest the article was immediately attributed to Murray in Buenos Aires, with the assumption that it represented official Irish ecclesiastical opinion.[141] Fahey, in responding to what he regarded as calumny, implied that the Irish Archbishop's reputation in Argentina was now in his hands and that public opinion would be calmed through his intervention alone.[142] Such conceited sentiment, although largely accurate, served only to justify Dublin's stance in reining in the Dominican priest. The article itself rationalised and legitimised its publication by espousing a desire to 'protect the extensive commercial interests of England and Ireland in Argentina by examining its merit as an emigrant destination'.[143] Whilst this may appear valid, it is not wholly convincing, as

the reader was swiftly informed of the dangers of despotism striking at the liberty of Catholicism under a 'monarchical form of government'.[144] The ensuing exposition of human barbarism was perhaps rendered all the more abhorrent to the *Dublin Review* given the
anticlerical environment in which it was committed and the
increasing isolationist approach adopted by Fahey.

Rosas' incursion into ecclesiastical pre-eminence had undoubtedly contributed to the timing and content of the article. The dictator's self-proclaimed title as head of the Church and the recent
decree that his portrait appear on all altars had led, once again, to
the suppression of the Jesuit order, which alone had refused to comply with the narcissistic edict.[145] Progressing further, the article
inflamed both religious and ethnic anxieties. It cited the execution
of a priest who had been overheard by a Rosas spy saying 'God
grant us better times!' The priest was 'marched into the square in
front of the cathedral and shot'.[146] It went on to once again quote
General O'Brien's assertion that the Irish needed shelter from the
'aggressions of Rosas (should he be inclined to attack men merely
because they were Irish emigrants)'.[147] O'Brien's view would, of
course, have been coloured by his own imprisonment at the hands
of Rosas, the implication that Irish immigrants were at risk by virtue
of their ethnicity amounting to little more than scaremongering.[148]

However, the overall intimation of the article was clear: not only
was Argentina unsafe for Catholics, but also for Irishmen. This was
ironic in the extreme, given that the community enjoyed the dictator's favour. Indeed, Fahey had charted the arrival of the Sisters of
Mercy during Rosas' reign, knowing that 'there would not be any
obstacles put in his way by the authorities'.[149] Paradoxically, it was
the putatively close relationship between Irish cleric and Argentine
dictator that had led to the article's publication. In presenting such
a blow-by-blow assassination of Rosas it is likely that its principal
aim was not to protect Irish immigrants, but to undermine Fahey's
personal credibility by exposing his assertion that Argentina was
'the finest country in the world.'[150] Fahey's counterattack was
unequivocal and vitriolic. In responding to Rosas' alleged misde-
meanours he stated that as a leader he had:

> ...restored the reign of order, and the splendour of the Catholic Religion. [...]
> The protection has been and is uniformly extended in the most ample man-
> ner to the Irish Catholics, to other British subjects, and to all foreigners, as well
> as natives of the country who in the late struggles were adversaries of the
> Government. [...] Ordinary crimes are few in number and those which do
> occur are punished. Commerce and population have increased and continue

to advance greatly. [...] The Catholic Religion is venerated and protected by General Rosas. [151]

Fahey further fulminated that the article was 'revolting libel [...] incorrect and deceitful', and requested that the Vicar Apostolic of London, Cardinal Wiseman, 'under whose auspices the *Dublin Review* is published' rectify the matter.[152] No such correction appeared in the pages of the periodical, underlining the extent of Fahey's disfavour. Similarly, complaints made by Rosas' government through diplomatic channels to British authorities were not acted upon.[153] As might be expected, relations between Fahey and Archbishop's House in Dublin continued to deteriorate from this point on. Strong requests that clerical documentation accompany the arrival of Irish priests in accordance with the Bishop of Buenos Aires' stipulation, went unheeded, under both Murray and his successor Cullen.[154] Thus, the extent of Fahey's disfavour transcended personal conflict with Murray, and was elevated to the office of archbishop irrespective of its incumbent. In failing to provide the required clerical credentials in Buenos Aires, Fahey was also subjected to Escalada's displeasure, a reminder of his political limitations in Argentina despite his elevated profile. Realising his compromised reputation with the archbishops of Dublin, Fahey increasingly addressed his correspondence to an intermediary, Dr Woodlock, President of All Hallows seminary, who wielded a 'good deal of influence' with the Archbishop.[155] Although continuing in his zeal to raise awareness of the South American mission, the exertion of endless political wrangles over a thirty-year period was not without consequence, and in 1870 Fahey conceded that having 'entered my sixty-fourth year I am nearly worn out'.[156]

If Fahey's intervention in the *Dublin Review* débâcle was met with derision in Dublin and London, it was handsomely rewarded in Buenos Aires. He was officially thanked by State Congress for his unflinching support and timely intervention further cementing his, and by extension the Irish community's, relationship with Rosas.[157] Having so clearly nailed his political colours to the mast, Fahey's diplomatic skills are demonstrated as all the more beguiling by the patronage he enjoyed from opposing political quarters. As an astute and assiduous community leader, he had used his political *savoir-faire* to court liberal *unitario* factions, commenting himself in 1856, post Rosas, that he enjoyed 'the confidence of the government'.[158] His judicious labours were finally rewarded in 1864, when he was

named a canon by the Mitre administration, diametrically and vehe-
mently opposed to Rosas politically.[159] The Irish community attributed his success to being held in 'respect' and 'esteem' by all factions as a consequence of his 'unrestricted benevolence'.[160]

Such an appraisal seems conveniently naive in a political environment that fostered polemical allegiance. To have achieved universal appeal in such dangerous waters demonstrates an acute
diplomatic deftness realised, no doubt in part, through compromise
and negotiation. Fahey alluded to as much by commenting that he
had 'made the greatest of sacrifices to obtain this [position]'.[161]
Whether such sacrifices were of a spiritual or political nature is difficult to determine. However, his ability to court cross-party support
within a nineteenth-century society where attitudes toward religion were at best ambivalent, at worst anticlerical, implies a level of
political bargaining that far exceeded 'benevolence'. Perhaps even
more significant was *unitario* politicians' implicit awareness of the
importance of European labour to economic growth. The Irish had
quickly established themselves as worthy émigrés by contributing
substantially to the expansion of the rural economy. Moreover, they
formed part of the socially superior '*Inglés*' group and were, superficially at least, the epitome of model immigrants. For liberal factions to have ostracised or disadvantaged Fahey, and by extension
the Irish Church and community, would have been to flout the very
essence of the new Constitution, which had been largely drawn
from their own ideology and extensively modelled by J.B. Alberdi
on that of the United States.

Fahey's adroit political skills were employed to similar effect in his
relations with the Church hierarchy in Buenos Aires. He expertly
navigated a course of relative independence, yet sustained patronage, from the native Church, with the result that the Irish were
'more fortunate than any other foreign community in obtaining
priests of their own flesh and blood'[162] Although unforgiving of the
native Church's inability to discipline itself and its members, Fahey
was careful not to apportion blame to its hierarchy, describing
Bishop Escalada in 1855 as a 'saintly man and well qualified to gov-
ern this country'.[163] Any ecclesiastical failings were not the Bishop's
and, indeed, 'if he had good priests there is no country in the world
where the Catholic religion would advance so rapidly'.[164] Fahey
differentiated between the ill trained, ill equipped priest of postrevolutionary Argentina and the 'old venerable ecclesiastics that

[...] would be an honour to any diocese in Europe'.[165] In this regard, Irish Catholicism dovetailed more than that of any other European Church with the conservative forces of Argentina's hierarchy, who upheld the traditional Christian orthodoxy of the Spanish era, modified only by its expression for a new nation.[166] This shared conservatism, coupled with Fahey's innate political ability, elevated the Irish Church beyond its fighting weight.

The fruit of such elevation was apparent at the inaugural celebrations of St Brendan's College, the first Irish Catholic educational institution in Argentina. The guest list included 'representatives of Church and state [...] and influential natives', and it was witnessed that 'never did civil and ecclesiastical authorities feel more gratified by harmonious intercourse with the foreigner.'[167] With the 'bone and sinew of a nation's wealth' in attendance, the Irish flaunted the 'wealth and beauty of the sheep farmers'.[168] In his address, Father John B. Leahy from County Kerry, recently ordained and based in Carmen de Areco,[169] outlined what could only be described as a social pact between immigrant and native, instructing the community on:

> [...] what the native had a right to expect and receive from them. An example of industry at all times, intelligence to prevent internecine broils, and maintain a respectable peace [...] The foreigner was not to look down on anything esteemed by his native fellow-citizen but unostentatiously exhibit to him, what a good, truly patriotic citizen ought to be, and then shoulder to shoulder, foreigner and native, lead the country to plenty and strength.[170]

Superficially at least, the Irish appeared to embody the ideal character for an immigrant labour force from the perspective of native political ideology. Leahy encapsulated this when he spoke of 'the necessity and congruity of foreigners understanding the obligations they contracted by domicile in a foreign land' and how 'without ceasing to belong to their natal country, they were bound to aid the nation that gave hospitality'.[171] The eloquence with which native sensibilities were massaged and yet Irish identity asserted is testament to the astute political construction of the address. Leahy delivered it, but he worked under the auspices of Fahey, for whom the annual reports of the institution were prepared.[172] It was likely, therefore, that, given the political and social eminence of the audience, as well as Fahey's obsession with control and Leahy's relative inexperience, that Fahey not Leahy was its principal scribe.

It may be, however, that the apparent 'control' consistently demonstrated and asserted by Fahey in this, and indeed all his dealings recorded above, may require an alternative interpretation than that of ambitious zeal for personal and ecclesiastical elevation. The nature of his mission was such that by 1870 a total of ten chaplaincies, accommodating twelve priests and administering to approximately 25,000 Irish immigrants and their offspring, spanned a terrain extending over 150,000 km. Given the vast dispersal of both his flock and clerics, a well co-ordinated and structured central administrative system would have been a logical necessity. Without it, a centrifugal and fissiparous fragmentation of the community and a demoralised and isolated clergy were surely dangerous possibilities. This threat would indeed have influenced Fahey's management style and should, to some extent, modify our reading of his behaviour. However, to suggest that Fahey's actions and achievements were largely a response to challenging terrains and limited resources would be to lessen the determined nature of his character and reduce the significance of his intellectual and political prowess. Perhaps the ultimate demonstration of native approval for Fahey came when the Bishop of Buenos Aires requested the role of chief mourner at the Irish priest's funeral in 1871.[173] Such an honour could be regarded as a just reward for Fahey's unflinching stage management of Irish and native relations. In the decades following Fahey's passing, however, the community's relationship with the native hierarchy became increasingly contradictory in nature. On the one hand, contemporary commentators remarked on how subsequent archbishops of Buenos Aires took 'the warmest and most kindly interest in the Irish, [never failing] to assist them, and to confer special honours and privileges on Irish priests'.[174] On the other, attempts to increasingly regulate the Irish ministry were exemplified by Archbishop Aneiros' instruction that Irish chaplains act in accordance with the duties of parish priests, as defined by the native hierarchy.[175] These two seemingly conflicting sentiments reflect the changing position, not only of the Irish Church in Argentina, but also of its native counterpart in the epoch after Fahey.

The 'special' patronage alluded to by contemporary commentators was certainly not without evidence. Aneiros had furthered lay proposals to establish a community of Irish priests following the death of Fahey by writing first to Archbishop Cullen in Dublin and then to the Papal Secretary in Rome, urging immediate attention to Irish-Argentina's religious needs:

> It is a well-known fact that the Irish population is undergoing a great change in their customs and ideas and this change, particularly among the young of both sexes is causing serious alarm for their spiritual good. The position of

the Irish is rendered more critical by the fact that they have accumulated immense wealth by their industry. The future of the Irish is sad if a timely remedy be not brought to them. Missions are most necessary in the camp [*campo*], in order that the people may be instructed in the faith, and taught to practice its most holy precepts.[176]

Such an apparently generous and supportive appeal, whilst no doubt representing hierarchical intervention on behalf of a 'special' community, was also, in no small part, a conscious investment in the future of native doctrinal instruction. The conservative nature of Irish Catholic dogma shored up a vulnerable native Church at a time when traditional values were systematically challenged by secular forces. Aneiros' fears of a 'sad future' for Irish Catholics reflected a broader fear that European immigrants were contributing to the secularisation of the Argentine Republic and the continued disintegration of its Church.[177] In servicing this small, but not insignificant, ethnic group, whose core religious values were compatible with the aims of the native Church, Aneiros was, by extension, protecting the greater good of the Church in Argentina. In this regard, the Irish community inadvertently functioned as an instrument of native ecclesiastical instruction. This most propitiously timed role was also appreciated by one of Aneiros' successors, Dr Mariano Antonio Espinosa, who with equal aplomb combined apparent patronage with political expedience.[178] On the eve of the first Irish pilgrimage to the shrine at Lujan, scheduled for St Patrick's Day 1901, Espinosa confirmed his presence at the head of the Irish procession.[179] The bestowed honour was preceded by a pastoral letter to be read 'on Sunday 3rd February during the hour of most numerous attendances in all the churches of the Archdiocese'.[180] It read:

We appreciate the religious spirit and patriotism of the Irish and from them we have ever received demonstrations of affection and respect which we shall always bear in grateful remembrance [...] At the same time we comply with a sacred duty in exhorting you to continue always loyal to your faith [...] The great evil of modern times is the religious indifference which saturates the ambient[181] in which we live [...]. We exhort you to take great care in preventing from entering your homes books, periodicals or newspapers which contain doctrines contrary to those professed by our Holy Mother the Church. Foster in your children religious vocations thus have the great glory of your family amongst the chosen of the land.[182]

At a time when Catholic propagandist rhetoric identified Freemasonry as the most immediate and perilous foe of the laity, the native hierarchy astutely employed the Irish community as a means of instructing the broader Catholic Church members.[183] In outlining religious perils, whether real or perceived, a lesson of conformity and spiritual purity was thus instilled. The Irish became the mechanism of transmitting a subtext aimed not at them, but the entire Catholic population of the archdiocese. Having suffered the humiliation of the Civil Marriage Act, and facing a determined secular campaign to eradicate Church primacy, Espinosa massaged the address to suit his own political agenda.

As a result, native patronage of the community, as described by contemporary Irish commentators, was largely of a superficial nature. Despite hierarchical rhetoric, the distinct Irish Catholic identity Fahey had so consciously and expertly forged was gradually subsumed into native institutional structures. Irish chapels, such as at Suipacha and Venado Tuerto, constructed using Irish finances in 1875 and 1883 respectively, increasingly functioned as parochial churches within the diocese.[184] More significantly, where chaplancies had survived, fewer and fewer Irish priests administered there.[185] Much later in 1925, a German Pallottine, Henry Weber, ordained in Rome and having previously served as parish priest in Suipacha, assumed the position of Irish chaplain of Capilla del Señor.[186]

By the early 1890s, many Irish chapels languished vacant, prompting Aneiros to approach the Pallottine Fathers – recently arrived in Buenos Aires and occupying the residence previously secured for the Sisters of Mercy in Mercedes – 'to perform the duties of chaplains to the Irish people'.[187] This was perceived as the best solution to a problem that had become irksome to the ecclesiastical authorities, duty bound to offer cursory appeasement to Irish disquiet.[188] Since the Pallottines' principal ministry was one of education, they were reluctant to become embroiled in pastoral care and viewed the very existence of Fahey's chaplaincies as a 'peculiar institution'.[189] In responding to the Archbishop's request to continue the practice where possible, many in turn fell under the permanent administrative control of the secular Church. Thus, as the Pallottine Fathers became increasingly integrated within the native diocesan structure, so too did many of the Irish chapels under their direction.[190]

Prominent Irish Pallottine Fathers such as John Dolan and Patrick O'Grady, the latter of whom became the third rector of the order in Argentina, viewed their personal ministry, and that of the order itself, as broader than servicing Irish chaplaincies, an obligation they increasingly believed should be fulfilled by local parish priests.[191] When Aneiros wrote to Fr. Dolan, a fluent Spanish speaker, to express his 'sorrow' at Dolan being sent by his superior to New

York, Anieros was not referring to his work within Irish chaplaincies but to his contribution in parishes across the diocese.[192] The difficulty for the Irish community in being reliant on any religious order was that their spiritual and temporal interests were ultimately of limited overall concern to the order itself. This denotes a most immediate departure from Fahey's governance. In the absence of his leadership, the welfare of the community was rapidly and starkly neglected in any considered form. In addition, it would appear that, having successfully expanded its own institutional structures, the native hierarchy was opposed to any one Irish cleric assuming Fahey's overtly prominent role. Anieros reportedly issued a circular to this effect, stating that all Irish chaplains now enjoyed equal standing: perhaps pre-empting any personal aspirations to inherit Fahey's political profile.[193]

Of all potential heirs, Patrick Dillon came closest to emulating Fahey's run at ecclesiastical power.[194] Born in Mayo and ordained at All Hallows, Dillon had been appointed by Fahey as chaplain to the southern districts of Chascomus, Ranchos and Magadena.[195] He rose through the ranks to be appointed canon in 1876 and dean of the Cathedral in 1881, and simultaneously chosen as domestic prelate by Pope Leo XIII.[196] Like Fahey, the ultimate position of bishop eluded him and he returned to Dublin in 1888 due to ill health.[197] Although Dillon's career can, in many ways, be described as more distinguished than that of Fahey, he failed to fill the shoes of the indefatigable leader convincingly. Other clerics of note included Fr. Samuel O'Reilly from Ardagh, granted the title of Apostolic Protonotary in recognition of fifty years' service in the districts of Lujan and Chivilcoy.[198] Michael and John Leahy from County Kerry were active community clerics, and responsible for building a chapel and founding a school in the district of Carmen de Areco.[199] Despite local and in some cases official recognition, none of the twelve Irish-born All Hallows priests ordained for the Argentine mission went on to grasp Fahey's mantle. In the absence of such leadership , the political profile and influence previously exerted by the Irish Church within native institutional structures steadily, but inevitably, diminished.

This demise cannot, of course, be attributed to any of these individual Irish clerics whose personal ministry did not perhaps extend to political ambition. It was, nonetheless, the lack of senior Irish representation, coupled with an isolated and archaic chaplaincy structure, that caused the Irish Church's failure to adapt to changes in native governance, which precipitated its decline. Unlike the

Irish communities in North America and Australia, where the emergence of a distinct Irish Catholic subculture was facilitated through the appointment of Irish bishops to diocesan sees; in Argentina, the Irish did not secure hierarchical ethnic representation.[200] In this can be found echoes of the Irish experience in Scotland, where, in spite of substantial representation, hierarchical appointments remained out of Irish ecclesiastical reach.[201] Any further comparison between the two destinations would be unwise, however, due to different Irish immigrant numbers and composition of native institutional structures.

In Argentina, the absence of senior Irish clerics left the community not only without a voice in Rome, but also dependent upon the whims of patronage bestowed by a native Church whose own political agenda took precedence. Thus, Fahey's fears of the isolation and subjugation of the Irish Church would appear well founded. Strategies employed to counter such threats through the expansion of institutional capabilities would, when viewed in this light, assume a resonance that transcended personal and political ambition. In the event, his elevation to canon was insufficient to secure the political longevity of Irish interests in the corridors of ecclesiastical power, or to prevent the community's exploitation at the hands of more powerful religious agencies. This is most clearly demonstrated in the establishment of the Passionist Fathers. Although the first order to administer to the Irish community, their arrival was fraught with controversy. The decision in 1880 to establish a house in Buenos Aires generated a misleadingly harmonious editorial in the Irish press:

> We are happy to inform our readers that the Passionist Fathers have at length made up their minds to establish a branch of their Order in this city. Father Martin has received letters from the Superior in Rome, stating that the priests will be sent out as soon as the Archbishop of Buenos Aires gives his approbation. [...] We sincerely congratulate the Irish community on so grand an acquisition as the Passionist Fathers. We always said a religious Order would be established here if our poor efforts to that end would be of any avail.[202]

The self-congratulatory tone adopted in announcing the 'acquisition' of the Fathers not only belied the acrimonious backdrop to proceedings, but also demonstrated the community's inflated self-importance in entering negotiations with the Passionists. As an order, their first foray into Argentina had occurred some years earlier, when in 1874 Fr. Pius Devine arrived in Buenos Aires with the purpose of:

[...] not to found a permanent mission here, but to collect alms for the English Province. It was known that Irish and English sheep farmers of this country were exceptionally prosperous and proposed here (as well as all over the rest of the world) to bestow liberal alms on religious institutions of the Mother country. Accordingly Fr. Pius Devine [who] came here in the seventies [and] found that accounts had not be exaggerated and soon returned to England with a generous contribution. He arrived in Buenos Aires on 4th May 1874.[203]

The missionary experience had been so financially rewarding that in 1879 the order instigated a second appeal through Fr. Martin Byrne. It was from this point that controversy engulfed relations between the Passionists and the Irish community. Whilst in Argentina, Fr. Byrne was approached by representatives of the Irish community to assist in the establishment of a permanent Passionist house, which he was assured would be 'liberally supported' financially by the community.[204] The general superior of the order approved Fr. Byrne's continued presence until such time as authorities in Rome could duly consider the proposition. During this time independent arrangements were struck between Fr. Byrne and the Irish, approved by Archbishop Aneiros, that the Passionists would be paid 'a large sum of money in exchange for a certain number of Irish priests, of their community, who were to come to Buenos Aires and establish a branch of their order in the city, and who would attend to the spiritual wants of Irish Catholics'.[205] However, the Irish accused the Passionists of foul play after monies were paid and the order announced its intent to create an international house and install Italian priests.[206] Outraged at such flagrant abuse of their patronage, the community produced a pamphlet in which it was stated:

> We consider that the Italian Passionists are as good as any other nationality; but we are strongly of the opinion that they or their Superiors should apply to their own countrymen for the means to build houses and churches for themselves and their Italian people whom they wish to minister. [...] it could not be expected that our small Irish community should be expected to build and support the Passionist houses for the benefit of the immensely numerous and immensely wealthy Italian population in Argentina.[207]

The necessity of the lay community to register their grievance through private means not only indicates the absence of representation within high ecclesiastical office, but also, more significantly, demonstrates the depth of their collective weakness in falling prey to Passionist designs. Even intervention by the Archbishop, albeit perfunctory, did not prevent the order from taking advantage of the opportunity presented by a susceptible but wealthy Irish community.

In its defence, the order attempted to remove itself from the emerging feud by attributing the misunderstanding to Fr. Byrne, stating:

> The real object of our Order was overlooked by Fr. Martin's proposal namely that we were not destined to do the work of Chaplains, that it was preposterous to establish a community merely for a kind of Parochial work, whereas it is the spirit of our Congregation to preach and not to Baptize and if we are to establish ourselves anywhere it is with the avowed object of giving missions as the principle aim of our Order. Here on the contrary there was very little prospect of giving missions if we were to establish a community exclusively for the English speaking community, in just one year, one or two priests could give all the mission needed for a decade. The largest congregation to be collected outside of the city would not amount to more than 150 or 200 people, to establish a community for these would be unwarrantable.[208]

The gulf that had developed between the two parties was largely one of perception. The Irish community considered itself worthy of an order to exclusively service their 'parochial needs', whilst the Passionists, in desiring a more ambitious mission, considered the Irish too insular and insignificant a community to satisfy their missionary zeal. In reality, the bargaining position of both parties was compromised through their inherent need of each other. The onslaught of Italian and Spanish immigrants and their Churches was rapidly eclipsing the potential influence of Irish Catholicism. Equally, the Passionist order, then housed in the Irish chapel at San Roque, was dependent on Irish benefactors for the continuation of its work. Indeed, Fr. Fedelis, a Passionist from North America sent to assess the situation, astutely reported that without the help of the Irish 'we cannot live in this country'.[209] He further concluded that, with regard to receiving financial support from other European groups, 'it would be necessary to commence with the Irish; there is nothing to hope from the others at present'.[210] It would seem, therefore, that there was some justification to Irish claims that the Passionists had misused their financial and spiritual support and were duplicitous in their dealings with them. Furthermore, Irish grievances were inflamed by reports that the Passionists had proclaimed them a 'nation of red-headed savages', describing Irish-Argentine women as 'a gang of Biddies'.[211] Whether reports of such insults were accurate or not, without representation within senior ecclesiastical circles and given their keenness to secure an order, the Irish community was exposed and vulnerable to Passionist ambitions.

On 14 May 1880, the Very Reverend Father General of the Passionists wrote a searing letter to Fr. Byrne, clearly stating the unacceptability of being dictated to by the Irish community:

Why again to ask only for Irish priests, and to take upon the responsibility of supporting Irish priests exclusively and to look after the spiritual or to say the national wants of the Irish (people). All this I think would be rather too much. [...] Please get out of any engagement you may have undertaken and come back to Europe and leave for some one else the charge of satisfying the exigencies of the Irish colony.[212]

Despite the eventual arrival of the order, disillusionment at inadequate pastoral representation had formed in the collective awareness of the Irish. This realisation encouraged the laity to form religious based social organisations that would more effectively provide a platform for an Irish Catholic voice. In part, this movement was reflective of broader ecclesiastical calls for lay social action in the years following Vatican Council I (1869–70). In particular, the pontificate of Leo XIII (1878–1903) encouraged Catholics to engage in movements of a confessional nature.[213] In his most explicit socially focused encyclical, *Rerum novarum*, 1891, the Pope emphasised the benefits of lay associations in furthering the aims of social action by empowering Christian action groups.[214] The unequivocal papal approval he expressed for what was an organic lay movement was advocated equally in the subsequent pontificates of Pius X (1903–14) and Benedict XV (1914–22). Their respective encyclicals *Il fermo proposito*, 1905, and *Ad beatissimi*, 1914, called for the Church's social teaching to be realised through the practical work of lay societies and the employment of Catholic social principles.[215] In North America and Britain, Catholic action groups such as that of Saint Vincent de Paul and the Ancient Order of Hibernians were created to complement established institutional structures.

Emergent lay associations in Argentina were, therefore, in keeping with Catholic social action worldwide. The Irish community's response, however, was not so much a call to arms by Catholic social action as a unification of Irish Catholic interests in the face of deficient ecclesiastical leadership. The most prominent example of this was the founding of the Irish Catholic Association (I.C.A.) in 1883. As an organisation, the I.C.A. set out to serve the 'spiritual and educational interests of the Irish community'.[216] Although the list of candidates for appointment to the committee included four prominent clerics, in the event, those appointed comprised sixteen lay Irish community members, all of whom were notable *estancieros..*[217] In spite of Dean Patrick Dillon assuming its initial presidency, institutional control belonged decidedly to the community. The statutes decreed that, should the association dissolve, all remaining funds and property were to be held 'in trust by 50 Irishmen or the descendants of

Irishmen'.[218] As a failsafe, the Archbishop of Buenos Aires was to be appointed trustee if implementing the above decree was impracticable.

In not deferring to an Irish cleric to administer affairs, the community starkly demonstrated the absence of a prominent, politically powerful Irish ecclesiastical voice. Furthermore, in stating that the association would 'take charge of' hospitals, schools and other charitable associations operated by the community', it was in effect assuming control over its own affairs within Argentina.[219] Thus, failure to craft a distinct Irish-Argentine ecclesiastical identity in the deepest sense had, in turn, narrowed and simplified the community's points of reference. In creating lay associations, a subcultural society emerged that was without reference to Dublin or Rome. Within an ostensibly wholly Irish-Argentine context, therefore, an increasingly inward-looking ethnic group was formed.

The unique social, political and religious climate Argentina proffered the Irish Church enhanced its standing in a way that was not observable in other nineteenth-century immigrant destinations. By assuming the generic 'Iglesia Inglesa' classification – the application of which carried deeper significance than the spoken language of its communicants – the Irish Church demonstrated an astute awareness of prevailing native influences. In securing an elevated social position, the forces of Irish Catholicism consciously and expertly massaged native political and ecclesiastical factions. Post Independence, political governance frequently and abruptly changed hands in the ebb and flow of liberalism versus conservatism. However, the deft courting of opposing political interests was finely balanced with the omnipresent sensibilities of Argentina's Church, to which Irish ecclesiastical conservatism, principally under Fahey's guidance, was aptly suited. If Fahey's politicking could be described as failing in any quarter, it was in relation to Dublin not Buenos Aires. The Irish hierarchy viewed his isolationist approach and controversial political allies as reprehensible. In so consuming himself with the institutional advancement of the Irish Church in Argentina, Fahey failed to court the patronage of his own ecclesiastical hierarchy, alienating himself and, ironically, the interests of his cherished mission in the process. Viewed retrospectively, Fahey's pre-emptive strike at institutional power within the Argentine religious structures, had it been successful, would have established early ecclesiastical authority for the Irish Church and its community. In the event, his death signalled the collapse of any considered pretensions to high office, as an increasingly confident native Church asserted its pre-eminence. More significantly, the inflated sense of importance the community attributed to itself and expected from others during the Fahey years was decisively shattered through its dealings with both the Pallottine and Passionist Fathers. Collective impotence and an inability to secure a dedicated religious ministry contributed to the community's growing institutional isolation. By establishing social action groups, however, the Irish not only responded to the broader Catholic teachings of Vatican Council I, but also assertively reacted to a new native ecclesiastical order in which they no longer had a significant voice. The future direction of the community, although still significantly influenced by Irish clergy at a local level, was, in the more general sense, now in the hands of the laity.

Although in the aftermath of Fahey the Irish were forced to reappraise its institutional and ecclesiastical influence, the style of the efficacious Dominican remained embedded in the fabric of the community. By enforcing a rigid social and moral code, the Irish Church, under Fahey's direction, contributed to a confused Irish identity within the framework of a dominant '*Inglés*' social order. The exacting communal insistence on conduct befitting an '*Inglés*' identity, in turn, created an intransigent legacy whereby collective response to social unorthodoxy was condemnatory and absolute. Treatment of those who succumbed to, or fell victim to, a less than perfect social ideal was subject to an extreme and often contradictory judgement from the Irish ethnic group.

Thus, as the self-appointed agency of social orthodoxy, it could be argued that a function of the Irish Catholic Church in Argentina was to suppress socially deviant behaviour. Although providing an imperfect mortar for Irish immigrants, which fractured under pressures of social and economic differentiation, the Church was, of course, but one agency amongst many that sought to facilitate Irish integration into the moneyed classes of Buenos Aires Province and render the community fit for elite society. Lay associations, commercial and landed interests, and cultural societies equally contributed.[220] And, although not easily established, it is necessary to explore the extent to which these combined forces were successful in easing the process of Irish assimilation.

NOTES

1. Tulio Halperín-Donghi, *Historia contemporánea de América Latina* (5th ed., Buenos Aires, 2004), esp. ch. 1.
2. Austen Ivereigh, *Catholicism and Politics in Argentina, 1810–1960* (New York and London, 1995), p. 39.
3. Guillermo Furlong Cardiff, 'El catolicismo Argentina entre 1860–1930' in R. Levene (ed.), *Historia de la nación Argentina*, vol. III (Buenos Aires, 1937), pp. 595–622.
4. Ivereigh (1995), p. 39. These dioceses were: Santa Fe in Paraná, Cordoba in Upper Peru and Buenos Aires in La Plata.
5. Leslie Bethell, 'A Note on the Church and the Independence of Latin America' in Leslie Bethell (ed.), *The Cambridge History of Latin America*, vol. III (Cambridge, 1995), pp. 229–234
6. Daniel Omar de Lucía, 'Iglesia, estado y secularización en la Argentina (1800–1890)' in *El Catoblepas*, no. 16 (June 2003), pp. 13–45.
7. Domingo Faustino Sarmiento, *Facundo: Civilización y barbarie* (2nd ed., Madrid, 1993), p. 108
8. Ibid.
9. Ivereigh (1995), p. 41.
10. Guillermo Furlong Cardiff, *Nacimiento y desarrollo de la filosofía en el rio de la Plata, 1536–1810* (Buenos Aires, 1952), p. 58.
11. John Lynch, 'The Catholic Church in Latin America, 1830–1930' in Leslie Bethell (ed.), *The Cambridge History of Latin America*, vol. IV (Cambridge, 1995), pp. 527–595.
12. Stanley G. Payne, *El catolicismo español* (Barcelona, 1984), pp. 88–92.
13. Austen Ivereigh, 'The Shape of the State: Liberals and Catholics in the Dispute over Law 1420 of 1884 in Argentina' in Austen Ivereigh (ed.), *The Politics of Religion in an Age of Revival*, (London, 2000), pp. 166–187.
14. Lynch (1985), p. 534.
15. Idem.
16. National Library of Ireland [hereafter NLI], William Bulfin Papers [hereafter Bulfin Papers]: Ms. 13, 804/11. For a discussion of priestly involvement in the revolution see also Monsignor Agustín Piaggio, *Influencia del clero en la Independencia Argentina, 1810–1820* (Barcelona, 1912).
17. J. Lloyd Mecham, *Church and State in Latin America: A History of Politico-Ecclesiastical Relations* (Chapel Hill, 1934), p. 278.
18. Ivereigh (2000), p. 170.
19. Translated as 'federation or death'. See Sarmiento (1993), p. 60.
20. De Lucía (2003), p. 18.
21. Mecham (1934), p. 284.
22. Ivan Vallier, *Catholicism, Social Control, and Modernization in Latin America* (New Jersey, 1970), p. 55.
23. Quoted in *The Southern Cross*, 5 July 1889, p. 2.
24. *Guía eclesiástica Argentina* [Hereafter *Guía eclesiástica*], (3rd ed., Buenos Aires, 2000), p. 87. It is important to note that these changes were linked to the world-wide reforms pressed by Pius IX in creating a distinctively diocesan ímpetu to reform, which was so influential in Ireland under Cullen and in the United States under the Kenricks, Hughes and their successors.
25. See E. Birschoff, *Historia de Córdoba* (Buenos Aires, 1979), pp. 281–338.
26. De Lucía (2003), p. 24.
27. Ivereigh (1995), p. 54. See also David Rock, *Authoritarian Argentina* (Berkeley, 1993), pp. 27–54.
28. Bruno Cayetano, *Historia de la Iglesia en la Argentina* (Buenos Aires, 1976), p. 153
29. Rock (1993), p. 31.
30. Ibid., pp. 32–34.
31. De Luaía (2003), p. 36.
32. Lynch (1985), p. 567.
33. Mecham (1934), p. 286.
34. Halperín-Donghi (2004), pp. 242–246.
35. Lynch (1985), p. 566.
36. Scobie (1971), p. 191.
37. For a complete account of the agreement see Woodbine Parish, *Buenos Ayres and the Provinces of the Rio de la Plata: from their Discovery of Conquest by the Spaniards to the Establishment of their Political Independence* (2nd ed., London, 1852), p. 401, appendix IV.

38. Alberto Kleiner, *Inmigración inglesa en la Argentina: El informe, 1875* (Buenos Aires, 1983).
39. M.G. Mulhall, *The English in South America* (Buenos Aires, 1878), p. 416.
40. Ivereigh (1995), p. 52.
41. Fernando J. Devoto, *Estudios sobre la emigración italiana en la Argentina en la segunda mitad del siglo XIX* (Rome, 1991), p. 199.
42. See J. Godio, *Historia del movimiento obrero argentino: Immigrantes, asalariados y lucha de clases, 1880–1910* (Buenos Aires, 1973); R. Entraigas, *Historia de los Salesianos en la Argentina* (Buenos Aires, 1972).
43. Devoto (1991), p. 200.
44. Translated as ' in America [Italians] lose their faith'. See Gianfausto Rosoli, 'Las organizaciones católicas en la Argentina' in Fernando J. Devoto and Gianfausto Rosoli (eds), *La inmigración italiana en la Argentina* (Buenos Aires, 1988), pp. 209–239.
45. Devoto (1991), p. 203. See also Tulio Halperín-Donghi, 'La integración de los inmigrantes italianos a la sociedad Argentina' in Devoto and Rosoli (1988), pp. 87–94.
46. *Censo de la Ciudad de Buenos Aires, 1855* and *Tercer censo nacional de la República Argentina, 1914* [hereafter *Tercer censo nacional, 1914*].
47. Devoto (1991), p. 205.
48. *Guía Eclesiástica*, p. 616.
49. Devoto (1991), p. 205.
50. Rosoli (1988), p. 215.
51. Quote from Bishop Mariano Antonio Espinosa of Buenos Aires, translated as 'other groups do not pose difficulties as their numbers are less substantial'. See Rosoli (1988), p. 214.
52. Ibid.
53. Fernando J. Devoto, *Historia de la inmigración en la Argentina* (Buenos Aires, 2003), p. 285.
54. All Hallows College: Fahey to Archbishop Cullen, 27 July 1864.
55. Devoto (2003), p. 285.
56. Rosoli (1988), p. 215.
57. Ronald C. Newton, *German Buenos Aires, 1900–1933: Social Change and Cultural Crisis* (Austin & London, 1977), p. 26.
58. *Segundo censo nacional de la República Argentina, 1895.*
59. M.G. and E.T. Mulhall, *Manual de las Repúblicas del Plata* (Buenos Aires and London, 1876), p. 29.
60. Newton (1977), p. 26.
61. Ibid.
62. Mecham (1934), p. 304.
63. Monsignor Santiago M. Ussher, *Los capellanes irlandeses en la colectividad hiberno-argentina durante el siglo XIX* (Buenos Aires, 1953), p. 31.
64. *The Southern Cross*, 21 March 1890, p. 5.
65. All Hallows College: Fahey to Moriarty, 2 June 1853.
66. Only the diocese of Córdoba was established earlier, in 1570. See *Guía Eclesiástica*, p. 145
67. Lynch (1985), p. 534.
68. *Catholic Encyclopaedia*, vol. I (New York, 1907), p. 704.
69. Ibid.
70. See Monsignor James M. Ussher, *Father Fahy* (Buenos Aires, 1951), pp. 35–37, 80–81, 420; Thomas Murray, *The Story of the Irish in Argentina* (New York, 1919), p. 87.
71. Mulhall, 1953, ch. VII.
72. *Una breve reseña de la acción católica irlandesa en la República Argentina* (Buenos Aires, 1932) [hereafter *Una breve reseña*]. Published for the '31st International Eucharistic Congress' at the request of the Central Committee, Dublin.
73. All Hallows College: Fahey to Woodlock, 3 March 1856.
74. Ussher (1953), chapter VII.
75. McKenna (1994), p. 128. The system of Irish chaplaincies was instigated by Fr. Anthony Dominic Fahey and is discussed at length below.
76. Ussher (1951), p. 83.
77. Ibid.
78. NLI, Bulfin Papers: Ms. 13, 804/11 n.d.
79. Keith Robbins, 'Religion and Community in Scotland and Wales since 1800' in Sheridan Gilley and W.J. Shiels (eds), *A History of Religion in Britain: Practice and Belief from Pre-Roman Times to the Present* (Oxford & Cambridge, Mass., 1994), pp. 363–380.

80. David Fitzpatrick, 'A Peculiar Tramping People: The Irish in Britain, 1801–70' in W.E. Vaughan (ed.), *A New History of Ireland: Ireland Under the Union, I, 1801–70*, vol. V (Oxford, 1989), pp. 623–660.
81. Sheridan Gilley, 'The Roman Catholic Church in England, 1780–1940' in Sheridan Gilley and W.J. Shiels (eds), *A History of Religion in Britain: Practice and Belief from Pre-Roman Times to the Present* (Oxford & Cambridge, Mass., 1994), pp. 346–362. See also John Bossy, *The English Catholic Community, 1570–1850* (3rd ed., London, 1979).
82. See David N. Doyle, 'The Remaking of Irish America, 1845–1880', in J.J. Lee and Marion R. Casey, *Making the Irish American* (New York, 2006), pp. 213–252, esp. pp. 213–215.
83. David N. Doyle, 'The Irish in North America, 1776–1845' in Lee and Casey (2006), pp. 171–212, esp. p. 200.
84. Kerby A. Miller, *Emigrants and Exiles* (Oxford, 1985), pp. 274–276.
85. Ussher (1951), p. 43.
86. Malcolm Campbell presented a similar thesis for San Francisco and Australia's east coast. See Campbell, Malcolm, *Ireland's New Worlds: Immigrants, Politics and Society in the United States and Australia, 1815–1922* (Wisconsin, 2008), pp. 99–100.
87. Edward F. Every, *The Anglican Church in South America* (London, 1915), p. 11. For a discussion on Judaism and Freemasonry see Devoto (2003), pp. 343–345 and Rock (1993), pp. 27, 59.
88. Every (1915), p. 18.
89. Lynch, 1985, p. 558. See also Frederick B. Pike, *Freedom and Reform in Latin America* (Notre Dame, 1967), pp. 33–38.
90. See Edmundo Murray, *Devenir irlandés* (Buenos Aires, 2004), esp. introduction.
91. Ibid.
92. Every (1915), p. 11.
93. All Hallows College: Fahey to Moriarty, 2 June 1853.
94. *The Southern Cross*, 5 July 1889, p. 2.
95. Murray (1919), p. 267.
96. *The Southern Cross*, 5 July 1889, p. 2.
97. Murray (1919), p. 87.
98. Ussher (1951), p. 420.
99. The spelling of 'Fahey' appears in Mulhall and Ussher as 'Fahy', but this book adheres to that cited in Murray (1919), p. 141. Murray remarks that Fahey himself always spelt his surname with an 'e', though examination of his correspondence does not fully support this as both spellings appear to have been used.
100. Ussher, Monsignor Santiago M. *A Biography of Anthony Dominic Fahy, O.P., Irish Missionary in Argentina, 1805–1871* (Buenos Aires, 1951), p. 30. Some ambiguity surrounds the exact period Fahy spent in Kentucky as it has been reported elsewhere as ten years. See *Una breve reseña* (1932), p. 14.
101. Murray (1919), p. 344.
102. Ibid.
103. Dublin Diocesan Archives, Murray Papers: 33/13/12a.
104. Ibid.
105. Ibid., Murray Papers: AB3/33/13.
106. All Hallows College: Fahey to Woodlock, 2 March 1855.
107. Ibid., Fahey to Moriarty, 2 June 1853.
108. Ibid., Fahey to Archbishop Cullen, 27 July 1864.
109. Ibid., Fahey to Woodlock, 3 April 1858.
110. Ibid., Fahey to Moriarty, 2 June 1853.
111. Ibid, Fahey to Woodlock, 2 March 1855.
112. Fahey would make all appointments of arriving priests to allotted parishes. See *Una breve reseña* (1932).
113. All Hallows College: Fahey to Woodlock, 26 June 1866.
114. Ibid.
115. Ibid., Fahey to Moriarty, 2 June 1853.
116. Ibid., Fahey to Moriarty, 1 December 1853 and 3 December 1853, also Fahey to Woodlock, 2 June 1863.
117. Ibid., Fahey to Woodlock, 14 January 1862.
118. Ibid., Fahey to Woodlock, 28 April 1861.

119. Ibid., Fahey to Woodlock, 2 July 1856. See also letter from Archbishop's House confirming power to ordain for the Buenos Aires mission, in ibid., Lyons to Woodlock, 15 March 1856. Escalada was made the first Archbishop of Buenos Aires in 1865.
120. Ibid., Fahey to Woodlock, 3 March 1856.
121. Ibid., Fahey to Woodlock, 28 December 1859
122. Dublin Diocesan Archives, Cullen Papers: 332/2/I (2).
123. All Hallows College: Fahey to Woodlock, 2 March 1855.
124. The £100 would have covered the cost of passage. Dublin Diocesan Archives, Murray Papers: AB3/33/13.
125. All Hallows College: John Cullen to Woodlock, 29 November 1855.
126. Sister Mary Josephine Gately, *The Sisters of Mercy* (New York, 1931), p. 489.
127. Dublin Diocesan Archives, Cullen Papers: 339/6/II/3.
128. Ibid.
129. Ibid., Murray Papers: AB3/33/13/2.
130. Ibid.
131. Ibid., Murray Papers: AB3/33/13/1.
132. Ibid., Murray Papers: B3/33/13/4.
133. Ibid., Cullen Papers: 339/6/II/2.
134. Maria Teresa Julianello and Maria Silvana Vazquez, 'The Story of Camila O'Gorman' in *Irish Roots*, no. 3 (1996), pp. 18–19.
135. See Maria Teresa Julianello, *The Scarlet Trinity* (Cork, 2000)
136. My translation: 'having more power than the Archbishop'. See Ussher (1953), p. 45
137. Murray (1919), p. 173.
138. Dublin Diocesan Archives, Murray Papers: 33/15/5a.
139. M. Chevalier de Saint Robert, 'Le General Rosas et la question de la Plata' (Paris, 1848), quoted in *Dublin Review*, vol. XXVI (1849), pp. 33–59.
140. Letter from General O'Brien to the Earl of Aberdeen, 9 December 1844, quoted in ibid. O'Brien had fought in the 'Wars of Independence' for the Argentine General San Martin. He was later imprisoned by Rosas under threat of execution for delivering a communiqué bearing the name of an adversary, General Santa Cruz. See Murray (1919), pp. 44, 117.
141. Mgr James M. Ussher, *Father Fahy: A Biography of Anthony Dominic Fahy O.P., Irish Missionary in Argentina, 1805–1871* (Buenos Aires, 1951), p. 66.
142. Dublin Diocesan Archives, Murray Papers: AB3/33/13.
143. *Dublin Review* (1849), p. 34.
144. Ibid., p. 35.
145. Murray (1919), pp. 110–112.
146. *Dublin Review* (1849), p. 54.
147. Ibid., p. 58.
148. See Murray (1919), pp. 81, 37–44.
149. Murray (1919), p. 174.
150. All Hallows College: Fahey to Woodlock, 2 October 1855.
151. Quoted in Murray (1919), pp. 130–131.
152. Ibid.
153. Ussher (1951), p. 71.
154. All Hallows College: Fahey to Cullen, 27 July 1864.
155. Ibid., Fahey to Woodlock, 28 October 1860.
156. Ibid., Fahey to Woodlock, 15 January 1870.
157. See Murray (1919), p. 164.
158. All Hallows College: Fahey to Woodlock, 2 February 1856.
159. Murray (1919), p. 319; Ussher (1951), p. 127–128.
160. See Murray (1919), pp. 318, 174.
161. All Hallows College: Fahey to Woodlock, 2 February 1856.
162. NLI, Bulfin Papers: Ms. 13, 804/11, n.d.
163. All Hallows College: Fahey to Woodlock, 2 October 1855.
164. Ibid., Fahey to Woodlock, 3 April 1858.
165. Dublin Diocesan Archives, Murray Papers: AB3/33/13/3.
166. Ussher (1953), p. 16.
167. *Saint Brendan's College, First Report* (December 1869). By kind permission of the Passionist Fathers, Holy Cross Church, Buenos Aires [hereafter *St Brendan's College, 1869*].

168. Ibid.
169. Ussher (1951), p. 166.
170. *St Brendan's College, 1869.*
171. Ibid.
172. Ibid.
173. Mulhall (1878), p. 424. Although Buenos Aires was by now an archdiocese, the previous Archbishop, Mariano Escalada, had died in 1870 and Frederico León Aneiros, Bishop of Buenos, was made Archbishop in 1873.
174. Murray (1919), p. 274.
175. Quoted in Ussher (1953), p. 58.
176. Quoted in Murray (1919), p. 402.
177. De Lucía, 2003, p. 31.
178. Espinosa was made Archbishop of Buenos Aires in 1900.
179. NLI, Bulfin Papers: Ms. 13,819, Archbishop Espinosa to William Bulfin, 16 March 1901.
180. Ibid.
181. The term 'ambient' is quoted directly from the original source and is presumably meant to read 'ambience'.
182. Ibid.
183. For an article outlining the dangers of Freemasonry see 'Catholics and Freemasonry' in *The Irish Ecclesiastical Record*, vol. VI (1899), pp. 309–326.
184. Ussher (1953), p. 55.
185. Rev. John S. Gaynor, *The History of St. Patrick's College in Mercedes* (Buenos Aires, 1957), p. 76 and Rev. John S. Gaynor, *The English-Speaking Pallottines* (Rome, 1962), p. 167
186. Gaynor (1957), p. 65.
187. *The Southern Cross*, 23 October 1891.
188. Gaynor (1962), p. 167.
189. Ibid., p. 166.
190. Ibid., pp. 56–59.
191. Rev. John S. Gaynor, *Memoir of Father Patrick O'Grady* (Buenos Aires, 1959), p. 12.
192. Quoted in Rev. John S. Gaynor, *Memoir of Father John Dolan* (Buenos Aires, 1958), p. 7.
193. See Ussher (1953), p. 58.
194. *Una breve reseña* (1932).
195. Ibid.
196. *La Asociación Católica Irlandesa en el centenario de su fundación, 1883–1983* (Buenos Aires, 1983).
197. *Una breve reseña* (1932).
198. Ibid., p. 169.
199. Ussher (1951), p. 168.
200. See David Noel Doyle, 'The Irish in North America, 1776–1845' in W.E. Vaughan (ed.), *A New History of Ireland: Ireland under the Union, I, 1801–70*, vol. V (Oxford, 1989), pp. 682–724; and Patrick J. O'Farrell, 'The Irish in Australia and New Zealand, 1791–1870' in ibid., pp. 661–681.
201. See James E. Handley, *The Navvy in Scotland* (Cork, 1970), pp. 324–326.
202. *The Southern Cross*, 2 April 1880, p. 1.
203. *Platea Chronicle of Holy Cross Church* [hereafter *Platea Chronicle*]. By kind permission of the Passionist Fathers, Buenos Aires. All extracts herewith are reproduced as originally written, without grammatical corrections.
204. Ibid.
205. Murray (1919), p. 404.
206. Ibid., p. 413.
207. Extract from a published pamphlet, *The Passionist Order in Argentina*, quoted in Murray (1919), p. 406.
208. *Platea Chronicle*. See note 203 for full citation.
209. See Murray (1919), pp. 411–416.
210. Quoted in ibid.
211. NLI, Bulfin Papers: Ms. 13, 815. Quoted in a letter from Jorge Manson to William Bulfin, 31 October 1909.
212. *Platea Chronicle*. See note 203 for full citation.
213. *New Catholic Encyclopedia*, vol. XIII (Washington, 1967), p. 311.

214. Ibid., vol. VIII, p. 647.
215. See ibid., vol. XI, p. 411; vol. II, p. 280.
216. *Associación Catolica Irlandesa, 1883–1983, Edición Centenario* (Buenos Aires, 1983).
217. NLI, Bulfin Papers: Ms. 13,818. See Irish Catholic Association Statutes [hereafter I.C.A. Statutes], 25 March 1900. See also Passionist Fathers, Buenos Aires, *Acta de la Ascociación Católica Irlandesa: Nuevo directorio* (Buenos Aires, 1925).
218. I.C.A. Statutes.
219. Ibid.
220. See Chapter 6 for a discussion on cultural expression.

CHAPTER FIVE

Falling from grace?
Integration and the myth of
Irish social deviancy

The process, pace and extent of integration is a central concern of immigration studies. But it is also among the most difficult to measure. Inevitably, given the silent nature of the most successful levels of integration, research on this topic has focused on the other, negative side of the scale of integration; that is to say, levels of 'deviancy'. 'Deviancy' in its variant forms has become, therefore, the most accessible and fruitful approach to assessing levels of integration amongst Irish immigrant communities. Within this broad category of sociological phenomenon several closely related manifestations of deviancy have been selected for examination, including mental health, disorder, crime and, above all, drunkenness. The discussion that follows considers each of these facets in so far as the evidence allows. But, because it is the most prominent feature of Irish immigrant behaviour and, more importantly, because it embodies in a particularly striking way the methodological and interpretative problems attached to all attempts to assess extensive deviancy (and influence levels of integration), it is best to begin with drunkenness.

A principal signifier of Irish slippage from social conformity within nineteenth-century immigrant destinations was a propensity for excessive alcohol consumption. Universal over-representation across time and space has led to a series of theses on causality, among which are ethnicity, class, neighbourhood and social conditions.[1] The marked propensity of the Irish to public drinking, which led to its early identification as a cultural stereotype, has for long been the subject of intense historical study. David Fitzpatrick noted that Irish criminality in Britain was largely fuelled by alcohol and was of a 'casual and unskilled' nature.[2] In Liverpool in 1877 a contemporary commentator estimated that 90 per cent of offences committed by Irish inmates of the borough gaol were drink related.[3] It was a much repeated pattern elsewhere. In Sydney, the 1887

Intoxicating Drink Inquiry Commission ascribed three quarters of all offences committed to drink; Irish born offenders in New South Wales were heavily represented across all recorded crime.[4] And, in New Zealand, the heavy representation of the Irish in drink related offences was not attributed to police harassment or local prejudice but to an established and traditional set of behavioural traits, exported from the homeland, and which provided a comforting defence to the challenges of immigrant existence.[5] Irish immigrants in Pittsburgh described such problems as physical hardship and psychological isolation, both of which fuelled their drinking habit and led to a stream of dysfunctional and pathological realities.[6]

But, in accounting for the Irish propensity to drink, one commentator has gone further. The pervasive nature of alcohol consumption within Irish immigrant groups led Richard Stivers to conclude that the level of recorded abuse was evidence of an institutionalised cultural stereotyping that they themselves were complicit in forming.[7] Hard drinking amongst Irish males in Ireland, Stivers argued, emerged as a symbol of masculinity, which commanded prestige within the local community and anchored male identity. It functioned as a cultural release from the restrictions imposed by nineteenth-century Irish society, a form of compensation for the 'paucity of customary opportunities to attain manhood: marriage, family and landownership.'[8] And commentators such as Robert F. Bales and Elizabeth Malcolm have broadly agreed that, for the male adolescent, drinking became a rite of passage that heralded the advent of adulthood with all its accompanying social frustrations.[9] Dependency upon it thus became germane to an adult status, a cultural expression symbolising solidarity with particular groups within the social system.[10]

But Stivers progressed further. He suggested that drinking became a national pathology, which once transported to America was disembodied from its original connotations and assumed renewed significance as a means of group identity. Excessive alcohol consumption differentiated the Irish, for whom arrests for drunkenness were higher than any other European group.[11] No longer the bastion of Irish masculinity, drinking became a collective symbol of Irish identity irrespective of gender.[12] Stivers concluded that the negative stereotype of the drunken Irishman was facilitated by the willingness of the Irish to embrace the role attributed to them, thus becoming 'both the stereotyper and stereotyped'.[13]

This relatively limited appraisal of the use and indeed abuse of alcohol has been contested. Critics of Stivers point to the limitations of explaining excessive alcohol consumption by means of a national characteristic endemic to the Irish race. His argument has been described as a stilted, artificial explanation for what is also a convivial pastime.[14] Furthermore, Stivers' thesis suggests that excessive drinking was consistent with patterns in Ireland and a response to anxiety and social instability.[15] But this is challenged by studies on Britain and the United States, which present a more complex interpretation. W.J. Lowe, in his study of Lancashire, recognised the tradition of drinking in Ireland but also identified the importance of alcohol amongst the English working class. Lowe stated that sprit consumption was actually slightly lower in Ireland than in Britain, and beer consumption significantly so.[16] This is largely supported by a study on New York, which identified that English and Scottish immigrants were as prone to excessive drinking as were the Irish.[17] Most significantly, Elizabeth Malcolm's study established that falls in consumption levels coincided with periods of economic decline or famine and that drinking was a luxury afforded only at times of affluence. She concluded that a 'complex interplay of forces' determined patterns of drink consumption.[18]

And this complexity is, perhaps, best demonstrated through regional studies. The danger of adopting a 'one size fits all' approach is increasingly clear thanks mainly to a growing historiography, which addresses the nature of local and regional settlement. The much quoted study of Oscar Handlin on Boston's immigrants identified the wretchedness of local conditions as a contributing factor to the consumption of alcohol.[19] Lowe later echoed this in his appraisal of nineteenth-century Lancashire. Drunkenness was recognised as the most significant problem facing Lancashire police, but Lowe asserted that those Irish frequenting public houses were not in fact drunks but were seeking respite from the drudgery and oppression of everyday existence.[20] And the traditional role alcohol played in Irish social life would almost certainly have influenced this natural gravitation. Celebrations, feast days and fair days were all associated with excessive drinking in the homeland, often resulting in drunken brawls. Any replication of such opens displays of misconduct within host societies undoubtedly rendered the community more visible and resulted in a more vigilant and sustained approach to policing.[21] In Wolverhampton, for example, local law enforcement officers closely observed Irish districts, reflecting a lack of tolerance for homeland customs within the local community.[22]

What emerges from these disparate Irish studies is that, despite a heightened propensity for drunk and disorderly behaviour, evidence is far from conclusive. A combination of prejudice, regionalism and deficiency of records obscures the discussion of Irish immigrant alcoholism and, thus, the assessment of Irish assimilation. But a further indicator of the extent of immigrant settlement is represented in more general crime. That nineteenth-century Irish immigrants demonstrated a heightened level of criminal activity has equally been widely documented. Mayhew and Binney, in their nineteenth-century appraisal of London prisons, arrived at a rather prosaic conclusion as to the cause and frequency of Irish criminality:

> As to what may be the cause of crime in Ireland we are not in a position to speak, not having given any special attention to the matter; but the reason why there appears a greater proportion of Irish among the thieves and vagrants of our own country admits a very ready explanation. The Irish constitute the poorest portion of our people. [...] He has learnt to consider trickery or 'artful dodgers' as he calls them, as the highest possible exercise of the intellect.[23]

And yet, Mayhew and Binney's reference to the homeland reflects more general commentary on immigrant assimilation. Many commentators have pointed to social and behavioural practices in the homeland as learnt and exported practices in their destination of choice. In the United States, immigrant origin was considered reliable evidence in ascertaining the ability to become 'American' and indeed informed the immigration legislation of 1917–24.[24] Immigrants arriving before 1880 from Northern and Western Europe were generally considered more suitable than later arriving immigrants from Southern or Eastern Europe. Handlin attributed this form of 'racism' to a widely held belief in the 1890s that Southern and Eastern European immigrants were from an inferior bloodline, which manifested itself in certain social behaviour.[25] Indeed, it was suggested that newly arrived 'Mediterranean basin' immigrants were composed of the 'weak, the broken, and the mentally crippled' who filled the 'jails, asylums, and almshouses'.[26]

Although such findings were fiercely debated and contested in the early 1890s, the Dillingham Commission conclusively endorsed the 'old' and 'new' immigrant divide. Having firmly established the varying degrees of suitability of European immigrants, it went on to attest to immigrant participation in crime, clearly stating that it was higher among the foreign born than the native born.[27] This thesis was not corroborated by the only available statistics of the day, the *United States Census Report on Prisoners*, which clearly stated that immigration had not increased the volume of crime, and that between 1890 and 1904 the percentage of immigrant incarcerations had fallen. Although the Dillingham Commission (1906) – which proceeded to commission its own statistical data in light of the contradictory evidence provided by the census report – did not accept such conclusions, Handlin emphasised that at no point did it present objective evidence to support the assertion that immigrants committed more criminal offences than natives. [28]

W.E. Vaughan has broadly substantiated this in the case of the Irish. While examining consistently high records of Irish criminal activity within immigrant host countries, Vaughan stated that the perception of a crime ridden Ireland whence immigrants came was grossly misrepresented. He argued that, from the early 1850s, serious crime in Ireland had in fact decreased 'faster than the population'.[29] Other studies have agreed. Rather than exporting these traits, it is suggested that the social conditions encountered on arrival fostered such behaviour.[30] And it is here that the development of provincial policing gains particular significance.

Successive legislative changes, commencing with Peel's Metropolitan Police Act of 1829 and culminating in the 1856 County and Borough Act, created a more structured, cohesive police force.[31] But, in spite of this, the nature and consistency of policing varied greatly from region to region. Local conditions largely governed and variants included police-to-population ratio and the prevailing attitude of the chief constable in charge.[32] In Coventry in the mid-1850s, a shortage of manpower and a general policy of leniency resulted in very few Irish arrests.[33] In contrast, in the nearby city of Birmingham the Irish represented approximately 20 per cent of all assaults on police officers between 1862 and 1877, although accounting for only 4 per cent of the population.[34]

David Fitzpatrick demonstrated that between 1871 and 1891 Irish settlers were over-represented in 'virtually all categories of crime' in Manchester and Liverpool.[35] Furthermore, between 1861 and 1911 Irish immigrants in Britain were five times as likely to go to prison as the English population.[36] Fitzpatrick concluded that the consistency of Irish criminal activity rendered it unlikely that arrests could be wholly attributable to police prejudice or hostility. But R.E. Swift warns of the danger of attributing too much weight to criminal statistics, where recorded data may not be simply interpreted as increases in criminal behaviour but, rather, may represent the willingness or ability of the legislature to prosecute.[37] In many cases this led to a targeting of working class areas where the Irish had settled in their droves, which may, in part, account for their statistical over-representation.[38] In addition, and as Frank Neal demonstrated in his study of Liverpool, the number of committals do not always represent the number of offenders, as some are imprisoned more than once each year.[39]

A further indicator of Irish assimilation in host societies is mental illness, and it is often closely associated with a heavy dependency on alcohol. The uniformity of Irish over-representation in alcohol related psychosis has prompted a range of hypotheses. One such study suggested that, in America, the Irish were the most exploited of all European groups and that disproportionately high levels of poverty, alcoholism and insanity were direct physical and psychological results.[40] Robert A. Burchell's analysis of San Francisco estimated that, between 1870 and 1890, 31 per cent of occupants of almshouses examined for insanity, and 24 per cent incarcerated in the House of Correction, were Irish born.[41] And Kerby Miller offered the sombre observation that 'a significant minority of Famine emigrants drifted into the relative haven of insanity'. In this connection Miller noted Edward Jarvis' 1855 report on insanity in the state of Massachusetts. Jarvis attributed high rates amongst Famine emigrants to insecurity and poverty brought on by the 'unsettling nature of the emigrants' experience'.[42] His report linked social class and ethnicity to mental illness, demonstrating 'the greater liability of the poor and the struggling classes to become insane'.[43] Jarvis concluded that insanity was higher among the foreign born than the native born and that of the foreign-born the Irish were most widely represented.[44]

For Jarvis, Irish mental illness was 'unquestionably due to intemperance, to which the Irish seem to be peculiarly prone'. Although current scholarly discourse has challenged the link between insanity and alcohol, there is still much disagreement and debate as to its significance.[45] This includes the work of Jarvis. Stoep and Link have challenged many of Jarvis' conclusions, attributing his findings to the mistaken idea that Irish ethnicity, foreign born status and poverty constituted a single construct. They argue that his apparent xenophobia and incorrect analysis of data was subject to the era's heightened concerns relating to social disharmony created by immigrants. This is also demonstrated by the findings of the Dillingham Commission, which found that, in relation to insanity, the longer the immigrant had been in the United States the higher the propensity. [46] But its prejudicial conclusions were informed largely by ethnicity, and expertly and systematically unmasked by Oscar Handlin.[47] Thus, it would appear that any discussion of mental illness within Irish immigrant communities is fraught with inconsistencies and complexities.

All these studies indicate that a comparative analysis across time and space is problematic not only because of enforcement of law and recording of offence, but also because of the varying social conditions encountered. The complexity of the issues involved in studying the nature of Irish immigrant communities abroad is neatly encapsulated in Malcolm Campbell's recent study of the Pacific rim countries.[48] Here, Campbell asserts that the US East Coast model, as presented by Handlin and others, only partly reflects the Irish immigrant experience, and that regional variations significantly depart from this traditional interpretation.

Campbell presents San Francisco as such an example. Here, nineteenth-century Irish immigrants responded to a more fluid society and economy in the years following the gold rush and experienced considerable benefits as a consequence. By establishing settlement during early development of the region, when political, economic and social structures were still relatively fluid and eagerly contested, the Irish settled in a distinctive way.[49] But against the dominance and extensive documentation of the East Coast model, the West Coast experience has been more difficult to assert. Campbell states that, rather than viewing San Francisco against US historiography, a more helpful comparison would be that of Australia's eastern seaboard. He argues that Irish immigrants in San Francisco and Australia shared a number of common characteristics, including demographic, social and economic. Australia's Irish did not consider themselves subject to hardships on the scale reported elsewhere, but instead, and in association with San Francisco, celebrated opportunities presented to them in their new homeland.[50]

Issues raised in Campbell's study are particularly pertinent to the distinctive and hitherto insufficiently studied character of Irish migration to Argentina. But, in approaching the topic of Irish deviant behaviour, as expressed through established indices, there are several factors that must first be taken into account. The pattern of Irish drinking in Argentina is different from that found either in Ireland or recipient countries of Irish immigrants. And the distribution of the Irish community, both socially and geographically, is distinct. But finally, and most importantly, the statistics are extremely problematic. Thus, an enquiry into the character and extent of Irish public drunkenness in Argentina will be of central importance to the understanding of 'deviancy' in general and, ultimately, the degree of Irish integration into Argentine society.

Unlike other recipient destinations where extensive and accurate empirical data forms the basis of discussion, a lack of comprehensive statistical evidence in Argentina impedes and frustrates final analysis in all but general terms. Thus, in assessing imperfect statistical sources, which in itself creates a number of interpretative dilemmas, findings should not, in the case of Argentina, be viewed as a means in itself but rather as a means to an end. That is to say, although the recording of official Argentine data does not adequately allow for rigorous scholarly interrogation, the wealth of raw material available, albeit imperfect, does provide an extensive opportunity to address two key issues: first, the extent to which the Irish in Argentina comfortably assimilated; and, second, to contribute to the broader debate of Irish immigrant deviancy.[51] Of course, official records support only a speculative argument in this regard, and so it is here that the importance of contemporary anecdotal evidence is most significant in establishing the nature of their assimilation. But it is to empirical evidence that this discussion first turns.

The established mode of assessing drunkenness in all social studies is the level of arrests and short to longer term incarceration. And it is here that the generic problem of statistical data concerning immigrant communities in Argentina as a whole become particularly acute. The statistics presented below were compiled from two sets of official data. The first relates to 'police cell arrests' and incorporates male and female activity between 1872 and 1886; the second examines the 'prison population' for male inmates from 1872 to 1887.[52] Both sets represent activity within Buenos Aires City and Province, and as such, are not fully representative of the national picture. Each table details the number of criminals recorded as well as the type of crime committed. All data are restricted to the years for which official records categorised European immigrants by ethnic group and not, as was the case from the late 1880s, under the collective category of '*extranjero*'.[53] Furthermore, official data was not available for each consecutive year, resulting in the omission of certain years within the period under examination. In each case this is clearly detailed in the accompanying appendices, which provide a year-by-year statistical breakdown for each of the summary tables presented.

Consequently, all results represent data accumulated from the available sample, which may not correspond to the stated period in its entirety. The conclusions drawn are based on statistical calculations of either under or over-representation in each dysfunctional category for each ethnic group, in accordance with corresponding census population data.[54] For the purpose of consistency with available statistics, the population of Buenos Aires Province has been isolated from total population in both the 1869 and 1895 census in order to represent an accurate point of comparison. Table 13 records gender distribution for the five principal European immigrant groups in the First and Second National Censuses within Buenos Aires Province.

Establishing a comparative crime model for the Irish in Argentina is, of course, hindered by the ambiguity of the '*Inglés*' classification. Equally problematic is determining the percentage of recorded statistics that applied to first or second generation immigrants. As previously discussed in Chapter 2, the definition of

TABLE 13: GENDER DISTRIBUTION OF FIVE PRINCIPAL IMMIGRANT GROUPS IN BUENOS AIRES PROVINCE, 1869 AND 1895

First National Non-Argentine male population			Census 1869 Non-Argentine female population		
Nativity group	No.	%	Nativity group	No.	%
Spanish	22,272	23.94	Spanish	6,262	17.60
French	18,492	19.88	French	8,649	24.31
'*Inglés*'	6,339	6.81	'*Inglés*'	2,713	7.63
Italian	43,550	46.81	Italian	17,136	48.16
German	2,373	2.55	German	819	2.30
Total	93,026	100%	Total	35,579	100%

Source: Compiled from *Primer censo nacional, 1869*, pp. 636–637[55]

Second National Non-Argentine male population			Census 1895 Non-Argentine female population		
Nativity group	No.	%	Nativity group	No.	%
Spanish	97,813	27.21	Spanish	52,542	25.60
French	39,952	11.12	French	28,372	13.82
'*Inglés*'	9,820	2.73	'*Inglés*'	5,782	2.82
Italian	206,493	57.45	Italian	115,449	56.25
German	5,344	1.49	German	3,107	1.51
Total	359,422	100%	Total	205,252	100%

Source: Compiled from *Segundo censo nacional, 1895*, vol. I, table VII[56]

nationality recorded in official data was particularly opaque. Whereas nativity was the criterion used in census material, official police and prison records did not provide clarification. It is reasonable to expect, therefore, that data presented in Figure 4 and Tables 14-16 – appearing under the collective heading 'Ethnic group' – were not limited to those of foreign birth, but included subsequent Argentine born generations who continued to record a homeland ethnic identity. In relation to Argentine data, for example, numbers of Argentines recorded in criminal activity significantly increased from 1881. The marked swell, demonstrated in Figure 4, would indicate that the definition of Argentine nationality changed from this point forward as a consequence of significant portions of second or third generation immigrant offspring recording themselves as Argentine.

The increase is largely reflected in the levels of all ethnic groups committed to police cells, which, as Appendix X demonstrates, registered declines from 1881. In the case of the Italian group this pattern would appear consistent with immigrant studies. It is suggested that Italians assimilated quicker in Argentina than their US counterparts, and that second generation Italians were classified as Argentine.[57] This may or may not be an accurate depiction of Italian assimilation, or indeed that of other groups; however, the apparent change in Argentine classification distorts the process of ethnic comparison. In light of these factors it is considered inappropriate to assess the

FIGURE 1: NUMBER OF MALE AND FEMALE ARGENTINE OFFENDERS COMMITTED
TO POLICE CELLS, 1872–86

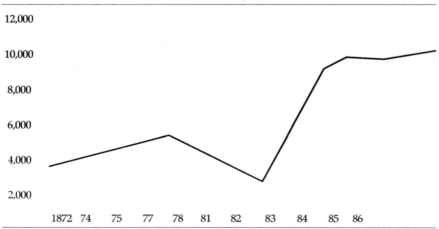

Source: Compiled from Registro estadistico, 1872–1886; see Appendix X.

TABLE 14: POLICE CELL ARRESTS IN BUENOS AIRES PROVINCE

Male offenders, 1872–86
% offences recorded by each of five ethnic groups[59]

	Total	Italian	*'Inglés'*	German	Spanish	French
Offence	No.	%	%	%	%	%
Homicide	574	60	5	1	25	9
Assault	3,047	56	5	2	27	10
Robbery	5,202	54	5	3	26	12
Fraud	108	58	0	0	29	13
Disturbing the peace	14,413	55	6	2	24	12
Intoxication	21,715	40	16	5	22	17
Total of above categories	45,059	48%	11%	3%	24%	14%

Source: Compiled from data in the Biblioteca Senado: *Registro estadistico, 1872–1886.*

TABLE 15: POLICE CELL ARRESTS IN BUENOS AIRES PROVINCE

Female offenders, 1872–86
% offences recorded by each of five ethnic groups[59]

	Total	Italian	*'Inglés'*	German	Spanish	French
Offence	No.	%	%	%	%	%
Homicide	16	69	0	0	12	19
Assault	55	49	0	0	20	31
Robbery	76	41	4	3	21	31
Fraud	1	0	0	0	0	100
Disturbing the peace	441	50	4	2	25	19
Intoxication	461	25	15	4	17	40
Total of above categories	1,050	39%	8%	3%	21%	29%

Source: Compiled from data in the Biblioteca Senado: *Registro estadistico, 1872–1886.*

TABLE 16: PRISON POPULATION IN BUENOS AIRES PROVINCE

Male offenders, 1872–87
% offences recorded by each of five ethnic groups[59]

	Total	Italian	*'Inglés'*	German	Spanish	French
Offence	No.	%	%	%	%	%
Homicide	352	58	7	1	24	10
Assault	603	63	4	1	25	7
Robbery	1,719	50	3	2	30	15
Fraud	38	42	3	8	29	18
Disturbing the peace	87	46	1	3	32	17
Intoxication	50	30	16	12	28	14
Total of above categories	2,849	53%	4%	2%	28%	13%

Source: Compiled from data in the Biblioteca Senado: *Registro estadistico, 1872–1887.*

crime statistics of the '*Inglés*' community against those of the total population. Once again, five principal European ethnic groups were examined, with levels of criminal activity established using the corresponding population percentage of each group within Buenos Aires Province. In spite of this adjustment, it is not possible to fully reconcile discrepancies between the nativity data of the census material and the ethnicity data of the police, prison and hospital material. And there is yet a further complication. The selection of terminal data presented in Tables 14–16 can significantly alter our perception of the levels of deviancy of the Irish community in Argentina due purely to the accidental availability of quantifiable sources.[58] Thus, it is important to note that any interpretation of statistical evidence requires a somewhat tentative, cautious approach and in this regard, findings must remain relatively speculative.

Tables 14–16 detail the police cell arrests and prison population in Buenos Aires Province. The specificity of offence demonstrates not only ethnic criminal propensities but also, more significantly, the extent to which the nature of Irish crime conformed to Irish type. Each table details the category of crime as a percentage of each group's activity, as well as total ethnic participation in all crime.

What is immediately evident from the limited data available is the impossibility of establishing changes in criminal activity over the specified time period. Although Appendices III and IV provide a year-by-year breakdown of these summary tables, they do so for a relatively short time frame, during which various random years are either missing or contain incomplete information.[60] Regarding comparative analysis against census material, the years for which statistics are available are distributed between the points of the two censuses. The population at risk, therefore, lay somewhere between 1869 and 1895 and, as such, no clear change in criminal propensity is evident. Although it is possible to compare levels of under or over-representation against the snapshot of either 1869 or 1895, a clear pattern cannot be established.

As previously stated, the non-serious category of offences recorded in Tables 14, 15 and 16 is demonstrated by the reduced number of male 'prison population' when compared to 'police cell arrests' across all five ethnic groups. This is particularly marked in the category of intoxication, where approximately 3,500 male '*Inglés*' offenders were placed in cells, but only eight imprisoned. Similarly for disturbing the peace: while just over 800 were arrested, only one was imprisoned.[61] Despite these low numerical representations, only the

'Inglés' ethnic group was substantially over-represented in alcohol related arrests and imprisonment against the census population data expressed in Table 13.[62] In contrast, Italian male and female data recorded a slight under-representation and conformed to the North American model of low Italian alcohol consumption. E.M Jellinek has argued that distilled spirits played an insignificant role in Italy, while in France they accounted for 14 per cent of total alcohol consumption.[63] In Argentina, data for French females in particular appeared consistent with this thesis, demonstrating a substantial over-representation in the category of intoxication.

But *'Inglés'* females were over-represented in counts of 'prison cell arrests'. Whereas disturbing the peace was only marginally so, intoxication levels were markedly more significant. Once again, the numerical representation was relatively small, with only seventeen women arrested for disturbing the peace and sixty-seven for intoxication; in the absence of 'prison population' data, corresponding rates of female incarceration cannot be ascertained. Thus, both male and female rates of intoxication within the generic *'Inglés'* group would appear to conform to the 'Irish' stereotype. And yet, the ambiguity of *'Inglés'* data supports a variety of conflicting hypotheses, not least of which is that the Irish were not dominant in levels of recorded *'Inglés'* intoxication: merely a more or less intoxicated component. Furthermore, although available data does not allow for rural versus urban geographical differentiation, it is reasonable to assume that the lion's share of drink related offences were committed in the city. Since Irish settlement was predominantly rural, English and Scottish immigrants would appear to be implicated.

Most significantly, male and female *'Inglés'* records for disturbing the peace did not demonstrate the same stereotypical consistency as other Irish models. Although comparison with 1869 and 1895 data produced the largely expected under and over-representation across respective censuses, male counts of disturbing the peace in 'prison population' data were, in contrast, under-represented against 1895. Although the non-serious nature of the crime may have accounted for the reduction, the *'Inglés'* percentage was still significantly lower than the equivalent figures for Italy, Spain or France. Since recorded levels of disorderly conduct for both sexes were substantially lower than corresponding levels of intoxication, it would appear that alcohol consumption was not typically accompanied by comparable acts of disorder. This suggests that, contrary to the association of the Irish with drunk and disorderly behaviour,

1 Bernard Fox, married to Mary Robbins on 24 January 1872.

2 José O´Neill and Margarita Harrington with their children Dolores, Santiago, Delia, Manuel, Eduardo and Daniel, 1918.

3 Margarita and Brígida Young Fennon c. 1885.

4 Fr. Pío Walsh, sometime in charge of St. Patrick's chapel.

5 Station at Arrecifes parish church, 17 March 1922 (a 'station' being a mission by Catholic priests in the countryside or in a rural town).

6 Teresa Porta Young at the storehouse.

7 Celtic crosses at the cemetery of Carmen de Areco, Buenos Aires province. Photo Edmundo Murray 2003.

8 Elena Kehoe Tyner and Tomás O´Riordon Young, c. 1910.

9 Luke Doyle and Catalina Gaynor with their children Santiago and Eduardo in Estancia Santa Catalina, 1875.

10 Station at St. Patrick's Chapel of Santa Lucía, 1890s.

11 Juan, Cristobal and Thomas Young Doran.

12 Juancito Young in his sulky.

13 Maria Kennedy, Carlos, Eduardo, Patricio, Marcos and Tomás, José Feeney of Co. Longford.

the Irish in Argentina were frequently drunk, but rarely disorderly. This may, of course, have been a facet of rural settlement, where distances between homesteads prohibited rowdy interaction and instead encouraged quiet drinking. But it may also have been a consequence of a deeper reflection. In an anglophile Argentina, assimilation and success of Irish immigrants was dependent upon their 'Britishness'. A stage Irish character akin to that in America did not emerge in Argentina, nor was it sought. The national stereotype existed more as a shadow over the community, not a construct of immigrant identity. The Irish did not create a nationalistic, alcohol related identity that would separate them from the English-speaking community; neither had they the desire to differentiate themselves through stereotypical labelling. Irish Anglophobia and resentment of authority, as described by R.B. Walker in nineteenth-century Australia, was not a component of Irish settlement in Argentina.[64] If then, as Stivers proposes, Irish alcohol consumption in North America became a conscious expression of nationalism and identity, whereby the more drunk the Irish were, the more Irish they became,[65] in Argentina, it would appear that the same conscious identity was inverted: the more sober the Irish were, the more '*Inglés*' they became.

And in Argentina, as elsewhere, public drunkenness was a subject on which opinion makers and commentators were apt to dilate, and from which spokesmen for the community sought to disassociate their more respectable members. In *The Southern Cross* newspaper, on St Patrick's Day, 1875, it was reported that not 'a single Irishman [had been] seen under the influence of intoxicating liquor during the entire day or night'.[66] It is probable that given the community's conservative aspirations these protestations reflected a desire to mask the stereotypical reputation of intemperance and present a respectable public image on this, its national day. But the intrinsic dilemma of alcohol abuse could not always be so ignored and prompted a warning from the provincial of the Passionist Fathers, Reverend Father Constantine, to 'beware of their greatest enemy, intemperance'.[67]

In spite of the cautionary words, the Irish community had little practical support to counter the vice. Although the Irish Argentine Society and the Knights of the Cross both included 'benevolence' in their statutes and cited aiding the poor and afflicted as objectives, neither organisation came into existence until c. 1920 and, more significantly, neither group openly referred to intemperance as a specific focus.[68] Both organisations solicited considerable joining fees and yearly subscriptions from their members, and in this regard were bastions of elite patronage. The Irish Argentine Society in particular obtained contributions of tens of thousands of pesos from the *estanciero* class.[69]

Thus, in founding and supporting such Irish associations, it might be suggested that the elite was reluctant to formally and officially recognise the prominence of alcohol abuse. Intemperance, and those who suffered from it, operated on the margins of communal society, isolated from the institutional concerns of the ethnic group. But an alternate thesis could also apply. It is possible that the spread of alcohol abuse was sufficiently limited as to not require intervention from established and more general community associations. If so, this would be very unusual indeed and quite distinct from other models. Although not fully supported by anecdotal evidence, it nevertheless may reflect two key issues: first, the limited nature of Irish drinking in Argentina; and, second, the rooting of the careful rural social classes in Westmeath and Wexford, amongst whom 'no hopers' were indeed rare.[70]

This absence of institutional response is in direct contrast to North America, where the Ancient Order of Hibernians had been established since 1836 with links to Church and temperance societies.[71] But in Argentina it was sporting groups that appeared to provide an alternative structure for containment, most notably hurling, played informally from 1887; a formal club was not established until 1922.[72] And yet anecdotal reports of alcohol consumption continued. Allegations of excessive drinking of *caña*[73] and of the 'scandalising' of neighbours, more commonly associated with gauchos, were made by the Irish, about the Irish.[74] In a letter to her cousin in 1867, Sally Moore wrote from Buenos Aires:

> I don't know the reason but it is a fact that a great number of young men coming from Europe get lost here, they turn to drink and it is not from the natives they learn it, for it is scarcely ever seen in the respectable classes, amongst the poor *'gauchos'*, yes, but *'Inglés borracho'* which means drunken Englishman is a common saying here.[75]

This provides a number of significant insights. First, the native term *'Inglés borracho'*, whilst not excluding the Irish, may also have included the English, Scottish and Welsh communities. But it would seem reasonable to assume that in writing to a family relation the reference was intended to describe Irish behaviour.[76] Second, its author struggles to account for the prevalence of alcohol misuse amongst young men. And it may well be that difficulties encountered through immigration and through a sense of being 'lost' in a foreign land contributed to their intemperance. This would certainly demonstrate some consistency with other models where immigrants combated the squalid social conditions by seeking refuge in local drinking establishments. But since such circumstances were not common factors in Argentina it is not a wholly adequate explanation. Furthermore, a native newspaper reporting on the dangers of alcohol abuse in both sexes singled out the '*Inglés*' group, commenting that in their homeland 'the number of intoxicated women is considerable'.[77] This was not a reference to '*Inglés*' who had immigrated and who had perhaps developed such traits as a consequence of being 'lost', but rather the behaviour of the '*Inglés*' in general. The implication was that, far from Argentina being the cause of their intemperance, they had, in fact, imported it from their native land. Whether an accurate appraisal of '*Inglés*' behaviour or not, anecdotal evidence of Irish intemperance stimulated communal concerns. In a letter to his brother in Wexford, John James Murphy wrote of the death of a neighbour:

> James Pender was buried on last week. He died of a broken down constitution caused by drink as is supposed. He leaves a family: a wife and five children, and badly provided for. Another Irishman from Westmeath threw himself into a well, and was drowned on the same day, all from grog.[78]

Both Moore's and Murphy's observations reflect, to varying degrees, the prevalence of alcohol problems among the Irish immigrants. And the apparent lack of any significant structural support by either the Irish Catholic Church or the broader community did not go unnoticed by contemporary observers. Drinking was identified as a threat to social cohesion and that allegedly stuck 'like the plague spot'.[79] The community was criticised from within for lacking any sense of 'public spirit', the 'demon of discord' contributing to a 'shapeless mass of struggling humanity'.[80] Culturally and anecdotally, therefore, it would seem that the Irish were at best aware of the dangers of alcohol; at worst, fearful of its destructive potential not only individually, but collectively.

But if, as anecdotal evidence suggests, drinking was a 'prominent vice of the Irishman'[81] it did not lead to estrangement within Argentine society. This, again, is quite unlike the experience elsewhere and may perhaps be explained, in part, by native Argentine drinking practices. Cafés and bars in Buenos Aires were popular establishments of social activity and, by 1870, over 230 of them sold alcohol and were hotbeds of native and immigrant disorder.[82] The backstreets of the city where taverns predominated were considered dens of iniquity where 'half-savage inhabitants' dwelt.[83] The clientèle consisted largely of male labourers and sailors, and female laundry workers and seamstresses. Sandra Gayol has argued that female patronage of the bars encouraged prostitution, which became an additional vice.[84] As a consequence, a public order act was passed in 1885 to enable law enforcement officers to maintain the peace on the streets of the city, particularly with regard to excessive alcohol consumption.[85] Thus, the proliferation of drinking establishments in Buenos Aires, along with native Argentine drinking practices, may have rendered any '*Inglés*' propensity for alcohol slightly less visible. It is also probable that urban café as well as pampas gaucho culture were reasonably tolerant of convivial drinking. But perhaps more significant was the absence of accompanying acts of actual disorder, thus avoiding extensive public censure.

Although it is not possible to satisfactorily conclude that the Irish in Argentina drank, it would appear that culturally there was an obvious disquiet. However, in this alone they were far removed from the models of excessive consumption found elsewhere. Furthermore, there is even less compelling evidence to suggest a frequency of drunken disorder either statistically or anecdotally. Those that did drink had apparently learnt to imbibe quietly and avoid rowdy public displays of violent inebriated behaviour. Although anecdotal commentary does, to some extent, counter the indeterminacy of statistics and highlight communal concerns, what is most interesting is its relatively limited nature. Thus, in the absence of sources presenting clear evidence of distinctively alcoholic conduct, the Irish in Argentina would appear to have been reasonably temperate. But as an indicator of settlement, drunk and disorderly behaviour only partly reflects the extent and ease of immigrant absorption into a host society. And in the case of Argentina, as in other countries, it is necessary to examine other indices of deviancy.

Assessing data relating to more general forms of deviancy present the same interpretative dilemmas encountered elsewhere. And in the case of the Irish, these statistical impediments restrict the measurement of deviancy as an indicator of immigrant settlement and assimilation. Nevertheless, the Figures 5 and 6 illustrate the distribution of 'police cell arrests' and 'prison population' among the five principal ethnic groups in 1872–86/7 within Buenos Aires Province.

FIGURE 2: DISTRIBUTION OF POLICE CELL ARRESTS, 1872–86

Male prisoners

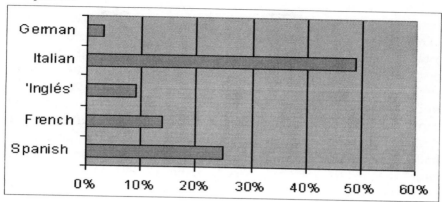

Female prisoners

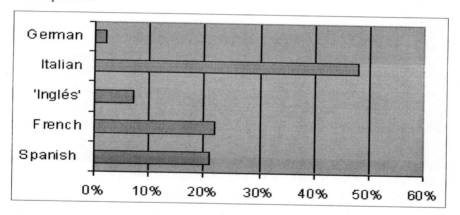

FIGURE 3: DISTRIBUTION OF MALE PRISON POPULATION, 1872–87 Male prisoners

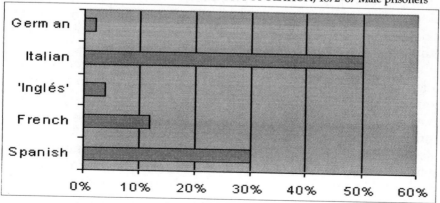

Source: Compiled from data in the Biblioteca Senado: *Registro estadistico, 1872–87.*

These figures demonstrate that the male percentages of 'police cell arrests' and 'prison population' were reasonably matched, although actual numbers incarcerated were significantly reduced. In each category, Italian men represented the highest percentage of total crime. Whilst this can largely be explained by their dominant representation in population figures, several commentators have attributed them with having 'the highest crime rates in the world'.[86] Indeed, a municipal official commenting in 1887 on immigrant propensity to commit offences in Argentina stated that 'the [Italians] enjoy the worst reputation'.[87] This claim would appear, at first glance, to be supported in these Buenos Aires Province data, in which, against the 1869 census, male Italians were over-represented in all categories of crime for 'police cell arrests', with a similar over-representation in 'prison population' for homicide, assault and robbery.[88] Similarly, Italian women, who again accounted for the highest percentage of crime across the groups examined, were over-represented in homicide and assault.[89]

As might be expected, the same analysis conducted against the 1895 census registered an under-representation in all Italian male categories except for homicide and fraud in 'police cell arrests', and homicide and assault in 'prison population'. Likewise, female Italian activity had reduced, only registering an over-representation in counts of homicide. In the closing decades of the century, the exponential increase in Italian immigration resulted in their accounting for a higher percentage of total Europeans compared with other groups. It would reasonably follow that available statistics for Italian offences would register a decline against increased 1895 population levels. However, rather than merely representing discrepancies in available comparative data, it is likely that any decline was also a by-product of changing recorded denominations from Italian to Argentine.

Figures 5 and 6, as could be anticipated, demonstrate that the aggregate comparison with census material for both male and female '*Inglés*' data was lower in 1869 than 1895. What is significant, however, is the huge discrepancy across all ethnic groups between numbers of 'police cell arrests' and numbers subsequently incarcerated in correctional facilities. Similarly to virtually all jurisdictions where only major offences gave rise to penal imprisonment, it is likely that in many cases in Argentina the nature of the crime was insufficient to warrant prison confinement. Inadequate facilities may also have contributed to low levels of incarceration since several prisons were officially recognised as needing extensive reform and modernisation. Insufficient and cramped amenities were combined with a lack of basic provisions such as clothing, food, drinking water and medical care.[90]

Prison conditions were to greatly improve following the construction of the Penitentiary in Buenos Aires City. Built in about 1877 and occupying 120,000 m, its oblong quadrangular construction housed approximately 845 prisoners in 1882.[91] By 1895 this figure had substantially increased to 3,755.[92] Its personnel comprised a governor, two deputy governors, seventeen wardens and thirty-two prison guards, and its facilities were hailed as rivalling any comparable European institution.[93] Prisoners awaiting trial were housed separately from convicted inmates and were allowed to receive food and clothing from visitors and mix openly with one another.[94] Convicts were permitted supervised daily exercise and taught a variety of trades in the workshops to facilitate long term rehabilitation.[95]

In spite of the obvious improvements the Penitentiary offered prisoners and detainees, failed governance of the legal and judicial system marred its effectiveness. Only the apathy of local *alcaldes*[96] and justices of the peace matched reports of the inadequacy of the judiciary, damningly described as 'false, useless and expensive'.[97] It was alleged that evidence proving a man's innocence would 'crawl through the courts for three years [as] *mañana* is the attitude in Argentina'.[98] In relation to local law enforcement, the provincial structure was such that the justice of the peace, with powers reminiscent of Spanish colonial rule, represented absolute authority and reported upward to the head of police and the legislature.[99] Structures were put in place to ensure that the appointment of *alcaldes* – who reported to the justice of the peace – and of the justice himself, were largely representative of the community they served, as such a high proportion of them were immigrant *estancieros*.[100] This token of communal representation did little to prevent accusations of negligence and corruption from within local jurisdictions, all of which was compounded by the lethargy employed by the legislature. Reports surfaced that prisoners were frequently incarcerated for an unlimited period, often years, without formal charge or prospect of trial.[101] In a dialogue with an 'English Speaking' prisoner incarcerated in the Penitentiary, the inmate was asked:

> - Why are you here?
>   I am accused of murder.
> - Who is your accuser?
>   I don't know.
> - Has there been any evidence brought against you?
>   None whatever.[102]

In extreme cases the flawed and corrupt system operated by the justice of the peace encouraged local law enforcers to act with apparent impunity, as when a drunken man resisting arrest was run through by the 'peace officers sword'.[103] Although the officer was taken into custody there was doubt in the press as to whether punishment would be administered.[104] In addition, anomalies in the proportionality of penalties to crimes committed were widely reported, inciting the charge that authorities played 'fast and loose with the law, [turning] its administration into ridicule'.[105] A homicide committed in self-defence, for example, received the same sentence as 'a murderer by profession who lies in wait for his neighbour and slaughters him in cold blood'.[106] In other instances, perceived over-zealousness employed to incarcerate without evidence, and the inadequacies of the judiciary thereafter, led observers to conclude that 'there is no justice, although there is plenty of law'.[107] As with other European groups, criminality within the '*Inglés*' community was not homogeneous across all categories, and amongst the most problematic to interpret is data relating to robbery. Whereas theft is associated with non-violent crime and is often under-represented in crime statistics, robbery is accompanied with violence and is over-represented.[108] Argentine statistics did not consistently record 'theft' and 'robbery' separately. Only in data relating to 'police cell arrests' was a distinction made between the two crimes, over a limited four year period.[109] Female data were not recorded; Table 17 analyses male activity regarding both offences from 1883 to 1886.[110]

TABLE 17: PERCENTAGE OF ARRESTS FOR ROBBERY AND THEFT BY EACH OF FIVE ETHNIC GROUPS

Male police cell arrests

1883–6	Total no.	Italian %	'*Inglés*' %	German %	Spanish %	French %
Robbery	1,263	55	6	1	27	11
Theft	329	50	6	1	23	19
Total	1,592	54%	6%	1%	26%	13%

Source: Compiled from data in the Biblioteca Senado: *Registro estadistico, 1872–1886.*[111]

For each ethnic group, the frequency of robbery and theft was calculated as a percentage of the combined total. In broad terms analysis of the relatively small sample shows that most groups conformed to type, registering lower participation in non-violent theft. The most notable exception to this was the French, although German data for theft appeared only in 1886 and is, thus, wholly inadequate for the purpose of comparative anaysis. Nevertheless, in respect of robbery the Italian, *'Inglés'* and French groups were all over-represented against population data. The limited time period available for assessment, however, prevents any conclusive findings.

Reliance on such flawed empirical data once again demonstrates the indeterminacy of statistical evidence and further limits analysis of Irish assimilation within broader Argentine society. In this regard, anecdotal evidence is instructive in establishing not only the nature of deviancy but is also a signifier of prevailing attitudes toward deviants. Evidence suggests that the socially superior position occupied by the *'Inglés'* in Argentina discouraged many within the Irish community, particularly amongst the elite, from acknowledging deviant or dysfunctional behaviour in their ranks. Indeed, the Irish-Argentine experience, as reflected within *The Southern Cross* newspaper, expressed ambivalence to Irish participation in crime.

On the one hand, articles deplored the frequency of Irish involvement yet, by the same token, editorial columns and letters pages contained frequent defences of the community as a whole, exonerating them as perpetrators and describing them as victims at the hands of 'savage *gauchos'*.[112] Private sources support this public view. A Christmas family letter in 1886 reported on the rarity of Irish crime, commenting that it was more likely 'amongst the natives in the camp [*campo*]'.[113] This perception was reflective of a deep rooted sense of conservative values fashioned from the time of Fahey. In instances where recognition of *'Inglés'* aberrancy was unavoidable, the community indulged its inflated sense of morality by suggesting a better 'class' of prisoner, commenting that 'the English-speaking prisoners always behaved well and gave no trouble to the authorities'.[114]

This sense of social elevation was so endemic that it was not unusual for criminals with Irish surnames to record themselves as *'Inglés'*, as in the case of Patrick Egan. Egan was arrested on 30

August 1850, charged with inflicting serious wounds on a Portuguese man. He had been in Argentina for eighteen months and was working as a peon.[115] Egan's police records described him as *'Inglés'*, white, single, twenty-six years old, able to read and write, and unable to ride a horse. When asked why he had committed the crime he replied that he had been heavily intoxicated. His signature at the bottom of the statement verifying its accuracy suggests that he declared himself *'Inglés'*, although his name, coupled with the short period he had been in the country, would imply that he was first generation Irish.[116] The extent to which it was customary for Irish immigrants to identify themselves as *'Inglés'* requires careful consideration and is explored in detail in Chapter 6 below. But it is significant to note that at the time of Egan's arrest Argentina was under the Rosas regime, and the Irish community under the influence of Fahey. It would seem reasonable, therefore, that in declaring himself *'Inglés'* Egan was responding to social and cultural forces more significant than merely linguistic or geographical differentiation.

This ambiguity of identity was further compounded in the reporting of Michael Casey's murder.[117] In 1850 Patrick McGinn and David Lynch[118] were arrested along with two *porteños*[119] for the murder of Michael Casey. Casey was recorded as an *'Inglés'* citizen, whilst McGinn and Lynch were recorded as *irlandeses*. Neither McGinn nor Lynch were able to read or write, and a letter from their prison cell written in Spanish was probably dictated to a third party:

> For three months now we have been in prison amongst people of a lower class, suffering all kinds of deprivations and illnesses. One of us (McGinn) has a flock of sheep with no-one to attend them. They are probably all lost by now. The other (Lynch) is very ill and will not last one more month if he remains in prison.[120]

McGinn and Lynch, the latter of whom died in prison, clearly considered themselves superior in social class to their fellow inmates. The flock of sheep referred to was probably acquired by the system of 'thirds' widely practised by Irish immigrants to obtain a foothold in the sheep farming industry.[121] Significantly, the victim of the crime was recorded as *'Inglés'* although clearly having an Irish name, whilst the perpetrators were *irlandés*. Patrick McKenna has argued that an ethnic divide was employed along class lines: *estanciero* regarded as English, and *peon* as Irish.[122] Although there may be some validity to this, evidence does not support a strict class divide.

Patrick Egan, for example, although a *peon*, referred to himself as '*Inglés*'. The separation appears to be more subjectively and randomly employed by the community in order to delineate social behaviour or desired social standing. In a letter to *The Southern Cross* newspaper one reader lamented the community's appraisal of itself:

> If Irishmen distinguish themselves by virtue, industry or other good qualities they are know as *Ingleses*. If, unfortunately, an Irishman turns aside from the path which duty and honour point out, then he is a 'bloody Irishman'.[123]

The Standard newspaper in particular appeared to propagate this differentiation by frequently referring to 'well-to-do' Irishmen as 'Englishmen'.[124] This may or may not have accurately reflected broader community views but, at the very least, it demonstrates a degree of social tension within the Irish subculture. In relation to crime, anomalies in identity further separated the two groups and exposed the fragmented nature of the Irish community itself. In 1875 an incident occurred whereby both the victim and the perpetrator of the crime were Irish. Edward Quinn was arrested for the murder of James Norris, about which, attesting his innocence, he stated:

> I am a humble, God fearing man and was never in prison before in my life. My name is Edward Quinn born at Multifarnham Co. Westmeath Ireland. Eight years ago I came out to my brothers William and Andrew Quinn in San Pedro. After putting in two years with Mr. John Harrington I moved to down here and took sheep on 3rds from Mr Michael Doherty. Would that I had remained there still; health, freedom, wealth and happiness were my lot. But in an evil hour I was tempted by my cousin to take sheep from Sr. Achaval on halves and here I am now, a helpless cripple, my sheep sold for half their value to my partner and myself condemned without a hearing – for what? For defending my own life against two armed men.[125]

Quinn claimed that Norris and his accomplice Michael Kelly, a known local 'ruffian', had arrived at his home drunk, brandishing guns and threatening his life. A fight ensued in which Quinn inflicted mortal wounds on Norris, who later died from his injuries. Norris' father, a native of County Kilkenny, had been in Argentina for thirty-five years, making his son, in all probability, second generation Irish. The Irish community did not rally to Quinn's defence but were 'too much taken up with their own business to look after him, a very good excuse where parties are not capable or able, or willing to aid a fellow countryman in distress'.[126] And similar communal ambivalence was reported in relation to two young men arrested for murder and referred to only as Egan and Ledwith. Widely reported in the press to be innocent, their friends '(if they had any) did but little in the way of justifying their innocence'.[127]

These case studies demonstrate the inconsistencies of group unity. The Irish community was not cohesive where aberrancy was concerned. Although cases did exist where neighbours rallied to the aid of fellow countrymen, more frequent were instances of indifference and disunity.[128] Individualism was the cornerstone of Irish-Argentine success, creating a false construct of collective identity within an ostensibly fragmented ethnic group. Deviance from a strict social code of morality and conservatism was not comfortably received, and it would appear that the accused experienced a distancing of the community irrespective of previous social standing. Guilt was established through implication, with the individual quickly disassociated from communal society: his actions and predicament lamented, but rarely supported in any practical way. Thus, it would appear that the Irish community were frequently united more through social propriety than ethnic solidarity.

In examining levels of 'deviancy' as a means of assessing Irish assimilation in Argentina it is useful to consider one further indicator: mental illness. In Argentina, provision for the mentally ill was considered as early as 1823, when Rivadavia founded the Society of Beneficence.[129] A philanthropic organisation, it was initially run by women and supported by government funds and private donations. As the century progressed, it expanded to become the administrator of Argentina's entire welfare system.[130] In the early decades of the twentieth century Argentine asylums were severely overcrowded, housing predominantly European patients.[131] Unlike North America or Canada, Argentina had not exercised rigorous vetting of arriving immigrants to ascertain mental or physical defects.[132] Contemporary psychiatrists had believed that psychological disorders were hereditary and that enforcement of a more stringent immigration policy would safeguard against future generations' affliction.[133]

In the case of Argentina it was argued that, on landing, immigrants were consumed by an obsession to acquire wealth. The pressures of modernity, which so preoccupied Argentina in the closing decades of the nineteenth century, were identified as contributing to a rapid deterioration of mental health within an immigrant community, which had experienced acute geographical and social dislocation.[134] In so stating, it is not clear whether the patients referred to were first or subsequent generations, although the inference of dislocation would imply first generation. It is likely, however, that theories of hereditary psychosis were supported more by the ideology of social Darwinism, which had so influenced Argentine intellectual circles, than by empirical research of patients' birthplace.[135]

As with previous statistical analysis, officially recorded mental health data by patients' ethnicity were opaque and precluded generational analysis. Inadequacies were further compounded in

FIGURE 4: MENTAL HEALTH DATA BY ETHNIC GROUP

Patients admitted to the hospital for 'demented women', 1858–86

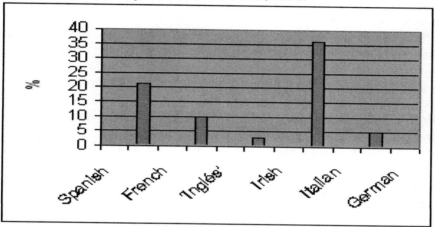

Sources: Biblioteca Senado, *Registro estadistico*, and Sociedad de Beneficiencia, Hospital Nacional de Aliendas, Legajo 218, 1858–86.[136]

Patients ('demented men') admitted to Hospital San Buena Ventura, 1863–9

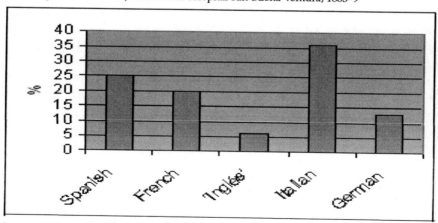

Source: Biblioteca Senado, *Registro estadistico*, 1863–69.

relation to male patients, as records covered only a seven year peri-od. Female data were more extensive, encompassing the years 1858 to 1886. Figure 8 expresses both sets of available statistics.

The data for 'demented women' were the only statistics where both the *'inglesa'* and *'irlandesa'* classifications appeared. However, only in 1880 were patients of both ethnicities recorded simultane-ously. The unlikely possibility of this being the only year when both nationalities were admitted would suggest that the ethnicities were sufficiently blurred to be used interchangeably.[137] For the purpose of consistency, the female *'Inglés'* percentage can be added to the recorded *'irlandesa'* figure to give a total of 13.9 per cent for the com-bined *'Inglés'* group. This was marginally over-represented against 1869 census material, then increasing to more than three and a half times the 1895 population level. The male statistics registered virtual parity with the 1869 census and, as might be expected, approxi-mately twice the 1895 population level. Commenting on asylum populations, the *La Prensa* newspaper reported in 1889 that the Italians represented the highest number of patients, followed by the Spanish, then equally by the French and *'Inglés'*.[138] As Figure 8 demonstrates, *'Inglés'* male and female levels were in fact consider-ably lower numerically than the French, although using the 1895 census both nationalities were typically over-represented. The Italians, despite accounting for the greatest proportion numerically, were under-represented in 1895, with the Spanish broadly consis-tent with population data.

The actual cause of mental illness amongst patients was not recorded officially by ethnic group, but alcohol related insanities and religious melancholy were prominent as collective causes of illness.[139] Contemporary medical professionals frequently referred to immi-grants' desire for alcohol as a prime cause of mental instability.[140] However, an analysis of mental disorder in Argentina between 1878 and 1882 was significant not only because it referred specifically to the Irish community in isolation from the *'Inglés'*, but also because of the causes of mental illness it identified:

> There are many Irish of both sexes in mental institutions suffering from men-tal derangement; all related to melancholy in various forms; more prevalent than other forms is religious melancholy, with a tendency for suicide.[141]

As argued in a previous chapter, Irish Catholicism did not experience alienation or cultural exclusion within the apparatus of Argentine society and, as such, it is unsatisfactory to attribute religion related insanity to confessional isolation. Its root more conceivably lay in the expectation by Church representatives that Irish Catholics conform to the behavioural practices of a non-Catholic *'Inglés'* community. Patrick McKenna suggests that the burgeoning sense of propriety and morality attached to the Irish community belied the experience of loneliness and solitude, which led to insanity and alcohol abuse.[142] However, with regard to pressures of religious observance, evidence does not support extensive breaching of the doctrinal code. Recorded statistics for incidences of infanticide, for example, are virtually non-existent. Between 1873 and 1886 only one *'Inglés'* arrest for infanticide was made, which was male, not female. Remarkably, not one single female was arrested for this reason over the entire period.[143]

Recorded levels of illegitimacy were also exceptionally low compared with total *'Inglés'* numbers documented.[144] Between 1864 and 1880 official statistics detail only two years when *'Inglés'* illegitimate births were registered: one in 1876 and two in 1878.[145] There is, of course, the possibility that inadequacies in the registration system, coupled with a reluctance to come forward on the part of the mother or family, resulted in inaccurate levels of recorded illegitimacy and infanticide. Nevertheless, these extraordinary statistics would suggest that, if indeed Catholic insistence on private morality did contribute to mental illness, its manifestations were not to be found in infanticide or illegitimacy. As an alternative explanation, high recorded levels of intoxication, particularly amongst *'Inglés'* females, could have provided the necessary outlet for social frustrations suffered as a result of strict doctrinal adherence, and thus contributed to the propensity for alcohol related insanities as well as religious melancholy.[146]

In Argentina, as everywhere else, it is not difficult to find evidence of dysfunctional and deviant Irish immigrant behaviour. Models in Britain and the United States in particular demonstrate that excessive drinking, social exclusion, crime and mental ill-health were indeed part of the immigrant experience. And yet, in every incidence, available literature is deeply divided as to the cause and universality of this stereotypical portrayal. But, in establishing the extent to which any given community conformed to the traditional Irish image, two key factors must be considered: first, the bias of different sources; and, second, the experience of different places. Swift argues that judicial records and policing techniques varied substantially between regions and significantly altered the immigrant experience. Added to this is the social, cultural and political climate identified by Campbell in San Francisco as facilitating a unique 'West Coast' experience distinct from the dominant models of the Eastern seaboard.

But in so far as these complexities and difficulties inform our perceptions of settlement elsewhere, in Argentina the deficiency of sources assumes a peculiar significance. The poverty of evidence appears to indicate that, rather than complying with the stereotype of the dysfunctional Irish immigrant, in Argentina there is no special case of deviancy. Rather, that the stereotypical elements of the community were marginalised by a far more dominant group that was engaged more successfully in the process of assimilation. The Irish in Argentina were thus not deviant Irish, but assimilating Irish. But it is the silence of this assimilation that necessitates an appraisal of the established indices of Irish integration: drink, crime and mental disorder.

Anecdotal and contemporary commentary indicates that drink in particular played a significant role within the community. This might be explained the immense loneliness of life on the *campo*, which itself made for an uncomfortable process of assimilation and encouraged a return to 'old' ways. Nevertheless, when the Irish did drink, they drank quietly. Unlike in other destinations the Irish stereotype of the drunken ruffian or the drunken fool did not emerge. Of course, it might be argued that rural holdings were so far apart that public houses could not be sustained and that camaraderie, which so fuelled disorder in many host countries, did not and could not emerge to anything like the same extent. But given the absolute deficiency of evidence it is more reasonable to conclude that rates of integration were largely higher than rates of deviancy and that Irish anecdotal evidence should be viewed in this light.

The dominant assimilating group within the community was actively engaged in disassociating itself from the stereotype of Irish deviancy. So it would follow that the severity of commentary on, and condemnation of, their fellow countrymen would reflect this desire. In other words, anecdotal evidence is engaging but flawed. And the seemingly low level of offending would indicate that established structures for containment, such as sporting clubs and the Irish Catholic Church, were in fact reasonably successful in easing the process of settlement. A significant indication of this is criminals recording themselves as *'Inglés'*, suggesting that despite their deviant activity they were, in fact, already engaged in a form of integration. Thus, it would appear that, in Argentina, an examination of established indices of Irish assimilation within host societies – drunkenness, disorder, general crime and mental illness – indicate an extraordinary lack of deviancy within a community that was striving silently and anxiously to be integrated.

All this, of course, contributed to the creation of a distinct Irish identity, which was perhaps also influenced by a strict '*Inglés*' social and moral code. It was, after all, an '*Inglés*' identity that had facilitated the accumulation of wealth and respectability, and the Irish community was certainly actively engaged in sustaining this elevated social standing. But fears of jeopardising an '*Inglés*' identity did not prevail indefinitely. As the century drew to a close the Irish, along with all the immigrant communities, became engulfed in a heated and controversial debate, which was to challenge established notions of identity. As a changing Argentina grappled with forging a sense of nation state, the Irish community struggled equally to reconcile its own internal conflict in reasserting an Irish identity – distinct from the generic '*Inglés*' – within the framework of an embryonic but dominant native national movement.

NOTES

1. See Roger Swift, 'Crime and the Irish in Nineteenth-Century Britain' in Roger Swift and Sheridan Gilley (eds), *The Irish in Britain, 1815–1939* (London, 1989), pp. 163–182, esp. p. 177; David Fitzpatrick, 'A Peculiar Tramping People: The Irish in Britain, 1801–70' in W.E. Vaughan (ed.), *A New History of Ireland: Ireland under the Union, I, 1801–70*, vol. V (Oxford, 1989), pp. 623–660, esp. p. 648. For a broader discussion see also Kevin Kenny, *The American Irish: A History* (Harlow, 2000), pp. 108, 147; David Fitzpatrick, 'A Curious Middle Place: The Irish in Britain, 1871–1921' in Swift and Gilley (London, 1989), pp. 10–59, esp. p. 25.
2. David Fitzpatrick in Vaughan (1989), p. 647.
3. Frank Neal, 'A Criminal Profile of the Liverpool Irish' in *Historic Society of Lancashire and Cheshire*, no. 140 (1991), pp. 161–199.
4. P. Grabosky, *Sydney in Ferment: Crime, Dissent and Official Reaction, 1788–1973* (Canberra, 1977), pp. 86, 90.
5. Miles Fairburn and Stephen Haslett, 'Violent Crime in Old and New Societies: A Case Study Based in New Zealand, 1853–1940', in *Journal of Social History*, vol. XX, no. 1 (1986), pp. 89–126, esp. p. 104.
6. Kerby A. Miller, *Emigrants and Exiles* (Oxford, 1985), p. 320.
7. Richard Stivers, *The Hair of the Dog*, (Pennsylvania, 1976), p. 93.
8. Ibid., p. 94.
9. See Robert F. Bales, 'Attitudes Toward Drinking in the Irish Culture', in David J. Pitman and Charles R. Snyder (eds), *Society, Culture and Drinking Patterns* (Carbondale, 1962), pp.157–187, esp. pp. 158–159; and Elizabeth Malcolm, 'The Rise of the Pub: A Study in the Disciplining of Popular Culture' in James S. Donnelly and Kerby A. Miller (eds), *Irish Popular Culture, 1650–1850* (Dublin, 1998), pp. 50–77, esp. p. 51.
10. Bales (1962), p. 158.
11. Kenny (2000), p. 108.
12. This is largely supported by Robin Room's analysis of ethnic rates of alcoholism, in which

he concluded that 'not only Irish bachelors, but also Irish spinsters, wives and husbands [demonstrated] higher rates than their equivalent status in other ethnic groups'. See Robin Room, 'Cultural Contingencies of Alcoholism: Variations between and within Nineteenth-Century Urban Ethnic Groups in Alcohol-Related Death Rates' in *Journal of Health and Social Behaviour*, vol. IX, no. 2 (1968), pp. 99–113, esp. p. 110.

13. Stivers (1976), p. 171.
14. Kenny (2000), p. 200.
15. See Malcolm (Dublin, 1986), p. 332.
16. W.J. Lowe, *The Irish in Mid-Victorian Lancashire: The Shaping of a Working Class Community* (New York, 1989), p. 128. See also Elizabeth Malcolm, *Ireland Sober, Ireland Free* (Dublin, 1986), pp. 323–324.
17. Robert Ernst, *Immigrant Life in New York City, 1825–1863* (New York, 1979), p. 57.
18. Ibid., p. 329.
19. Oscar Handlin, Oscar, *Boston's Immigrants, 1790–1880* (New York, 1970), p. 121.
20. W.J. Lowe (1989), p. 126.
21. See Swift (1989), pp. 169, 177.
22. R.E. Swift, 'Another Stafford Street Row: Law and Order and the Irish Presence in Mid-Victorian Wolverhampton' in *Immigrants and Minorities*, vol. III, no. 1 (1984), pp. 5–29, esp. p. 11.
23. See Henry Mayhew and John Binney, *The Criminal Prisons of London* (London, 1862).
24. Oscar Handlin, *Race and Nationality in American Life* (Boston, 1957), p. 94.
25. Ibid., p. 96.
26. Handlin was quoting from a contemporary commentator, Madison Grant; see ibid., p. 97. Handlin goes on to discuss the impact of the Laughlin report commissioned ten years after Dillingham but largely supporting its predecessor's findings.
27. Handlin (1957), p. 124.
28. For a discussion of the compromised nature of this data see ibid., pp. 125–138.
29. W.E. Vaughan, 'Ireland c. 1870' in Vaughan (1989), pp. 727–800, esp. p. 764.
30. See Miles Fairburn and Stephen Haslett, 'Violent Crime in Old and New Societies – A Case Study Based on New Zealand 1853?1940' in *Journal of Social History*, vol. XX, no. 1 (1986), pp. 89–126.
31. David Taylor, *Crime, Policing and Punishment in England, 1750–1914* (London, 1998), p. 71.
32. Ibid., pp. 80–81.
33. Paul Mulkern, 'Irish Immigrants and Public Disorder in Coventry, 1845–1875' in *Midland History*, no. 21 (1996), pp. 119–135, esp. 124.
34. Quoted in Swift (1989), p. 170.
35. Fitzpatrick (1989), p. 26.
36. Ibid., p. 25.
37. Taylor (1998), p. 21.
38. Swift (1989).
39. F. Neal (1991), esp. p. 172.
40. Kenny (2000), p. 145.
41. Robert A. Burchell, *The San Francisco Irish, 1848–1880* (Manchester, 1979), p. 155.
42. Miller (1985), p. 320.
43. Ibid.
44. Cited in Ann Vander Stoep and Bruce Link, 'Social Class, Ethnicity, and Mental Illness: The Importance of Being more than Earnest' in *American Journal of Public Health*, vol. 88, no. 9 (1998), pp. 1396–1402, esp. p. 1397.
45. See as an example Liam Greenslade, Maggie Pearson and Moss Madden, 'A Good Man's Fault: Alcohol and Irish People at Home and Abroad' in *Alcohol & Alcoholism*, Vol. 30, No. 4 (1995), p. 407–417, esp. p. 409.
46. Oscar Handlin, *Race and Nationality in American Life* (Boston, 1957), p. 129.
47. Ibid., p. 124.
48. Malcolm Campbell, *Ireland's New Worlds: Immigrants, Politics and Society in the United States and Australia, 1815–1922* (Wisconsin, 2008), see ch. 4, esp. pp. 85–87
49. Ibid., p. 89. For a favourable account of the Irish experience see also Burchell (1980), esp. p. 184.
50. David Fitzpatrick, 'Irish emigration in the later nineteenth-century' in Irish Historical Studies, Vol. XXII, No. 86 (1980), pp. 126–43, esp. pp. 136–137.

51. See as an example Fitzpatrick in Swift and Gilley (1989), esp. p .25; Kevin Kenny, *The American Irish: A History* (Harlow, 2000), pp. 108, 147; Grabosky (1977), pp. 86–90.
52. See Appendices III and IV for breakdown of 'police cell arrests' and 'prison population' by ethnicity.
53. Translated as 'foreigner'.
54. An explanation of what is defined by 'Ethnic group', as well as discrepancies arising from comparative analysis with census material, are presented later in this chapter.
55. Hereafter *Primer censo nacional, 1869*.
56. Hereafter *Segundo censo nacional, 1895*.
57. See Herbert Klein, 'The Integration of Italian Immigrants into the United States and Argentina: A Comparative Analysis' in *The American Historical Review*, vol. 88, No. 2 (1983), pp. 306–329, esp. 318, 329. See also Samuel L. Baily, 'Italian Immigrants in Buenos Aires and New York City, 1870–1914: A Comparative Analysis of Adjustment' in Samuel L. Baily and Eduardo José Míguez (eds), *Mass Migration to Modern Latin America* (Wilmington, 2003), pp. 69–80, esp. pp. 76–78.
58. I owe this important note to discussions with David N. Doyle.
59. All percentages have been rounded up or down as appropriate.
60. Statistics in Appendix IV relating to 'prison population' did not, from 1879, include data for intoxication or disturbing the peace. Equally, statistics for 1886 and 1887 did not detail levels of German incarceration.
61. See Appendices V and VI.
62. Germany was also over-represented in both censuses but to a lesser extent. Spain was over-represented against 1869 but was comparable to 1895 population levels.
63. E. M. Jellinek, 'Cultural Differences in the Meaning of Alcoholism' in David J. Pittman and Charles R. Synder, *Society, Culture and Drinking Patterns* (Carbondale, 1962), pp. 382–388.
64. R.B. Walker, 'Bushranging in Fact and Legend', in *Historical Studies of Australia and New Zealand*, vol. XI, no. 42 (1964), pp. 206–221.
65. See Stivers (1976), p. 190.
66. *The Southern Cross*, 25 March 1875, n.p.
67. Ibid., 21 March 1890, p. 5.
68. *Irish Argentine Society Statutes* (Buenos Aires, 1919) and *Outline of the New Social Organisation of the Knights of the White Cross* (n.d.), by kind permission of the Passionist Fathers, Buenos Aires.
69. Irish Argentine Society, *Donaciones Recibidas*. By kind permission of the Passionist Fathers, Buenos Aire.
70. I am grateful to David N. Doyle for his contribution to this discussion.
71. For a discussion on the Ancient Order of Hibernians in North America see David Noel Doyle, 'The Irish in North America, 1776–?1845' in W.E. Vaughan (1989), pp. 682–725, esp. 704–705. From the 1850s the Irish Catholic Church in Canada also concerned itself, with varying degrees of success, with the promotion of parochial temperance societies. See Brian P. Clarke, *Piety and Nationalism: Lay Voluntary Associations and the Creation of an Irish-Catholic Community in Toronto, 1850–1895* (Montreal & Kingston, 1993), ch. 6.
72. *Festejos del Cincuentenario del Hurling Club* (Buenos Aires, 1972), by kind permission of The Hurling Club, Buenos Aires.
73. Sugar cane alcohol, also called *aguardiente* or firewater.
74. See as an example *The Southern Cross*, 1 February 1878, n.p.
75. Letter from Sally Moore to John James Petit, 25 November 1867, quoted in Murray (2004), p. 175.
76. Sally Moore's cousin had, like her, been born in Argentina but his family had subsequently re-emigrated to Australia. See Murray (2004), p. 155–156.
77. My translation. *La Prensa*, 18 November 1897, p. 6.
78. Letter from John James Murphy to Martin Murphy, June 1865, quoted in Murray (2004), p. 111.
79. *The Southern Cross*, 17 June 1875, n.p.
80. Ibid., 15 March 1875, n.p.
81. *The Southern Cross*, 22 July 1875, n.p.
82. See Sandra Gayol, *Sociabilidad en Buenos Aires: Hombres, honor y cafés, 1862–1910* (Buenos Aires, 2000), esp. ch. I.
83. *The Southern Cross*, 7 March 1890, p. 2.

84. See Gayol (2000), ch. III.
85. Ibid. See also E. Zimmermann, *Los Liberals Reformistas: La cuestión social en la Argentina 1890–1916* (Buenos Aires, 1995), p. 64.
86. For a discussion on theories of criminal activity within immigrant groups in Argentina, see Carl Solberg, *Immigration and Nationalism: Argentina and Chile, 1890–1914* (Austin & London, 1970), pp. 93–102. See also Zimmermann (1992), p. 33.
87. Quoted in José C. Moya, *Cousins and Strangers: Spanish Immigrants in Buenos Aires, 1850–1930* (Berkeley & London, 1998), p. 348.
88. See Tables 14 and 16 above.
89. See Table 15 above.
90. *Segundo censo nacional, 1895.*
91. Report conducted on behalf of the British community appraising the State Penitentiary and reported in *The Southern Cross*, 7 April 1882 [hereafter, Penitentiary Report (1882)], pp. 4–5.
92. *Segundo censo nacional, 1895.*
93. Ibid.
94. Penitentiary Report, 1882.
95. Ibid.
96. Translated as mayors.
97. *The Standard*, 1 February 1870.
98. National Library Dublin, Bulfin Papers: Ms. 13,804. Lecture given by William Bulfin in Buenos Aires.
99. Juan Carlos Garavaglia, *Poder, conflicto y relaciones socials: El río de la Plata, XVIII–XIX* (Rosario, 1999), p. 101.
100. Carlos Cansenello, 'Domiciliarios, transeúntes en el proceso de formación estadal Bonaerense, 1820–1832' in *Entrepasados*, vol. IV, no. 6 (1994), pp. 7–22.
101. Penitentiary Report (1882).
102. Ibid.
103. *The Southern Cross*, 8 February 1878, no pagination [hereafter n.p.].
104. Ibid.
105. Penitentiary Report (1882).
106. Ibid.
107. *The Southern Cross*, 8 February 1878.
108. David Fitzpatrick in Vaughan (1989), esp. pp. 647–649.
109. 1883 did not separately record the crimes.
110. See Appendix VII for yearly analysis.
111. All percentages have been rounded up or down as appropriate. For a statistical breakdown see Appendix VII.
112. *The Southern Cross*, 8 February 1878, n.p.
113. Sally Moore to John James Petit, 26 December 1866, quoted in Edmundo Murray, *Devenir irlandés* (Buenos Aires, 2004), p. 168.
114. Penitentiary Report (1882).
115. Farm labourer.
116. Archivo General de la Nación [hereafter AGN], Buenos Aires: Sala X, 43-7-6.
117. Recorded as Miguel Casey.
118. Recorded as Patricio Miquin and Diego Lynch.
119. Resident of Buenos Aires.
120. My translation of original letter. AGN, Buenos Aires: Sala X, 43-7-6.
121. See Chapter 3 above for a full exposition of this practice.
122. Translated as 'land owner' and 'farm labourer'.
123. *The Southern Cross*, 1 September 1882, p. 4.
124. Thomas Murray, *The Story of the Irish in Argentina* (New York, 1919), p. 304.
125. *The Southern Cross*, 8 February 1878, n.p. The murder of James Norris was reported in *The Southern Cross*, 25 January 1878, n.p.
126. Ibid., 25 August 1878, n.p.
127. Ibid., 5 April 1878, n.p.
128. As in the case of a man recorded only as Mr Allen, who was accused of the murder of John Brennan. Neighbours pleaded his innocence and bailed him out of jail. See *The Southern Cross*, 15 March 1878, n.p.

129. M. Carlson, *Feminismo, The Women's Movement: Argentina from its Beginnings to Eva Peron* (Chicago, 1988), pp. 49–53.
130. Ibid.
131. Jonathan Ablard, 'The Limits of Psychiatric Reform in Argentina, 1890–1946' in Roy Porter and David Wright (eds), *The Confinement of the Insane: International Perspectives, 1800–1965* (Cambridge, 2003), pp. 226–247, esp. pp. 226–229.
132. E.A. Zimmerman, 'Racial Ideas and Social Reform: Argentina, 1890–1916' in *Hispanic American Historical Review*, vol. 72 (1992), pp. 23–46, esp. p. 37.
133. Ibid., p. 36.
134. Ablard (2003), p. 232.
135. See Marcelo Monserrat, 'La mentalidad evolunionista: Una ideología del progresso' in Gustavo Ferrari and Ezequiel Gallo (eds), *La Argentina del ochenta al centenario* (Buenos Aires, 1980), pp. 785–818.
136. All percentages have been rounded up or down as appropriate. Percentages are calculated from a total of 764 recorded 'demented women' across stated groups and 775 'demented men'. For a detailed breakdown please see Appendices VIII and IX.
137. See Appendix VIII.
138. *La Prensa*, 1 January 1889.
139. AGN, Sociedad de Beneficiencia, Hospital Nacionál de Alienados: Sala X, Leg. 218.
140. See Ablard (2003), p. 232.
141. My translation of José M. Ramos Mejía, *Las neurosis de los hombres célebres en la historia, Argentina, 1878–1882* (Buenos Aires, 1915), p. 15.
142. See Patrick McKenna, *Nineteenth-Century Irish Emigration to, and Settlement in, Argentina* (unpublished MA thesis, St Patrick's College, Maynooth, 1994), p. 307.
143. *Registro estadistico*, 1873–1887.
144. Across Catholic and Protestant parishes within Buenos Aires, 7,517 illegitimate births were registered between 1864 and 1880.
145. *Registro estadistico*, 1864–1880.
146. For levels of intoxication see Tables 14–16 above.

CHAPTER SIX

Immigrant newspapers and the emergence of an Irish-Argentine identity

> Want of Irish spirit amongst our wealthy countrymen of Argentina is not, by any means, a new characteristic. As soon as our people began to get wealthy, some of them began to get snobbish. To be of the English, to be with the English, to be thought English, in a word condescending smiles of recognition, would seem to have been the aim, laboriously and at large cost, sought by many of those and by their children as far back as fifty or sixty years ago.[1]

To an economically and culturally fractured group such as the Irish immigrant community was in the mid-nineteenth century, acceptance and passive adherence to the generic term '*Inglés*' appeared, at times, to be its only mode of sustained cohesion. It was a superficial effect as its adoption further dismantled group identity, creating class and behavioural chasms in the process. These profound gaps in experience were accentuated by the contemptuous indifference, by parts of those Irish who considered themselves '*Inglés*', towards those who had fallen through the cracks of social orthodoxy.

In the closing decades of the nineteenth century, however, the advantageous social and economic position enjoyed by European immigrants was challenged by native political forces, which, while seeking to emulate the European ideology of the nation state, sought to create a distinctly Latin model. Faced with increasing native rejection of dominant European culture, the Irish recognised the political expediency of reformulating their own allegiance and identity. Simultaneously, political events in the homeland were inciting Irish nationalistic sentiment in Argentina, gradually reopening Old World divisions that the collective '*Inglés*' identity had been outwardly successful in camouflaging. By the late 1800s, the Irish community was faced with the acute dilemma of responding to nationalising forces within Argentina whilst sustaining its own distinct sense of nationalism. In either case this would not be easily achieved. Political forces in Argentina had already established a clear vision of the Old World as well as those from it. Since the Irish were complicit in forming an '*Inglés*' ethnic synthesis, the creation of an embryonic Irish-Argentine consciousness whereby Irish and native sensibilities were satisfied would entail a clear severance from the past '*Inglés*' ideal. Although feasible, this was complicated not only by the powerful forces of native Argentine nationalism, but also by the fragmented nature of the Irish community itself.

The administration of General Julio A. Roca (1880–6) adopted a style of governance that has been described as an 'imperceptible' transition from liberal to positivist political ideology, and which facilitated a series of anticlerical reforms.[2] The sea of ecclesiastical opposition it incited rallied antiliberal political factions at a time when traditional *federalismo* ideologies were resurging.[3] Problems of immigrant social integration increasingly aroused the native elite's anxieties.[4] Thus, with shades of a postrevolutionary clerical and provincial alliance, an organic nationalist movement began to emerge that sought to re-establish ecclesiastical pre-eminence; challenge the central policies of Buenos Aires; and, most significantly, address the fragmented nature of the immigrant population.[5]

From the late 1880s, a forceful ideology of New World nationalism versus Old World allegiance permeated native and immigrant discourse.[6] Ethnic entrenchment of immigrant groups had alienated the native populace and threatened societal unity at a point when political forces sought to champion ideological and cultural unification.[7] Nationalist factions advocated a departure from the ties of the Old World to embrace a new, inclusive identity and national allegiance. At its vanguard were organs of native conservatism, most notably the *La Prensa* and *El Diario* newspapers, the latter of which published a series of articles in 1889 denouncing the ills of immigration.[8] In addition, elite political groups such as Ideas proved a hot house for budding nationalist thinkers in the form of writer Manuel Gálvez and politician Estanislao Zeballos.[9] In 1887 Zeballos, a seasoned parliamentarian and former university professor, addressed Congress on the challenges facing the fledging republic:

> The question of immigration is a most serious issue for the Republic of Argentina. Congress must adopt prudential measures to deal with the two key issues: to attract immigrants who wish to settle permanently in Argentina, and to instil in the hearts of foreigners a firm sense of our own national identity.[10]

These 'two key issues' had underpinned the nature of European immigration to Argentina in previous decades, and were now at the heart of political and social disquiet. Economic expansion, previously associated with the acquisition of European labour, was now used effectively by nationalist forces to create a xenophobic view of transient, avaricious 'foreigners' who viewed Argentina, according to *La Prensa*, through purely 'commercial eyes, amassing a colossal fortune for their benefit. Why do we not secure our own fortune?'[11] As demonstrated in Chapter 2, this was, in part, an accurate appraisal. A large proportion of immigrants had indeed fully intended to leave, their seasonal or temporary labour status limiting their contribution to national growth.

Historians have observed that, amongst those that did remain, the German group in particular directed their economic activity toward nurturing a German import-export enclave, rather than demonstrating any desire to expand the Argentine economy.[12] However, *La Prensa's* rather tendentious portrayal is challenged by other examples of immigrant behaviour. Herbert Klein's study demonstrated that Italian immigrants, the largest of all European groups, favoured investment in the expanding local economy to that of their homeland.[13] Similarly, private returns notwithstanding, *'Inglés'* investment had substantially contributed to commercial sector growth and infrastructure development.[14] It would seem, therefore, that immigrant plundering of native resources was not as unequivocal as propagandist rhetoric maintained.

A more convincing aspect of the nationalist argument as presented by Zeballos was the failure of immigrants to cast off their Old World allegiance for a New World identity. In highlighting this, Zeballos was joined by a most vociferous supporter of nationalist principles, ex-President of the Republic, Domingo Faustino Sarmiento (1869–74).[15] Sarmiento clearly highlighted the ominous refusal of immigrants to adopt Argentine citizenship. Jointly, both he and Zeballos argued that the future cohesion of the Argentine state was in jeopardy and that every immigrant who continued to support his own culture weakened that of Argentina.[16] In spite of the 1853 Constitution and the citizen's law of 1869, which provided ample opportunity for immigrants to naturalise, few converted their European citizenship.[17] Of the meagre 39,553 immigrants between 1906 and 1915 that did, 14,769 were Spanish, 12,214 Italian, 854 French, 587 German and 147 *'Inglés'*.[18] By the third census in 1914 only 2.25 per cent of the foreign born population had opted for Argentine citizenship.[19] A spokesman for the German community underlined immigrant determination to remain separate, stating in 1884 that:

> Here the immigrant German, in the midst of an overwhelmingly Latin pop-
> ulation, runs far less danger of giving up his nationality, customs, language,
> habits – in short, of being *de*nationalised – than in North America.[20]

Whilst the relative exclusivity and novelty of native rural and higher society was important, in part, the decision to remain culturally separate was a consequence of immigrant desire to remain ethnically cohesive. Native nationalists accused previous immigrant generations of adversely influencing their offspring into not becoming Argentine citizens. Sarmiento was among those who observed the 'ungrateful spirit of certain immigrant groups who sought to mislead their children in relation to adopting citizenship'.[21] Central to this was the problem of military conscription. Border conflicts, continental wars and civil unrest meant that Argentina was constantly raising armies and felt obliged in 1852 to impose a form of conscription.[22] A National Guard was formed in Buenos Aires and adopted throughout the Confederation by 1854.[23] Legislation decreed that all male Argentines between the ages of 17 and 60 must participate, at some level, in military service.[24] Nationalist factions increasingly portrayed immigrant reluctance to serve as a sinister motivation for the 'masses to remain foreign'.[25] In so doing, immigrants not only avoided military conscription, but also direct political involvement in state affairs at any but a local level.[26] In 1878, it was reported that the national government had 'no representation from among the foreign element'.[27] An article in *The Times* in London expressed the limited nature of the immigrant contribution to Argentine society:

> A very singular fact and quite different from United States experience in this,
> is that none of these foreigners become naturalized. Some of them, it is true,
> come only to accumulate a little money and return home with it, but many,
> at the same time, intend to make the country their home, but never their
> home politically. The circumstance of revolutions and the fear lest they may
> be called on for military duty in suppressing these risings deter them from
> this. The result is that this foreign element which constitutes from one-third
> to two-fifths of the population, which creates nearly all the wealth of the
> country, has but no part in its political control.[28]

Nationalist forces believed that, to counter this development, by teaching Spanish in schools and, by extension, raising awareness of Argentine history and culture, a natural allegiance would develop within immigrant communities, which in turn, would stimulate a desire for naturalisation and ultimately lead to political participation.[29] Other factors also applied. Torcuato Di Tella has argued that elite conservative circles were preoccupied by fears that the politicisation of a largely working class immigrant group would ostensibly bolster the political agenda of left wing socialist parties.[30] These concerns were not totally unfounded. German immigrants, who had since the reign of Rosas practised an apolitical non-interventionist approach to native affairs, were now encouraged, as a consequence of increased working class immigration, to become politically active.[31] Through the recently established socialist organisation Vorwärts and its periodical *Buenos Aires Vorwärts* (1886–97), German acquisition of Argentine citizenship for political purposes was strongly advocated.[32] Similarly, from the 1870s, growing numbers of Italian working class migrants significantly contributed to the emergence of an organised labour movement within Buenos Aires, although remaining politically inactive until the turn of the century.[33] However, native elite fears, as described by Di Tella, were largely exaggerated. The evidence suggests that immigrant participation in the trade union movement was no more militant than the native element.[34] The almost universal rejection of Argentine citizenship by immigrant groups indicated that any intent to subvert the existing social order was muted.[35]

The native press was not alone in examining the contribution and motivation of immigrants to remain in Argentina whilst not adopting its citizenship. Organs of immigrant interest equally probed the practice. The *Buenos Aires Herald*, an English-speaking newspaper established in 1876 by the son of a Scottish immigrant but sold thereafter to an American, posed the question:[36]

> Why are we here? […] We may answer, self interest […] We are here because of what we can get or hope to get out of the country. […]We even make a boast of our indifference to political and public questions which have no concession in them. We sneer at public discussion and belittle public men. […] We cling to home, we remain citizens of our native land, and never think or intend to become identified with or citizens of this country although we may intend to remain here through life.[37]

In retaining such a defined allegiance to homeland identity, such immigrants not only differentiated themselves from other immigrants within Argentina but also, most significantly, from native Argentines. As Solberg has observed, the vernacular usage of *'extranjero'* (foreigner), rather than *'immigrante'* (immigrant), underlined the concept of 'other' as applied to immigrants.[38] In many ways, this separateness complemented immigrant perceptions of Old World superiority, which, according to Di Tella, was accompanied by a determination to maintain ethnic and cultural traditions.[39] It would seem, therefore, that the evident reluctance of Argentine born children to naturalise was symptomatic of a cultural detachment, which did indeed impede national transition.

Most compellingly, language was identified as a prime barrier to the future cohesion of an Argentine state. Nationalist leaders stoked native anxieties with predictions that 'we will find ourselves one day transformed into a nation that is without a national language, tradition, character, or flag'.[40] Such apocalyptic rhetoric was echoed within native press editorials, which further inflamed national disquiet:

> We are an independent nation for the last three quarters of a century, as independent as Italy, France, Germany or the United Kingdom. We do not want colonies of various European languages forming inside our territories. They are foreign populations, yielding and abiding by the laws of the Republic; laws just as valid as those enforced by Italy on its own citizens.[41]

Although referring to a number of European groups, native preoccupations focused on Italian immigrants. Perceptions of Italian reluctance to integrate; insistence on celebrating national heroes such as Mazzini and Garibaldi; and the strength and number of ethnic associations, were of increasing social and political concern within elite Argentine circles.[42] But it was in relation to Italian emphasis on language preservation that concerns were most vociferously aroused. In commenting on the importance of linguistic heritage an Italian spokesman stated:

> Without protecting our language, it will be abandoned to foreign influence, and little by little the remembrance of its origins will be lost and with it, the dignity and honour of the Italian name.[43]

Such anxieties were echoed amongst the native populace in Italy. From the late 1880s, Italian citizens overseas had been of growing political interest to government officials in the parent country. Newspapers in the homeland reported that the 'colony' in Argentina was confronted with a native population that was hostile to 'Italians and all that is Italian', and that the continuance of the Italian language would foster knowledge of 'Italy in all her glory'.[44] Franceso Crispi's administration, 1887–1896, espoused a decidedly expansionist foreign policy.[45] He believed that the propagation of Italian culture and language in immigrant destinations would, in turn, provide an effective tool of political and commercial infiltration in foreign institutions.[46] Thus, proposals from Italy to administer the Italian 'colony' in Argentina apparently justified Sarmiento's alarming prophecy of immigrant demands for self-governance.[47]

In order to facilitate cultural and linguistic attachment to the homeland a number of Italian newspapers emerged in Argentina. In the early 1870s, the politically moderate *L'Italiano* was founded as a result of the merger of two earlier competing newspapers, *La Nazione Italia* and *Eco d'Italia*. Editorial differences between the respective proprietors contributed to its early demise, however.[48] *La Nazione* had been edited by the irrepressible and charismatic Basilio Cittadini, who has been described as the 'dean' of Italian language journalism in Argentina.[49] He was directly involved in the establishment in 1872 of what was to become one of two principal Italian language newspapers, *L' Operaio Italiano*. Published until 1898, this was a decidedly monarchist daily, which quickly established a loyal readership.[50] However, from 1876 the establishment of the republican, anticlerical *La Patria* challenged its dominance.[51] Under the editorship of Cittadini its popularity amongst the working class was such that its circulation reached more than half the Italian community.[52] By the early 1900s, its readership had increased to 40,000, with its extent doubling to twelve pages.[53] These two competing and politically opposed newspapers adopted conflicting positions on key national debates within Argentina, such as preservation of Italian culture and language, immigration, state intervention in economic markets and labour protection.[54] *La Patria*, which by 1893 had become *La Patria degli Italiani*, was the 'self-appointed guardian of the Italian language and culture' and most vociferous opponent of naturalisation, stating 'we are not against Argentina, but how can we love Argentina if we deny our heritage?'.[55]

The monarchist versus republican split found in the Italian press was replicated within the community's associations. In 1866, two mutual benefit societies were formed in Buenos Aires: Unione e Benevolenza founded by monarchists, and Nazionale Italiano by republicans.[56] Within the next decade branches of both societies had been established in all major locations of Italian settlement. Although ideological rivals, the popularity of the associations significantly contributed to the promulgation of a distinct Italian culture. By 1891 the community had organised itself sufficiently to form a total of 215 societies of various natures, attracting over 76,000 members.[57] These included an elite business, economic and political club, Circolo Italiano, intellectually independent from the political affiliations previously outlined; as well as an Italian hospital founded in 1872.[58] From the 1880s, the creation of an Italy outside of Italy, whereby 'its strength, its numbers, but above all its union and attachment to the parent country', was widely recognised and discussed within the editorial columns of both the native and immigrant press.[59]

The Italian community was not alone in establishing organs of cultural expression. A German-speaking newspaper emerged tentatively in the 1860s and was consolidated in 1878 as the daily *Deutsche La-Plata Zeitung*. This was joined in 1889 by a second daily, *Argentinisches Tageblatt*.[60] Both newspapers published a weekly edition directed toward a rural readership.[61] The previous editor-in-chief of *Deutsche La-Plata Zeitung*, Ernst Bachmann, went on to become editor of the *Kunz Yearbook and Address Calendar of the German Colony in Buenos Aires*, in which he candidly wrote in the early 1880s about German commercial, social and political interests. Prior to the establishment of German newspapers, however, early community spirit was demonstrated by the founding of a number of associations, including an athletics club (1855), German hospital (1878), German orphanage (1909) and a variety of music and social clubs.[62] Similarly, French immigrants had catered for their own medical needs by forming the very first immigrant mutual aid society, L'Union et Secours Mutuels, in 1854.[63]

Of all immigrant communities the Spanish were less immediately visible due to a language shared with their hosts. Nonetheless, their determination to maintain a clear and separate ethnic identity led to the phrase *colectividad española* permeating native discourse.[64] As with other ethnic groups this was facilitated in the first instance through the establishment of the daily Spanish newspaper *El Español* in 1854, followed later that year by *Revista Española*.[65] The former, founded by the republican Benito Hortelano, espoused a separatist ideology that advocated non-intervention in Argentine political affairs, a stance adopted by the majority of Spanish publications thereafter.[66] The most significant of these, *El Correo Español*, continued the tradition of a republican editorial throughout the 1870s, during which time Enrique Romero was its editor.[67] A policy of political 'non-intervention' did not prevent an increasingly confident Spanish press from tackling what it viewed as insulting native symbols of hostility toward the legacy of Spanish rule. *Revista Española* forthrightly denounced Argentine nationalist leaders' damning depictions of Spanish colonialism as backward, inciting fierce clashes between the newspaper and Sarmiento, who through his writings had established himself as a particular critic of Spanish political and cultural emblems.[68]

Like other immigrant groups, the Spanish formed a series of associations. In 1857 it followed the example of the French and established the Sociedad Española de Beneficiencia for the purpose of providing medical services and administering the Spanish Hospital in Buenos Aires.[69] These provisions were further expanded when from 1883 branches of Sociedad Española de Socorros Mutos, assisting with medical and interment issues, were formed in various *barrios* within the capital.[70] Organisations were not only concerned with issues of benevolence, however, and the elite Club Español was formed in 1866 as a social and recreational society, followed in 1912 by the politically motivated La Asociación Patriótica Española.[71] Similarly, the Basque contingent within Spanish immigration asserted its own political agenda through the creation of two associations in 1895, Centre Basque Francais and Centro Navarro, both concerned with Basque politics in the homeland.[72] Euskal Eche, an organisation with the broader remit of maintaining Basque culture in Argentina, followed at the turn of the century.[73]

In the case of the *'Inglés'* community, sport was one of several early expressions of intracommunal activity.[74] Although a Buenos Aires cricket club was established in 1831, it apparently first played in 1806 following the capture of British officers in the failed invasion of the same year.[75] The first organised horseracing event was held in 1826 by a group of foreigners, largely *'Inglés'*, the success of which quickly spread to provide an important social link with elite native society.[76] From the 1840s, Newmarket rules were adopted and the first meeting of the Foreign Amateurs' Race Sporting Society, the predecessor of the elite Jockey Club, was held in 1849.[77] The Irish community were willing participators in the sport, regularly holding race meets attended by 'all nationalities' and reportedly equalling 'the best ever held in Mullingar'.[78] Athletics also figured, with the first Irish club, Brehon Athletic, established in Carmen de Areco in 1867.[79] By 1899, the growth in 'camp [*campo*] clubs' necessitated a handicap system at sports days to ensure 'fair play'.[80]

This early community social spirit was matched by the first *'Inglés'* foray into the world of print. In 1826 Thomas George Love founded *The British Packet and Argentine News*. Love was born in England in 1793 and is reported to have arrived in Argentina sometime between 1815 and 1819.[81] Until its closure in 1858 the newspaper provided commercial and social news to the English-speaking community, its success encouraging the rise of a number of short lived competitors.[82]

As witnesses to community development and cultural expression, newspapers, although providing a constant source of commentary, nonetheless offer only limited and at times biased views of public opinion. In discussing the '*Inglés*' and Irish communities using this medium, there is a danger of over-reliance on views presented in cultural and political slices of editorial comment. However, there are a number of indicators to suggest that the two most prominent and influential newspapers to emerge within the '*Inglés*' community, *The Standard* and *The Southern Cross*, were thriving enterprises. Both enjoyed impressive longevity – *The Standard* published until 1959[83] and *The Southern Cross* to this day – implying a popularity and success that accompanies only serious organs of public opinion. Furthermore, in the absence of hard evidence, the vibrancy of advertising pages and the contribution of readers through letters pages allows for both sources to be treated as significant. With this in mind, the following discussion focuses on the divergent political standpoints that emerged between the two newspapers in nineteenth-century Argentina.

The Standard was established in 1861 by two Dublin born brothers, Edward and Michael Mulhall. Edward Mulhall had arrived in Argentina in 1854 via New York, where he had worked as a solicitor. Some months after the establishment of the newspaper his brother Michael, who had been studying for the priesthood in Rome, joined him as joint editor. The first issue was a weekly, four page broadsheet printed in both English and French. In December 1861 the brothers increased production to a daily, maintaining its four-page layout but discarding the French language. A weekly was produced for the interior of the republic and a fortnightly shipped to Europe.[84] By 1900, the newspaper's extent had doubled. Editorial comment was offered under the heading 'Editor's Table', which expressed opinion on political, commercial and social affairs. This focused predominantly on '*Inglés*' community interests but also included foreign news stories. Contributing correspondents were not named individually but referred to as 'our own correspondent' under the features 'The London Letter' or 'The Paris Letter'.

In the first year of publication the newspaper boasted an impressive circulation of 3,000.[85] Of this it was estimated that 1,500 were paid subscribers.[86] A contemporary report suggested that *The Standard's* influence was such that it was 'quoted by all the London newspapers'.[87] The general tone was decidedly imperialist, as demonstrated on St Patrick's Day in 1875, when editorial comment declared that emigration had been the 'saving of Irish people', and that without the British Empire, Irishmen could 'hardly have attained eminence in so many fields of renown. Moore and Goldsmith might have sung in Celtic but their beauties would be unknown to the world [and] Wellington would have been a colonel of militia in Tipperary'.[88]

By the 1870s, issues contained extensive advertising, which dominated the four-page newspaper. Spanning seven columns, the front page was dedicated solely to advertisers of a predominantly commercial nature such as banks, insurance houses and shipping companies.[89] The first two columns of the second page contained smaller notices of rooms and offices to let, but maintained a commercial bias with many entries targeting the financial sector by advertising premises 'alongside the Bolsa'.[90] The first three columns of page three were devoted to commercial market reports, with the remainder taken up by a variety of minor advertisements featuring individuals seeking either employment or staff. These were of a largely urban nature, with one young man recently arrived from England promoting himself as having 'had considerable experience in some of the first offices and open to an engagement in town'.[91] Another, a bricklayer, also sought employment but recommended himself as 'understanding setting boilers to heat with economy of fuel furnaces and ovens etc.'.[92] Those advertising employment opportunities included those for a 'dispensing Chemists assistant'[93] and a 'respectable female to accompany an English family, with two children, to Europe'.[94]

The last page of each issue was once again devoted entirely to advertising, attracting significant corporate and industrial concerns such as London commercial houses, engineering companies and ironwork manufacturers.[95] The size and variety of companies investing in the pages of *The Standard* would suggest that the readership it attracted was not only predominantly urban but was also of a certain socio-economic class. 'English draperies' and beauty products such as perfumery and soap from 'Old Bond Street London' for female readership, accompanied European travel and investment opportunities.[96] Editorials reported on cricket matches and forthcoming events at the Opera House, all of which helped shape community attitudes toward an '*Inglés*' identity in Argentina. The first edition explained the newspaper's intended objective:

> Today *The Standard* is unfurled to the four winds of heaven, not as the emblem of a party or the watchword of rivalry, but as the bond of fellowship between the various members of our Anglo-Celtic race. [...] *The Standard* shall be interesting to all who read our language: offensive to none. Liberty without anarchy, religion without sectarianism, fusion without confusion is our motto. Bold yet not chimerical, our policy regarding this country as well as England can be neither set down as wholly Ministerial, nor as factious Opposition.[97]

At the time of its founding, such noble aspirations of unity were certainly in keeping with the '*Inglés*' portrayal of a community at one with itself. It was in the interests of the 'Anglo-Celtic race', as *The Standard* termed it, to share the social spoils bestowed by native society upon '*Ingleses*'. Maintenance of a separate Irish identity had, perhaps understandably, been subordinate to the more immediate and attractive proposal of integrating into an existing system of social and cultural superiority at an unusually advantageous level. Indeed, such was Irish determination in this regard that Thomas Murray described their masquerading as '*Britanicos*' as slavish.[98] The resultant portrayal of group identity significantly contributed to native perceptions of the '*Inglés*' community as a homogeneous group. Subtleties of Irish ethnicity were not appreciated, as a letter describing the view held of Ireland by a young native Argentine illustrates:

> I enquired what he really knew about Ireland, he said it was remarkable for its geysers and volcanoes. I saw at once that he mistook Ireland for Iceland. Our South American friends have but a very indefinite idea of Ireland or the Irish.[99]

As previously indicated, however, '*Inglés*' group cohesion all too easily fractured under pressure, and so did the ideology initially espoused by *The Standard*. Although declaring an inoffensive editorial position, its style of reporting quickly demonstrated a decidedly pro-British bias, despite the owners' ethnicity. Indeed, the British coat of arms emblem decorated the masthead: the lion rampant and the unicorn.[100] Of its two editors, Michael Mulhall in particular was described as 'not a good nationalist' and 'deeply loyal to our Gracious Queen', at all times constant to the interests of the British establishment.[101] As such, potentially divisive political or cultural issues were reported from the perspective of the imperial power, and presented within the pages of the *The Standard* as the opinion of the '*Inglés*' community in Argentina. This assumption was to ultimately contribute to nascent Irish nationalism at the close of the century. But, for the time being, the absence of an alternative,

dissenting organ of Irish political, social and cultural interests, coupled with the desire within the Irish community to appear as *'Inglés'*,
ensured that *The Standard* enjoyed a captive and submissive audience within the 'Anglo-Celtic' population. An Irish landowner writing to a family member in Wexford in 1862 approvingly commented:

> Our invincible "Standard" I hope you have the pleasure of seeing for it gives
> a full and true account of everything most interesting to foreigners in this
> country and their friends in the old land.[102]

Thus, *The Standard's* political interpretation of domestic as well as
international events remained unchallenged for the first fourteen
years of its existence. Any attempt to separate or reposition Irish
interests within this established and successful forum might desta-
bilise the community and lead to conflict. As *The Standard* opined,
'the general destinies of both countries are inseparable'.[103]

On 16 January 1875 *The Southern Cross* newspaper was established. Although facilitating a distinct Irish voice, its initial agenda
was not intentionally divisive. On the contrary, its mission statement outlined a rather innocuous, if not somewhat naive, purpose:

> To supply the want of an Irish and Catholic organ in the country. (…) I hope
> the paper will be found on the table of every Irish and English house in the
> Argentine Confederation. (…) The tone of the paper will be liberal. The paper
> will not adhere to any particular party in this country. The events of the week
> will be narrated with those comments, which proceed from a strictly impartial
> pen. The paper will contain general Irish, English, and North American news,
> and the Catholic news of the world, as well as the news of the country in
> which we live in.[104]

Like its predecessor, its expression of intent demonstrated a desire
to be an apolitical, non-partisan community newspaper, which
sought to complement rather than compete with its already established counterpart. As if to reinforce the benign nature of its birth,
the first issues were printed using the presses of *The Standard*.
Editorials of *The Southern Cross*, under the initial editorship of
Canon Patrick Dillon, went to great lengths not to antagonise *The
Standard* or its readers, stressing the solidarity of the English and
Irish communities and proclaiming 'we are united with each other.
(May we long continue!)'.[105] Indeed, Dillon had himself previously
supplied articles for *The Standard* from Rome when acting as theo-
logical consultant to the Vatican Council in 1869.[106]

Published as a weekly, *The Southern Cross* rapidly grew from four
to eight pages by the late 1870s, increasing to over twenty by the
close of the century. Like *The Standard*, the first issue devoted its
entire front page to advertisements but, in contrast, this represented

the sum of advertising space. This steadily increased to develop into a loyal, albeit relatively small, advertising base, with many products and services appearing in issues over a number of years. From the outset, however, *The Southern Cross* did not attract the same level of corporate business advertising as *The Standard*. The services of individual Irish wool brokers, such as Patrick Ham, Thomas Kenny and Edward Casey, appeared alongside drapers, grocers and general mercantile stores. Larger advertisements, when they did appear, underlined the distinct rural readership: promoting sheep dip, well machinery for watering livestock and fencing wire.[107] In further contrast to *The Standard*, relatively few personal advertisements appeared from those either seeking or providing employment. One hopeful exception saw fit to emphasise that he was 'a Roman Catholic young man' seeking the position of 'teacher in the city or the camp', perhaps aiming to alleviate any denominational concerns from the outset. The absence of extensive advertisements for rural employment would suggest that, whatever the networks operating to secure work or attract labour, the advertising pages of *The Southern Cross* were not a primary source.

Nevertheless, the agrarian nature of Irish immigration was fully reflected in the editorial of *The Southern Cross*, with its back page devoted to commercial reports on land values, land agents, dry and salted hide prices and the fluctuating wool market. The centre pages included editorial comment on the economic and social position of the Irish sheep farmer in Argentina, as well reporting homeland political news and reports on the Pope and the Church in general.[108] Despite its increased extent, the newspaper's basic structure was to remain largely unchanged well into the early decades of the new century. In the 1890s, commercial advertisements shared the front page with railway timetables and steam navigation companies, and grain production increasingly figured in market news. Ladies' fashion enjoyed its own column with patterns of the latest designs, and 'telegrams of the week' reported international news.[109] Its pages served as a social record of births, deaths and marriages and were a source of information for distant family and friends. Commenting on a family wedding in Buenos Aires, a relative writing from Mullingar remarked, 'I heard of the marriage before they were six weeks wed, I happened to see *The Southern Cross* and came on it.'[110] Above all, *The Southern Cross* transformed itself, over its first three decades, from being a non-controversial publication into representing the at times partisan and controversial interests of a distinct Irish community.

Both newspapers ultimately and predictably failed in their original intent to adhere to a harmonious and inclusive editorial position. As issues of Home Rule heightened political tensions in the homeland, opposing nationalist and loyalist sentiment divided editorial coverage in Argentina and splintered readers' loyalties. The extent to which either newspaper formed or indeed changed public opinion raises the central issue of the effectiveness of the press in this regard. This was of particular importance from the 1890s, when respective editorial columns expressed vociferously divergent political views. Although discussed at length below, it is important here to note the difficulty in assessing collective public opinion through the pages of newspapers, given the tenuous nature of press influence. Nevertheless, an Irishman, criticising *The Standard*'s increasingly anti-Irish tone and referring to the change in readership it thus attracted, wrote:

> I am, of course, well aware that the vast majority of *The Standard*'s present readers belong not to the nationality of those whose names were to be found on its subscription-list in the "days of its infancy", and, therefore, that it need not now pay much heed to the protest of a mere Irishman.[111]

This shift in political consciousness, defined by what was now the pro-British *Standard* and the Irish-Argentine *Southern Cross*, coincided with the nationalist debate within Argentina. Under pressure from native nationalising forces and against the rising culture of linguistic concern, the Irish community began to emerge from its early *'Inglés'* submergence. In addressing the issue of language and the acquisition of Spanish, *The Southern Cross* was initially as measured as *The Standard*, both viewing the native vernacular in practical and rational terms. But by the late 1880s a subtle divergence began to appear. An article published in *The Southern Cross* on 10 November 1887 began by articulating the relatively innocuous view hitherto echoed by its companion *The Standard*. It stated:

> The language we speak is one of the chains, which binds us to the past, and a word expressed in our native language will often recall a bygone scene that might otherwise be buried in oblivion. There is (however) no reason why we should not be true to parents, country and friends and at the same time acquire a knowledge of foreign language and customs.[112]

As the article progressed, a somewhat more controversial tone began to emerge as it proceeded to assess the character of the English language in relation to the Irish community and the paradox of it being their spoken tongue whilst not their native one:

> The Italians teach their children Italian in the schools, and they grow up
> Italians in heart and soul. The German children will shed tears when you
> speak to them of the Fatherland, which they never saw. The Welsh will learn
> no language but their own. But the Irish learn English; and we know the
> consequences. The knowledge of Spanish should not lessen our attachment
> to Irish nationality. In fact it is doubtful whether the preservation of the
> English language among us tends to inspire a love for Ireland.[113]

The Southern Cross argued that the Irish did not experience the same
passion or fervour for the protection of the English language as
their respective European counterparts. Whilst other ethnic groups
were fiercely nationalistic regarding the preservation of their language and by extension their identity, the Irish did not share the
same attachment to English. The newspaper implied that Irish
immigrants' native experience separated their love for their home
from the language they spoke. Although the majority of Irish in
Argentina had hailed from eastern counties in Ireland where the
Irish language had been redundant for some time, the maintenance
of English did not carry nationalistic connotations. Whilst not advocating a complete departure from English, its continuance was not
a principle of ethnic identity for *The Southern Cross*. In regard to the
broader '*Inglés*' community and distinct from other European
groups, safeguarding the English vernacular did not facilitate
nationalistic unity. *The Southern Cross* challenged the community to
compare its attitude toward the English language with that adopted
by the Welsh:

> The Welsh left their own country to preserve their language and customs.
> Some of our native colleagues complain of this; but they should remember
> that the Welsh, though British subjects, look upon the English language and
> customs with the same horror as they do the Spanish.[114]

Historians have described Welsh commitment to their language as
an ethnic marker in Argentina aimed at limiting the threat of assimilation. Indeed, a Welsh-language newspaper, *Y Drafod*, was established in 1891 to further consolidate vernacular preservation.[115] The
Irish newspaper's observation denotes a sense of admiration that
the Welsh should so steadfastly defend their linguistic heritage in
relation not only toward Spanish, but also toward the traditional
dominance of English. In so discussing, *The Southern Cross* was not
so much slighting Spanish culture as it was commenting on '*Inglés*'
identity. Paradoxically, whereas Welsh ethnicity was reaffirmed
through the preservation of the Welsh language, an assertion of
Irish ethnicity could only be achieved through casting off the
English vernacular and acquiring Spanish. In contrast to the Welsh,

any assertion of a distinct Irish identity, separate from the '*Inglés*' group, was dependent upon a cultural and linguistic fusion with native Argentine forces. Only through partially reverting to Old World ethnic entrenchment and rejecting new world '*Inglés*' synthesis could a hybrid Irish-Argentine identity emerge. In relation to the Spanish language, it was not so much its acquisition that separated the Irish from the '*Inglés*' position, but rather the political symbolism that rejection of English represented.

An organ of conservatism, *The Standard* viewed Spanish language acquisition as a logical necessity to function in the native environment, not an opportunity to assert ethnic obduracy. Conversely, *The Southern Cross* increasingly portrayed the native Spanish vernacular as a nationalist tool with which to segregate the Irish community from a dominant English language. At this juncture, however, its editorial stopped short of advocating the total demise of English, perhaps realising that it was not only impractical but also ideologically premature. Be that as it may, the future of the English language was by no means secure. In a Rattigan family letter written between cousins living in distant parts of Buenos Aires Province and probably without extensive contact, the writer began in English only to slip into Spanish; seamlessly reverting to English and then once again to Spanish with an apology which questioned their linguistic abilities: 'Expreso que me disculpa por esta carta mal escrito, no se si pude leer en inglés o no' [Apologies for this poorly written letter, I'm not sure if you can read English or not].[116] The uncertainty demonstrates that by the early 1900s, knowledge of the English language was no longer taken for granted amongst the Irish community and, in this regard, nationalist forces within *The Southern Cross* were at least partially successful.

The growing sense of Irish nationalism within Argentina at the close of the nineteenth century cannot, of course, be solely attributed to the establishment of a single newspaper. Explanations for the change in ideology are not easily arrived at but political developments in Ireland itself undoubtedly played a part. Editorial columns of *The Southern Cross* were dominated by political events at home, such as the 1886 Home Rule crisis; the fall of Parnell; feuds within the Independent Irish party, and these in turn provided a medium for the expression of a nationalist sentiment previously submerged in Argentina within the catch-all '*Inglés*' group.[117] Articles in *The Standard* entitled 'this miserable cry of Home Rule' created its own nationalistic backlash. In tandem came a series of social and legal reforms within Ireland that changed the landown-ership rights of tenant farmers. Amendments to the Land Act were widely reported amongst the English-speaking press in Argentina, and might have contributed to a sense of solidarity between the Irish-Argentine farming experience and land acquisition at home. The relative importance of the political or economic developments of a far away homeland in contributing to the natural evolution of an Irish-Argentine sense of identity is difficult to estimate. Yet the evidence suggests that by the turn of the century a process of closer identification with the issues of political and ideological conflict in Ireland was emerging, at least amongst the readers of *The Southern Cross*.

It was in this context that the outbreak of colonial conflict in South Africa known as the Boer War acquired its peculiar signifi-cance for the Irish-Argentine community. And it was also against this background that a change of management in *The Southern Cross*, which saw the arrival of a new proprietor and editor, William Bulfin, was to be of particular importance. Bulfin was born in County Offaly in 1864 and had arrived in Argentina in 1884. His uncle, the provincial of the Passionist Fathers in Buenos Aires, had encouraged the young Bulfin to emigrate. He worked initially as a sheep farmer, eventually selling his livestock in order to acquire *The Southern Cross* in 1896. Bulfin was a fervent nationalist who later became a member of Sinn Fein, and his arrival marked a firm depar-ture from previous editorial policy. His stewardship not only attempted to separate the Irish community from the '*Inglés*', but also highlighted uncomfortable divides among the Irish between nationalist and pro-British sympathies.

As editor, Bulfin had penned several nationalistic editorials since acquiring the newspapers, but political events in 1899 were to polarise Irish public opinion and define its own and its competitor's national allegiances. In Ireland, as in other parts of the British Empire, the war between Britain and two South African republics, the Transvaal and the Orange Free State, was to generate consider-able interest. The spectacle of the Empire experiencing embarrass-ing military defeats at the hands of two small South African states invigorated Irish nationalism at a time when it was still suffering from the effects of the Parnellite split. A parallel debate emerged amongst the Irish community in Argentina, initiated in part by the decidedly imperialist stance of *The Standard*. On the eve of the war, *The Standard* wrote an editorial asserting that the majority of Irish in

South Africa had denounced the view held by their countrymen elsewhere condemning the British Empire and its proposed act of war. It read:

> large meeting was held at Kimberley at which a unanimous motion of censure was passed on the conduct of those Irishmen who sympathise with the half civilized Boers. (...) Is it to count for nothing, in putting an end to the eternal political abuse of England by a section of Irishmen that never in the history of the British Empire, which their valour and talents have done so much to build up, have there been so many brilliant Irishmen in the service of Great Britain?[118]

The Standard's intervention constituted nothing less than a challenge to emergent nationalist opinion within the Irish community, one that Bulfin was happy to accept. In the very next issue of *The Southern Cross*, Bulfin wrote and signed a lengthy reply under the headline 'Irish and English: *The Standard* Propaganda'. Its opening remarks were '*The Standard* has never been representative of the Irish people here; but of late it has made more than usual efforts to mis-represent them.'[119] In this one statement Bulfin set the tone for his editorial and drove a wedge between the '*Inglés*' and Irish communities rarely so clearly expressed. His spirited and passionate reply went on to refute the 'unanimous motion' allegedly passed by the South African Irish, stating:

> The natural post for any 'brilliant man' is not in the ranks of those who build for other nations, but in the ranks of those who are building up his native land. What is it to Ireland with her vanished trade, with her dwindling population, and with her vacant fields that her children are building up the glory of other peoples?[120]

Bulfin argued that not only were the majority of Irishmen in South Africa against the war, but that amongst the press in Argentina only *The Standard* 'expressed a wish to see blood flow'. In stating this he isolated British policy both in relation to the Irish community and the broader Spanish-speaking native press.[121] Despite its antiwar stance, *The Southern Cross* gave ample editorial space to the progress of the Transvaal Irish Brigade once battle had commenced. A published letter from an Irishman in Pretoria:

> John MacBride, who is now Major MacBride, carried the flag, the real Irish flag, into the enemy's country. I can tell you he was proud to do so. [...] The Jingoes are naturally more furious against the Irish Brigade than all the rest but that will not prevent us having 3,000 Irishmen in line before long.[122]

In contrast, *The Standard* presented a united pro-British front. In announcing a requiem Mass to be held in Buenos Aires it spoke of the 'brave soldiers killed on the battlefield while doing their duty to their country and their God', of which the 'bravest of the brave were sons of Erin'.[123] It went on to confirm the presence of the British minister and the consular authorities at the service. Their proposed attendance caused irritated confusion within the columns of *The Southern Cross* as to whom the Mass was for, soliciting the sardonic assumption that it was to be for 'soldiers who had fallen in the ranks of the British army and for them alone, since the British minister would scarcely be expected to attend a service for those who had fallen in arms against his country'.[124]

Bulfin's heightened nationalistic rhetoric was, no doubt, partly informed by his relations with one of Sinn Fein's founding members, Arthur Griffith. In a letter to Bulfin, Griffith had commented on the importance *The Southern Cross* had assumed in stirring Irish nationalist politics in Argentina, writing that he 'should be glad of a note now and then from Argentina which is immensely popular here since *The Southern Cross* has worked up the Gaelic movement there'.[125] Certainly the establishment of the Buenos Aires branch of the Gaelic League, formed in 1899 under Bulfin's auspices, had raised awareness and improved links with Dublin's nationalist factions.[126] Bulfin himself had corresponded regularly with Douglas Hyde, exchanging literary works. Hyde had favourably appraised Bulfin's *Tales of the Pampas*, remarking that he had 'never read anything like it', and equally solicited Bulfin's opinion, declaring 'I have just written a new play satirizing Trinity College which I should like you to see!'[127] Their correspondence, however, surpassed mutual appreciation of literary expertise to discuss Hyde's aspirations for the League:

> I shall do all I can to strengthen the Gaelic League, re-organise it if possible, and heal the split between east and west. [...] If I go to the States [...] I will speak on Gaelic League principles which are radically nationalist without being political in the sense of espousing any party or any line of policy.[128]

For Bulfin's part, he wrote several editorials outlining the aims of the League in Buenos Aires and promoting its membership. More importantly, he demonstrated an acute awareness of the fragility of Irish nationalism in Argentina, which, still in its infancy, had the potential to arouse intense communal conflict. In attempting to establish a branch of the Gaelic League, this eventuality was sufficiently real to incline Bulfin to comment acerbically:

> The Gaelic movement is not political. The branch of the Gaelic League which we hope to see founded here need not, therefore, frighten anyone who may feel inclined to dread that conspiracy is in the wind.[129]

Resistance to its establishment led Bulfin to reappraise required membership levels, stating that 'if fifty members cannot be found it could begin with twenty or less'.[130] Bulfin's dogged perseverance was ultimately rewarded and the first remittance from Argentina to Dublin, totalling '£51.2.9 (fifty-one pounds, two shilling and nine pence sterling)' was sent on 4 July 1899, having been collected through a series of fundraising events within the province.[131] Encouraged by the new source of income and facing a financial deficit of 'close on £1000', Hyde was persuaded to enquire 'whether our good friends in Argentina might not come to our assistance [...] Is there a possibility of *The Southern Cross* raising some [funds] for us?'[132] Bulfin duly obliged by 'splendidly sending £150 in no short a time'.[133] It would seem, therefore, that under Bulfin's 'leadership' and in spite of some reticence at local level, the Irish community in Argentina came to the attention of both Griffith and Hyde in a way that had previously been absent.

It is difficult to estimate whether Griffith's flattery of *The Southern Cross* in raising nationalistic awareness in Argentina, as well as Hyde's comment, 'what a lot of fine matters you have in *The Southern Cross*', were calculated compliments designed to encourage continued remittances, or a genuine reflection of attitudes within Dublin circles. The size of the community in Argentina and its relatively low level of politicisation would suggest that both Griffith and Hyde spoke more out of their personal relationship and admiration for Bulfin than from any real political ambition for the Irish community. A letter published in *The Southern Cross* from the Secretary of the Gaelic League in Dublin, Charles M. Neil, directly acknowledged Bulfin's contribution, stating that the League had 'passed unanimously a resolution of special thanks to the proprietor and editor of *The Southern Cross*'.[134] Indeed, so established were Bulfin's links with nationalist Dublin that in 1909 Sinn Fein nominated him for the role of vice president, which he duly turned down, offering instead:

> In writing for the Daily Sinn Fein I shall try to do my best to help the good cause. But for various private reasons I cannot take any office and am therefore unable to allow my name to go forward.[135]

Bulfin's protestations went largely unheeded, and a second letter to the National Council just five days later necessitated a further refusal:

> While thanking those who wish to put me forward as candidate for election to non-resident Executive of Sinn Fein, I regret that the same reasons which obliged me to decline the position of the Vice-Presidency, oblige me to decline this.[136]

His continued reluctance to assume an official office within the organisation was perhaps an indication that, ultimately, Bulfin saw himself as a writer and journalist not a politician.[137] Nevertheless, in Argentina his nationalistic assault against *The Standard* continued unabated. Commenting on the fundamental identity of the Irish, he wrote:

> If we are to be English let us be frank about it, and cease to speak about being Irish. If we are to be Irish let us be consistent. If we are to be Irish we ought to be that, and not compromise on it.[138]

The Boer War had acted as the catalyst for Bulfin to attack the political position of the pro-British *Standard* whilst simultaneously asserting Irish nationalism. In so doing, he challenged the community's dual identity and demanded a departure from selective ethnicity. It was a theme to which he would regularly return. Some years later, during a lecture given in Buenos Aires following a visit to Ireland, Bulfin examined the Irish relationship with the 'Englishman' by asking, 'if we despise him why do we imitate him? Why do we speak his language, sing his songs and adopt his social life?'[139] In this he directly charged the owners of *The Standard* with subjugating Irish interests:

> The Standard has always believed that the only way to ingratiate itself with Englishmen is to throw cold water on Irish national claims, and sacrifice Irish principle for English applause. At the same time it has endeavoured to keep a hold on the Irish community.[140]

It cannot, of course, be argued that Bulfin's nationalistic, anti-British rhetoric was solely responsible for harnessing universal support for Irish nationalism across the entire Irish community. Given the paucity of subscription lists the influence of Bulfin's paper is difficult to establish.[141] But other evidence in the columns of the paper allows for some examination both of the character of the readership that the editor hoped to attract and the kind of readers who were attracted. Through assessment of the corresponding advertisements within *The Standard* and *The Southern Cross*, it is likely that the former invited a significantly larger urban based readership than the latter. Whereas *The Standard* drew advertisements from investment banks and engineering companies, more common in *The Southern Cross* were grocery stores and wool brokers. The lack of diversity in its advertising base, and the absence of larger advertising interests in general, may well be an indication of *The Southern Cross'* reduced market appeal compared with that of *The Standard*. Nevertheless, *The Southern Cross* clearly had a loyal readership, as its expansion from four to over twenty pages demonstrates. The two newspapers were clearly in competition, fighting for market share. Bulfin's persistent attacks on *The Standard* and its owners suggests a confidence that his prominent nationalist rhetoric would not prove detrimental to the future of the newspaper, a belief largely validated by its continued upward progress under his editorship. But none of this is conclusive. Although highly probable that *The Southern Cross* attracted and exerted influence over a substantial body of the Irish immigrant community, it is also clear that many remained loyal to *The Standard* and its politics.

Amongst those who were persuaded, the political climate in which Bulfin operated, in relation to events both in Argentina and in Ireland, was apt to facilitate a reappraisal of Irish identity irrespective of his intervention. Nonetheless, support gained within segments of the *estanciero* class, who had themselves directly benefited from the social and economic trappings afforded an *'Inglés'* identity, compellingly confirms Bulfin's skill as an orator and a nationalist. Whilst the apparent change in attitude of segments of the *estanciero* class is perhaps open to the plausible if not cynical interpretation of it being propitiously timed to suit their own best interests, nationalistic discourse within this socially advantaged group reflects, at least in part, the success and effectiveness of Bulfin's campaign:

> Be Argentine by all means but at present remember you are only so by birth, your blood and colour will for another few generations be Irish and white and while that blood remains don't disgrace it nor let your children do so. God put that Irish blood in your veins and you have no right to ignore it, so don't be ashamed of and never ought anyone so blessed wish to change. The question is which is the better of the two, Irish or Argentine? Let us rise them up and form a good Irish Argentine, which has done and ever will do more for this country than the Argentine alone.[142]

Appearing in a letter to Bulfin, this sharp shift in perspective by an Irish *estanciero* represented a fundamental reappraisal of ethnic allegiance. In a changing Argentina, the catch-all *'Inglés'* identity no longer served Irish interests. Similarly, nationalist sentiment espoused by Bulfin demanded the separation and reassertion of Irishness. By repositioning Irishness within an Argentine framework, both native and Irish sensibilities were accommodated and the *'Inglés'* 'hold' to which Bulfin had previously referred was, to some extent, loosened.

Be that as it may, Bulfin's disdain for *The Standard* and its owners did not subside. In 1899, the *Irish Times* published the obituary of one of *The Standard's* proprietors, Edward T. Mulhall, writing that 'thousands of Irishmen, guided by his words, emigrated to Buenos Aires and have established themselves with profit on the wide pampas. He was their truest friend.'[143] Correcting the newspaper's appraisal, Bulfin defensively, and somewhat churlishly given the circumstances, stated that 'the eulogistic obituary literature [...] cannot be commended. We venture to censure it as being both misleading and disedifying.'[144] He went on to offer his own reminiscences, describing Mulhall as:

> [...] not by any means a man of altruism. He lacked high ideals. No great moral purpose is anywhere observable in his writings. The Irish community looked upon [him] as the mouth-piece of English commercial enterprise and interests; and never for one moment as an Irish resident or an Irish journalist specially devoting himself to the maintenance of a single Irish principle, religious, political or social.[145]

Bulfin's verbal attack on the character of Mulhall and, by extension, *The Standard*, demonstrates the extent of his departure from the innocuous editorial beginnings of *The Southern Cross*. Although directing his hostility toward the late proprietor, he was equally addressing those portions of the Irish community who had themselves supported a pro-British doctrine for several decades. Bulfin's rhetoric was reflective of a change in attitude within the community, not only toward the English but also toward itself. He ultimately, however, acknowledged the limitations of emergent Irish nationalism under his guidance, and of its peculiarity to Argentina: a localised type of Irish patriotism constructed within, and as a consequence of, Argentine society:

> The overwhelming majority of the Irish people here and their children are in Irish matters as nationalist as they are Catholic. [However], we cannot and do not expect Irish-Argentines to feel as strongly on Irish affairs as Irishmen, although in many cases to their honour be it said, they are no less true to Irish national principles than to Argentine. While however, no-one expects to see Irish-Argentines as much attached to Irish traditions as Irishmen, very few people expect to see them more English in sympathy than Irish. The Standard does of course, but it is mistaken.[146]

With the emergence of the nation state in Argentina, Bulfin cleverly exerted an Irish national position whilst at the same time declaring loyalty to Argentina. He not only separated the community from the '*Ingleses*', but also, with equal subtlety, differentiated the Irish community in Argentina from the Irish in the most general sense, by his original and crucial coinage of the term 'Irish-Argentine' in a political context. Bulfin's neologism thus symbolised a watershed in the evolution of the Irish community in Argentina. However, in not becoming citizens, Irish political involvement remained on the fringes, 'excluded from all national and provincial offices and honours'.[147] Whilst recognising 'mal-administration and extortion [which was] so intolerable' within the republic, any attempt to mobilise a collective political voice ended in disagreement, acrimony and inertia. An example of this came in 1899 when a proposal was floated within the community to form a political party. After several meetings and much debate in the columns of *The Southern Cross*, agreement could not be reached as to whether the new party should be open to all who shared the same political ideology irrespective of ethnicity, or whether it should be limited to 'Irish and Anglo-Argentines'.[148]

Here the community revealed what it lacked most: leadership. Retrospectively, the most effective leader was Bulfin himself. Through his nationalistic editorials and support of the Gaelic League, Bulfin had achieved the momentum of 'leadership' amongst a community that was not 'easy to influence or lead'.[149] Thomas Murray has argued that only his death in 1910 prevented Bulfin from assuming political control. Prior to this point, however, Bulfin had left Argentina several times to return to Ireland and, in so doing, had consciously stepped back from the brink. During his often prolonged periods of absence, nationalist support wavered and it was reported that contributions to the 'Gaelic League [were] very slow'.[150] Furthermore, as news of the potential visit of Michael Davitt to Argentina circulated around the community, the provincial of the Passionist order, Father Vincent Grogan, wrote to Bulfin in Dublin asking that he dissuade Davitt from making his tour. Talking of Davitt, his letter read:

> No doubt the Irish member will receive a warm welcome if he comes (though I doubt if he is the best man for the mission). But I fear that he will be disappointed as to the financial results of his visits. Just now I am glad to say there is a very strong inclination to send no more money out of the country. At the very last meeting of the I.C.A. [Irish Catholic Association] the matter was spoken of and the feeling against doing so was very general.
>
> The girls' orphanage showed a large deficit in the accounts of last year. Now there are two orphanages to support. An Irish hospital and home for the girls badly needed and the St Vincent Society should also be supported to help distressed Irish here within the city. In the face of these necessities and aware of the hard times, is it not imprudent – to use a mild term – to send money away even though the cause be good.

What I would suggest is that you should manage to come across Don Miguel somehow and if your mind on this matter conforms with mine, give him a piece of it. Tell him that if he could postpone his visit till better times he would surely receive a warmer welcome and a heavier purse.[151]

The tone of the letter was one of measured restraint, which thinly veiled the cleric's irritation at the prospect of fundraising for what was ostensibly an external cause. In so firmly detailing and prioritising internal issues, he bluntly countermanded the nationalistic agenda espoused by Bulfin and his Sinn Fein comrades in Dublin. Without the influencing voice of the nationalistic Bulfin, the Irish in Argentina rapidly returned to their more natural position as a culturally and politically inward looking group.

Donald Akenson has argued that the Irish community in South Africa escaped the cultural hegemony of the Old World to create a new Anglo-Celtic culture of the 'British South African'.[152] In many ways, in the period between 1840 and 1880 the Irish in Argentina could be said to have undergone a similar process; but in Argentina there was a further complication. The early partial submergence of the Irish within a collective '*Inglés*' identity necessarily entailed that the assertion of a distinctive Irish identity could not be achieved without some reversion to the traditional cultural and historical divides of old Ireland. Under pressure from the nationalising forces of Argentina's political leadership, the entrenched identification of the Irish with the '*Inglés*' became increasingly problematic, and the need to secure a niche in the new political framework required an escape from that early submergence. Bulfin aptly appreciated this and capitalised on the split created as a result of the Boer War. In this he contributed significantly to the emergence of a hybrid Irish-Argentine identity, which ultimately combined Irish sensibilities with a loyalty to the developing Argentine nation state.

Despite Bulfin's opportunistic intervention the incipient nationalistic movement that he sought to exploit amongst the Irish in Argentina did not mature. Although achieving short term resonance, Irish nationalist sentiment was largely of a superficial nature, spurred on by the momentum of native nationalising forces, homeland political events, and the vigour and passion of Bulfin himself. In the absence of a central figure under whose auspices an organic movement could flourish, attempts to generate broader community political involvement, other than at a local or individual level, were likely to fail. For Bulfin's part, his contribution as a nationalist

188   *Irish 'Ingleses'*

'leader' was hampered by the dominant, inward looking priorities identified and supported by the Irish community. Thus, his political commitment to nationalism was never fully reflected in, or representative of, the community he sought to influence. In this regard, Murray's observation that their collective failure would ensure they remained forever *'Ingleses'* would appear to carry particular resonance.[153]

NOTES

1. Thomas Murray, *The Story of the Irish in Argentina* (New York, 1919), p. 320.
2. Charles A. Hale, 'Political and Social Ideas in Latin America, 1870–1930' in Leslie Bethell (ed.), *The Cambridge History of Latin America*, vol. IV (Cambridge, 1985), pp. 367–441. For an outline of clerical reforms see Chapter 4 above.
3. David Rock, *Authoritarian Argentina* (Berkeley, 1993), p. 41.
4. Fernando J. Devoto, *Historia de la inmigración en la Argentina* (Buenos Aires, 2003), p. 254
5. Rock (1993), p. 44.
6. Lilia Ana Bertoni, *Patriotas, cosmopolitas y nacionalistas: La construcción de la nacionalidad Argentina a fines del siglo XIX* (Buenos Aires, 2001), pp. 9–12.
7. Ibid., pp. 9–13.
8. See as an example *El Diario*: 'Inmigración Prejudicial', 8 May 1889; 'Inmigrantes and Mendigos', 8 July 1889; 'La Mendicidad en la República', 9 October 1889.
9. Rock (1993), pp. 37–54. Although a nationalist, Gálvez's writing was, at times, imbued with fervour about the beneficial effects immigration had on the Argentine race and the republic's future. See Manuel Gálvez, *El solar de la raza* (Madrid, n.d.), pp. 61–62.
10. My translation. Congreso Nacional, Cámara de Diputados, Diario de Sesiones, 21 October 1887, quoted in Bertoni (2003), p. 17.
11. My translation, *La Prensa*, 1 January 1889.
12. Ronald C. Newton, *German Buenos Aires, 1900–1933: Social Change and Cultural Crisis* (Austin and London, 1977), p. 18.
13. Herbert S. Klein, 'The Integration of Italian Immigrants into the United States and Argentina: A Comparative Analysis' in *The American Historical Review*, vol. 88, no. 2 (1983), pp. 306–329.
14. See Chapter 2.
15. Devoto (2003), p. 255.
16. Bertoni (2001), p. 1.
17. Ibid., p. 121.
18. *Tercer censo nacional de la Republica Argentina, 1914* [hereafter *Tercer censo nacional, 1895*], vol. 1
19. Quoted in Carl Solberg, *Immigration and Nationalism: Argentina and Chile, 1890–1914* (Austin and London, 1970), p. 42.
20. Quoted in Newton (1977), p. 4.
21. My translation. Quoted in Luigi Favero, 'Las escuelas de las sociedades italianas en la Argentina' (1866–1914), in Fernando J. Devoto and Gianfranco Rosoli (eds), *La inmigración italiana en la Argentina* (Buenos Aires, 1998), pp. 165–205, esp. p. 179. For further discussion of this subject see also Torcuato S. di Tella, *Historia social de la Argentina* (Buenos Aires, 1998), p. 52.
22. For a discussion on the necessity of augmenting military forces, see Solberg (1970), pp. 22–24.
23. Bertoni (2001), p. 214.
24. Idem.
25. My translation of Estanislao Zeballos, quoted in Bertoni (2001), p. 23.
26. For a discussion on immigrant involvement in native politics see Hilda Sábato, *La política en las calles: Entre el voto y la movilización, 1862–1880* (Buenos Aires, 1998).
27. *The Buenos Aires Herald*, 31 January 1878, p. 4.

28. Cited in *The Standard*, 25 May 1886, p. 2.
29. See Devoto (2003), pp. 247–261.
30. See Di Tella (1998), pp. 53–54.
31. Newton (1977), p. 26.
32. Ibid.
33. Samuel L. Baily, 'Italian Immigrants in Buenos Aires and New York City, 1870–1914: A Comparative Analysis of Adjustment' in Samuel L. Baily and Eduardo José Míguez (eds), *Mass Migration to Modern Latin America* (Wilmington, 2003), pp. 69–80.
34. See José C. Moya, *Cousins and Strangers: Spanish Immigrants in Buenos Aires, 1850–1930* (Berkeley & London, 1998), p. 313 and Devoto (2003), pp. 306–310.
35. See Di Tella (1998), pp. 53–54; For a general discussion see also David Rock, *Politics in Argentina 1890–1930: The Rise and Fall of Radicalism* (Cambridge, 1975); Paula Alonso, *Between Revolution and the Ballot Box: The Origins of the Argentine Radical Party in the 1890s* (Cambridge, 2000).
36. Oliver Marshall, *The English Language Press in Latin America* (London, 1996), p. 5.
37. *The Buenos Aires Herald*, 6 February 1878, p. 5.
38. Solberg (1970), p. 42.
39. Di Tella (1998), p. 53.
40. My translation. Estanislao Zeballos quoted in *El Diario*, 16 November 1887.
41. My translation. *La Prensa*, 18 March 1886.
42. Devoto (2003), p. 19.
43. My translation. 'I.MARTIGNETTI', 1906, quoted in Favero (1998), esp. p. 174.
44. My translation and paraphrase of *Italica Gens* as detailed ibid., p. 223.
45. Favero (1998), p. 188; see also Bertoni (2001), p. 67.
46. Ibid.
47. See David Rock's review of Bertoni (2001) in *Hispanic American Historical Review*, vol. 83 (May 2003), pp. 437–438.
48. Fernando J. Devoto, *Estudios sobre la emigración italiana a la Argentina en la segundo mitad del siglo XIX* (Rome, 1991), p. 194.
49. Samuel L. Baily, 'The Role of Two Newspapers in the Assimilation of Italians in Buenos Aires and Sao Paulo, 1893–1913' in *International Migration Review*, vol. XII, no. 3 (1978), pp. 321–340.
50. Devoto (1991), p. 193.
51. Grazia Dore, 'Un periodico italiano en Buenos Aires, 1911–1913' in Devoto and Rosoli (1998), pp. 127–140.
52. Baily (2003), p. 73.
53. Ibid., p. 326.
54. Devoto (1991), p. 195.
55. See Baily (1978), pp. 328, 335.
56. Devoto (2003), p. 243.
57. Favero (1998).
58. Ibid, p. 245.
59. *The Buenos Aires Herald*, 10 November 1882, p. 7.
60. Newton (1977), p. 10.
61. Ibid., p. 11.
62. Ibid., p. 10
63. Devoto (2003), p. 241.
64. Hugo José Rodino, *Inmigrantes españolas en Argentina: Adapción e identidad* (Buenos Aires, 1999), pp.13, 16.
65. Devoto (2003), p. 241.
66. Moya (1998), p. 279.
67. Ángel Duarte, *La república del emigrante* (Buenos Aires, 1998), p. 25
68. Moya (1998), pp. 340–344.
69. Alejandro Enrique Fernández, 'Los españoles de Buenos Aires y sus asociaciones en la época de inmigración masiva' in Hebe Clementi (ed.), *Inmigración española en la Argentina* (Buenos Aires, 1991), pp. 59–83.
70. Maria Liliana da Orden, 'Liderazgo étnico y redes socials: Una approximación a la participación política de los españoles en la Argentina, 1880–1912' in Alejandro Enrique Fernández and José E. Moya (eds), *La inmigración española en la Argentina* (Buenos Aires,

1999), pp. 167–187.
71. Fernández (1991), p. 71.
72. Hugo José Rodrigo, *Immigrates Españoles en Argentina: Adepción e Identidad* (Buenos Aires, 1999), p. 19.
73. Ibid.
74. Maintaining close relations with British consular authorities such as Woodbine Parish, and the establishment and maintenance of English (Anglican) churches and schools were other early examples of social cohesion.
75. Andrew Graham-Yooll, *The Forgotten Colony: A History of the English-Speaking Communities in Argentina* (London, 1981), p. 189.
76. Ibid., p. 191.
77. The Jockey Club was formally established on 15 April, 1882. See *Acta de la sessión de instalación del Jockey Club*. By kind permission of The Jockey Club, Buenos Aires.
78. Murray (1919), pp. 248–249.
79. Ibid., p. 234.
80. *The Southern Cross*, 11 August 1899, p. 11.
81. Graham-Yooll (1981), p. 111.
82. For a list of various English-speaking titles see ibid., pp. 210–211, and Oliver Marshall, *The English Language Press in Latin America* (London, 1996), pp. 1–18.
83. Marshall (1996), p. 14.
84. Ibid., p. 15.
85. The most widely read Spanish-speaking newspaper, *La Tribuna*, had a circulation of only 5,000 in comparison. See Marshall (1996), p. 16.
86. Murray (1919), p. 303.
87. Report by Father John Cullen, 1888, reproduced in Edward Walsh, 'The Irish in the Argentine Republic: John Cullen's 1888 Report' in *Collectanea Hibernica*, vol. 43 (2002), pp. 239–247.
88. *The Standard*, 17 March 1875, p. 2.
89. See as an example ibid., 7 January 1875, p. 1.
90. The Bolsa is the stock exchange. See ibid., 4 February 1870, p. 3.
91. *The Standard*, 2 February 1870, p. 3.
92. Ibid.
93. Ibid.
94. *The Standard*, 8 February 1870, p. 3.
95. Ibid., 1 January 1875, p. 4.
96. Ibid., 8 January 1875, p. 4.
97. *The Standard*, 1 May 1861, p. 2.
98. Murray (1919), p. 497.
99. *The Southern Cross*, 1 September 1882, p. 4.
100. I am grateful to Edward Walsh for our discussions in this regard.
101. Murray (1919), p. 303.
102. Letter from William Murphy to Martin Murphy, 20 July 1862, quoted in Murray (2004), p. 85.
103. *The Southern Cross*, 17 March 1875, n.p.
104. Marshall (1996), p. 12.
105. *The Southern Cross*, 25 March 1875, n.p.
106. Marshall (1996), p. 12
107. See as an example *The Southern Cross*, 21 January 1875; 18 February 1875.
108. See as an example ibid., 16 January 1875.
109. See as an example ibid., 21 April 1899.
110. Letter from Rattigan family, 24 July 1903, by kind permission of the Rattigan family, Buenos Aires.
111. *The Southern Cross*, 16 June 1882, p. 1.
112. *The Southern Cross*, 10 November 1882, p. 4.
113. Ibid.
114. *The Southern Cross*, 27 October 1882, p. 5.
115. Glyn Williams, *The Welsh in Patagonia: Critical Bibliographic Review* (Cardiff, 1979), p. 32.
116. Rattigan family correspondence, September 1916: by kind permission of the Rattigan family, Buenos Aires.

117. See as an example *The Southern Cross*, 'Home Rule Club', 30 January 1878; 'Parnell Arrest', 21 October 1881; 'Irish Land League', 30 June 1882; 'Home Rule League', 9 December 1901.
118. *The Standard*, 7 October 1899, p. 2.
119. *The Southern Cross*, 13 October 1899, p. 13.
120. Ibid.
121. David Rock has stated that native political factions identified worrying parallels between the position of immigrants within Argentina and that of uitlanders in South Africa. The Boer War was a model they sought to avoid. See David Rock's review of Bertoni (2001), in *Hispanic American Historical Review*, vol. 83 (May 2003), pp. 437–438
122. *The Southern Cross*, 9 February 1900, p. 14.
123. *The Standard*, 1 April 1900, p. 2.
124. *The Southern Cross*, 6 April 1900, p. 12.
125. National Library of Ireland [hereafter NLI], William Bulfin Papers [hereafter Bulfin Papers]: Ms.13,810/12. Letter from Arthur Griffith to William Bulfin, 11 July, 1901.
126. *The Southern Cross*, 11 August, 1899, p. 11.
127. NLI, Bulfin Papers: Ms. 13,810 (14). Letters from Douglas Hyde to William Bulfin, 27 December 1902, 2 September 1902.
128. Ibid., Letter from Hyde to Bulfin, n.d.
129. *The Southern Cross*, 14 April 1899, p. 11.
130. Ibid.
131. *The Southern Cross*, 11 August 1899, p. 10.
132. NLI, Bulfin Papers: Ms. 13,810 (14). Letter from Hyde to Bulfin, 17 October 1903.
133. Ibid. Letter from Hyde to Bulfin, 2 March 1904.
134. *The Southern Cross*, 29 September 1899, p. 4.
135. NLI, Bulfin Papers: Ms. 13,811(1). Letter from William Bulfin to Sinn Fein National Council, 11 August 1909.
136. Ibid. Letter from William Bulfin to Sinn Fein National Council, 16 August 1909.
137. University College Dublin, Department of Archives and Manuscripts, Eamon de Valera Papers: P150/1398. Bulfin's son, Eamon Bulfin, went on to be appointed, in 1921, the Irish Republic's representative in Argentina.
138. *The Southern Cross*, 13 October 1899, p. 14.
139. NLI, Bulfin Papers: Ms. 13,804/3. Lecture given by Bulfin in Argentina, 1905.
140. *The Southern Cross*, 13 October 1899, p. 13.
141. Subscription lists were published intermittently in the pages of *The Southern Cross* but contained inconsistent and limited information. On 11 August 1899, p. 20, for example, a total of forty-three names appeared. Some three weeks later, on 1 September 1899, p. 15, this had been reduced to twelve names, three of which were recorded as deceased. It is thus difficult to establish a clear indication of readership numbers.
142. NLI, Bulfin Papers: Ms. 13,810/13. Letter from Laurence Gahan to William Bulfin, 2 Dec 1900. Gahan was an *estanciero* in Navarro.
143. *The Irish Times*, 8 March 1899.
144. *The Southern Cross*, 21 April 1899, p. 11.
145. Ibid.
146. *The Southern Cross*, 13 October 1899, p. 14.
147. Ibid., 30 May 1890, p. 4. Similar attempts to mobilise an American Catholic lobby group, with political overtones, were made in the United States at this time. But, as in Argentina, the idea was largely rejected by Irish Americans as socially isolating and religiously divisive. See David N. Doyle, *Irish Americans, Native Rights, and National Empires* (New York, 1976), pp. 299–301.
148. *The Southern Cross*, 11 August 1899, p. 10.
149. Murray (1919), p. 496.
150. NLI, Bulfin Papers: Ms. 13,815. Letter from G. Foley to Bulfin, 28 October 1902.
151. NLI, Bulfin Papers: Ms. 13,818. Letter from Father Vincent Grogan to William Bulfin, 17 October 1902.
152. D.H. Akenson, *The Irish in South Africa* (Grahamstown, 1991), pp. 41–43.
153. Murray (1919), p. 497.

Conclusion

Both in absolute and in relative terms, the total number emigrating from Ireland to Argentina in the nineteenth century constituted a very small group. And likewise, as a component of European immigration to Argentina the Irish born accounted for less than 1 per cent.[1] Issuing predominantly from the eastern counties of Westmeath, Longford and Wexford, their homeland experience of small scale farming was acutely at variance with the vast, nomadic plains of the pampas on which so many staked their future livelihood. A distinctive group with a distinctive experience ahead of them, the importance of regionalism in the homeland was of equal relevance to settlement in Argentina. And distance, enormous distance, applied as it did elsewhere. But, in Argentina, the processes of arrival and dispersal were unique. In the absence of long standing networks of connection and assimilation, the channels receiving immigrant arrivals multiplied in diverse and unexpected ways, distributing them far away from the urban environment so characteristic of the Irish immigrant experience elsewhere.

And for the arriving Irish immigrant in Argentina there was a further complication. The widespread adoption of the generic '*Inglés*' classification obscured ethnic differentiation. Irish immigrants, however diverse they were in origin, tended to be fused into a community that was, from the outset, distinctly separate. And yet, over time, their settlement contrasted sharply with, and reflected a lack of integration, in any real sense, with urban '*Inglés*' immigration. By contrast, however, their steady acquisition of land and continued farming success happily coincided with the expansion of Argentina's agricultural economy and the increasing desirability of landownership within elite native circles. Consequences for the development of the Irish community within the '*Inglés*' group were considerable. Superficially integrated by virtue of language and 'ethnicity', the achievement of an elevated economic and social status by segments of the Irish community helped to transcend Old

World divides and cement a greater sense of cohesion within a class conscious '*Inglés*' group. The accumulation of wealth by a substantial number of individuals from an Irish immigrant background facilitated greater alignment with the '*Inglés*' social ideal, the significance of which far exceeded financial gain. A growing awareness of the expanding social and cultural benefits of an '*Inglés*' identity created a desire to be '*Inglés*', which, in turn, engendered a complex of conflicting identities with multiplying and sometimes competing choices.

Having secured a prominent and affluent status within '*Inglés*' ranks, the Irish swiftly and adeptly adjusted to '*Inglés*' behaviour, aided unsurprisingly by the Argentinian Irish Catholic Church. With social and political ambitions of its own, the Church of the immigrant Irish, principally under Fahey's tutelage, fully recognised and took advantage of native partiality to all things '*Inglés*' to further its own advancement. In so doing, it contributed considerably to the merging and blurring of Irish and '*Inglés*' identities. In seeking to enforce a stringent moral and social code, the Church helped stifle any sense of cultural uniformity that might be described as Irish within an immigrant group that had become markedly stratified in sociological terms.

A climate of religious oppression may, in part, be adduced to explain the character of such deviant behaviour as has been attributed to the Irish. But any such assumption must be treated with caution. Since official statistics allow for examination of '*Inglés*' data only, it has proved impossible specifically to identify distinctively Irish deviant conduct. But, in spite of its pretensions, the '*Inglés*' group as a whole was statistically recorded as intemperate. It is with some irony that, in desiring the social elevation of an '*Inglés*' identity, the Irish community, as members of the generic classification, were represented as drunkards. Whether this was an accurate portrayal of Irish behaviour or a composite of all the ethnicities subsumed within the '*Inglés*' group, must remain delightfully ambiguous. Anecdotal evidence inevitably confirms the stereotypical pattern of Irish intoxication. But it may also be suggestive of a deeper reflex.

It is possible that, as a culturally impoverished community within a group dominated by '*Inglés*' values, drunkenness may well have been the easiest avenue toward an assertion of independence. Manifestations of cultural dysfunction, which asserted ethnic differentiation by reverting to stereotypical expressions of Irishness, were, it might be suggested, an unconscious rebellion against the protocol of received *'Inglés'* culture. But all of this is speculative. Equally so, but no less likely, is the prospect that those aspiring with the Irish immigrant community to find a place within the *'Inglés'* community, and anxious to differentiate themselves from the more socially coarse segments of the Irish group, would have been happy to contribute to pre-existing stereotypes by supplementary anecdote and complaint. But given the intractable nature of the statistical sources, there is no need to give this prejudicial anecdotal evidence exceptional weight.

Evidence of a stereotypical Irish immigrant dysfunction is, therefore, far from complete. But what is clear is that a significant change is discernible from the late 1880s. The emergence of a native Argentine national movement sparked an exploration of Irish nationalism, which in earlier decades was incompatible with *'Inglés'* circles. In a host country where national and ethnic identity was under intense scrutiny, segments of the Irish community were now at liberty to explore ethnic priorities and loyalties without fear of jeopardising a societal *'Inglés'* position. The fact that in Argentina, and in contrast to the United States, an embryonic nationalist ideology did not develop into a full blown form of Irish nationalism reflects, most clearly, the extent and success of early *'Inglés'* imprinting.

This outcome was also influenced by the failure of the community to maintain its foothold in the corridors of ecclesiastical and political power in Ireland or Argentina. Perceiving no advantage in future reliance upon external forces in either location, the community reserved its most sustained patronage for internal causes such as the establishment of an Irish orphanage and hospital. Thus, a politically, culturally and economically inward looking community formed, which was both self-sufficient and self-reliant. Although achieving degrees of separation from the constraints of an *'Inglés'* identity, the community as a whole never attained a distinctive position between the two identities. Nor, it must be conceded, did they ever concertedly strive to achieve one. Instead, the Irish-Argentines were content ultimately to adopt a position that was at once culturally recognisable, but socially and politically comfortable within the fabric of Argentine society.

This study has attempted nothing more than an initial probe into the development of Irish immigrants in Argentina over the course of the nineteenth century. The methodological problems that it has encountered in relation to the separation of the Irish from the *'Ingleses'* have, in themselves, been centrally important. To the frustration of the present writer they have impeded statistical analysis and presented formidable archival dilemmas but, none the less, particularly reflect the cultural and conceptual difficulties experienced by the Irish immigrant community itself. It remains to be seen how further and broader analysis of the character of the ethnically diverse migration to Argentina will contribute to a deeper analysis of that deeply ambiguous term, *'Inglés'*. But for the present, with regard to the Irish, it is possible to conclude that this small but distinctive group played a small but distinctive role in the evolution of Argentina as a whole.

NOTE

1. Computed from data in *Segundo censo nacional de la República Argentina, 1895,* vol. I, pp. 643–647, and Eduardo Coghlan, *El aporte de los irlandeses a la formación de la nación Argentina* (Buenos Aires, 1982), pp. 18–20.

Appendices

POPULATION DECREASE WITHIN IRISH COUNTIES, 1841–51

County	Population 1841	Population 1851	% Decrease
Roscommon	253,591	173,436	31.61%
Mayo	388,887	274,499	29.41%
Monaghan	200,442	141,823	29.24%
Sligo	180,886	128,515	28.95%
Longford	115,491	82,348	28.70%
Cavan	243,158	174,064	28.42%
Leitrim	155,297	111,897	27.95%
Queens Co.	153,930	111,664	27.46%
Galway	440,198	321,684	26.92%
Fermanagh	156,481	116,047	25.84%
Clare	286,394	212,440	25.82%
Cork	854,118	649,308	23.98%
Tipperary	435,553	331,567	23.87%
Kings Co.	146,857	112,076	23.68%
Meath	183,828	140,748	23.43%
Kilkenny	202,420	158,748	21.57%
Wicklow	126,143	98,979	21.53%
Westmeath	141,300	111,407	21.16%
Carlow	86,228	68,078	21.05%
Limerick	330,029	262,132	20.57%
Kerry	293,880	238,254	18.93%
Tyrone	312,956	255,661	18.31%
Waterford	196,187	164,035	16.39%
Kildare	114,488	95,723	16.39%
Louth	128,240	107,662	16.05%
Armagh	232,393	196,084	15.62%
Donegal	296,448	255,158	13.93%
Londonderry	222,174	192,022	13.57%
Down	361,446	320,817	11.24%
Wexford	202,033	180,158	10.83%
Antrim	285,567	259,903	8.99%
Dublin Co.	140,047	146,778	-4.81%
Dublin City	232,726	258,369	-11.02%
Belfast	70,447	87,062	-23.59%
Connacht	1,418,859	1,010,031	28.81%
Munster	2,396,161	1,857,736	22.47%
Ulster	2,386,373	2,011,880	15.69%
Leinster	1,973,731	1,672,738	15.25%

Source: Vaughan, W.E. and Fitzpatrick, A.J. (eds), *Irish Historical Statistics: Population, 1821–1971* (Dublin, 1978)

APPENDIX II
POPULATION DECREASE WITHIN IRISH COUNTIES, 1851–91

County	Population 1851	Population 1891	% Decrease
Tipperary	331,567	173,188	47.77%
Meath	140,748	76,987	45.30%
Kilkenny	158,748	87,261	45.03%
Queens Co.	111,664	64,883	41.89%
Westmeath	111,407	65,109	41.56%
Kings Co.	112,076	65,563	41.50%
Clare	212,440	124,483	41.40%
Waterford	164,035	98,251	40.10%
Carlow	68,078	40,936	39.87%
Limerick	262,132	158,912	39.38%
Monaghan	141,823	86,206	39.22%
Wexford	180,158	111,778	37.96%
Wicklow	98,979	62,136	37.22%
Fermanagh	116,047	74,170	36.09%
Longford	82,348	52,647	36.07%
Cavan	174,064	111,917	35.70%
Roscommon	173,436	114,397	34.04%
Louth	107,662	71,038	34.02%
Galway	321,684	214,712	33.25%
Tyrone	255,661	171,401	32.96%
Cork	649,308	438,432	32.48%
Down	320,817	224,008	30.18%
Leitrim	111,897	78,618	29.74%
Donegal	255,158	185,635	27.25%
Armagh	196,084	143,289	26.92%
Kildare	95,723	70,206	26.66%
Kerry	238,254	179,136	24.81%
Sligo	128,515	98,013	23.73%
Londonderry	192,022	152,009	20.84%
Mayo	274,499	219,034	20.21%
Antrim	259,903	215,229	17.19%
Dublin City	258,369	245,00	15.17%
Dublin Co.	146,778	174,215	-18.69%
Belfast	87,062	255,950	-193.99%
Munster	1857736	1,172,402	36.89%
Leinster	1672738	1,187,760	28.99%
Connacht	1010031	724,774	28.24%
Ulster	2011880	1,619,814	19.49%

Source: Vaughan and Fitzpatrick (1978)

APPENDIX III

POLICE CELL ARRESTS IN BUENOS AIRES PROVINCE BY ETHNIC GROUP, 1872-86

Year: 1872

Ethnic group	Men	Women	% of total Men	% of total Women
Spanish	1,289	-	28.93	-
French	676	-	15.17	-
'Inglés'	323	-	7.25	-
Italian	2,003	-	44.95	-
German	165	-	3.70	-
Total	4,456	-	100%	-

Year: 1874

Ethnic group	Men	Women	% of total Men	% of total Women
Spanish	1,597	47	28.41	23.74
French	590	59	10.49	29.80
'Inglés'	500	19	8.89	9.60
Italian	2,751	71	48.93	35.86
German	184	2	3.27	1.01
Total	5,622	198	100%	100%

Year: 1877

Ethnic group	Men	Women	% of total Men	% of total Women
Spanish	1,789	75	26.41	24.92
French	890	77	13.14	25.58
'Inglés'	441	11	6.51	3.65
Italian	3,436	133	50.72	44.19
German	218	5	3.22	1.66
Total	6,774	301	100%	100%

Year: 1875

Ethnic group	Men	Women	% of total Men	% of total Women
Spanish	2,094	66	28.78	22.84
French	985	86	13.54	29.76
'Inglés'	548	28	7.53	9.69
Italian	3426	100	47.09	34.60
German	223	9	3.06	3.11
Total	7,276	289	100%	100%

Year: 1878

Ethnic group	Men	Women	% of total Men	% of total Women
Spanish	1,496	66	25.00	24.81
French	724	45	12.10	16.92
'Inglés'	359	27	6.00	10.15
Italian	3,194	124	53.37	46.62
German	212	4	3.54	1.50
Total	5,985	266	100%	100%

Year: 1881

Ethnic group	Men	Women	% of total Men	% of total Women
Spanish	2,338	6	26.59	9.38
French	1,155	-	13.14	-
'Inglés'	1,082	-	12.31	-
Italian	3,685	58	41.91	90.63
German	532	-	6.05	-
Total	8,792	64	100%	100%

Appendix III cont

Year: 1882

Ethnic group	Men	Women	% of total Men	% of total Women
Spanish	1,241	12	22.38	14.81
French	808	8	14.57	9.88
'Inglés'	594	8	10.71	9.88
Italian	2,797	46	50.44	56.79
German	105	7	1.89	8.64
Total	5,545	81	100%	100%

Year: 1883

Ethnic group	Men	Women	% of total Men	% of total Women
Spanish	1,438	16	27.32	18.18
French	879	17	16.70	19.32
'Inglés'	572	2	10.87	2.27
Italian	2,299	50	43.67	56.82
German	76	3	1.44	3.41
Total	5,264	88	100%	100%

Year: 1884

Ethnic group	Men	Women	% of total Men	% of total Women
Spanish	1,378	10	20.73	11.49
French	915	14	13.77	16.09
'Inglés'	746	8	11.22	9.20
Italian	3,490	51	52.50	58.62
German	118	4	1.78	4.60
Total	6,647	87	100%	100%

Year: 1885

Ethnic group	Men	Women	% of total Men	% of total Women
Spanish	1,352	23	21.75	19.83
French	837	14	13.47	12.07
'Inglés'	523	7	8.41	6.03
Italian	3,402	71	54.73	61.21
German	102	1	1.64	0.86
Total	6,216	116	100%	100%

Year: 1886

Ethnic group	Men	Women	% of total Men	% of total Women
Spanish	1,310	12	20.48	14.81
French	834	18	13.04	22.22
'Inglés'	534	3	8.35	3.70
Italian	3,619	46	56.58	56.79
German	99	2	1.55	2.47
Total	6,396	81	100%	100%

Source: Compiled from data in Bibliotecca Senado: *Registro Estadistio, 1872–1886*

APPENDIX IV:
MALE PRISON POPULATION IN BUENOS AIRES PROVINCE BY ETHNIC GROUP, 1872–87

Ethnic group	Year: 1872 No.	%	Year: 1873 No.	%	Year: 1874 No.	%	Year: 1875 No.	%	Year: 1876 No.	%	Year: 1877 No.	%
Spanish	67	25.67	193	31.33	121	31.19	163	31.90	63	29.44	247	31.39
French	26	9.96	79	12.82	58	14.95	64	12.52	32	14.95	82	10.42
'Inglés'	11	4.21	33	5.36	15	3.87	14	2.74	6	2.80	19	2.41
Italian	146	55.94	298	48.38	187	48.20	261	51.08	109	50.93	418	53.11
German	11	4.21	13	2.11	7	1.80	9	1.76	4	1.87	21	2.67
Total	261	100%	616	100%	388	100%	511	100%	214	100%	787	100%

Ethnic Group	Year: 1879 No.	%	Year: 1880 No.	%	Year: 1881 No.	%	Year: 1882 No.	%	Year: 1883 No.	%	Year: 1884 No.	%
Spanish	71	29.22	62	22.96	25	25.51	25	20.49	76	35.35	65	28.14
French	21	8.64	29	10.74	10	10.20	17	13.93	19	8.84	27	11.69
'Inglés'	5	2.06	9	3.33	2	2.04	8	6.56	21	9.77	14	6.06
Italian	138	56.79	168	62.22	59	60.20	70	57.38	97	45.12	124	53.68
German	8	3.29	2	0.74	2	2.04	2	1.64	2	0.93	1	0.43
Total	243	100%	270	100%	98	100%	122	100%	215	100%	231	100%

Ethnic group	Year: 1885 No.	%	Year: 1886 No.	%	Year: 1887 No.	%
Spanish	57	25.00	32	27.12	26	25.74
French	27	11.84	20	16.95	7	6.93
'Inglés'	11	4.82	6	5.08	6	5.94
Italian	132	57.89	60	50.85	62	61.39
German	1	0.44	-	-	-	-
Total	228	100%	118	100%	101	100%

Source: Compiled from data in Bibliotecca Senado: *Registro Estadistio, 1872–1886*

APPENDIX V:
POLICE CELL ARRESTS IN BUENOS AIRES PROVINCE BY ETHNIC GROUP AND CRIME, 1872–86

1872: Male

Crime:	Italian	'Inglés'	German	Spanish	French	Total
	No.	No.	No.	No.	No.	No.
Homicide	16	2	1	8	3	30
Assault	132	14	7	90	25	268
Robbery	230	15	17	108	68	438
Fraud	-	-	-	2	1	3
Disturbing the peace	340	41	29	194	108	712
Intoxication	351	118	58	220	202	949
Total	1,069	190	112	622	407	2,400

1873: Male

Crime:	Italian	'Inglés'	German	Spanish	French	Total
	No.	No.	No.	No.	No.	No.
Homicide	30	2	-	9	7	48
Assault	170	15	2	92	45	324
Robbery	239	23	1	28	32	323
Fraud	5	-	-	3	1	9
Disturbing the peace	511	51	33	298	130	1,023
Intoxication	560	312	84	407	314	1,677
Total	1,515	403	120	837	529	3,404

1873: Female

Crime:	Italian	'Inglés'	German	Spanish	French	Total
	No.	No.	No.	No.	No.	No.
Homicide	3	-	-	1	-	4
Assault	2	-	-	1	3	6
Robbery	6	2	-	4	7	19
Fraud	-	-	-	-	-	-
Disturbing the peace	19	2	2	12	12	45
Intoxication	3	12	2	11	19	47
Total	33	16	2	29	41	121

Appendix V Cont

1874: Male

Crime:	Italian	'Inglés'	German	Spanish	French	Total
	No.	No.	No.	No.	No.	No.
Homicide	40	2	1	18	7	68
Assault	182	19	3	95	29	328
Robbery	404	39	19	209	117	788
Fraud	24	-	-	4	5	33
Disturbing the peace	525	45	18	258	142	988
Intoxication	516	229	76	332	291	1,444
Total	1,691	334	117	916	591	3,649

1874: Female

Crime:	Italian	'Inglés'	German	Spanish	French	Total
	No.	No.	No.	No.	No.	No.
Homicide	1	-	-	-	-	1
Assault	4	-	-	1	2	7
Robbery	6	-	1	4	5	16
Fraud	-	-	-	-	1	1
Disturbing the peace	6	1	-	5	5	17
Intoxication	4	7	1	8	10	29
Total	21	8	1	18	23	71

1875: Male

Crime:	Italian	'Inglés'	German	Spanish	French	Total
	No.	No.	No.	No.	No.	No.
Homicide	26	-	-	17	5	48
Assault	194	15	4	109	39	361
Robbery	410	14	21	184	96	725
Fraud	22	-	-	13	3	38
Disturbing the peace	684	36	24	394	142	1,280
Intoxication	663	335	117	479	330	1,924
Total	1,999	400	166	1,196	615	4,376

1875: Female

Crime:	Italian	'Inglés'	German	Spanish	French	Total
	No.	No.	No.	No.	No.	No.
Homicide	3	-	-	-	-	3
Assault	5	-	-	2	2	9
Robbery	3	-	-	5	2	10
Fraud	-	-	-	-	-	-
Disturbing the peace	16	-	5	14	1	36
Intoxication	21	8	9	17	58	113
Total	48	8	14	38	63	171

Appendix V Cont

1877: Male

Crime:	Italian No.	'Inglés' No.	German No.	Spanish No.	French No.	Total No.
Homicide	23	1	-	1	2	27
Assault	149	6	3	70	35	263
Robbery	300	12	17	153	61	543
Fraud	8	-	-	5	2	15
Disturbing the peace	1,095	47	48	504	177	1,871
Intoxication	606	288	111	497	307	1,809
Total	**2,181**	**354**	**179**	**1,230**	**584**	**4,528**

1877: Female

Crime:	Italian No.	'Inglés' No.	German No.	Spanish No.	French No.	Total No.
Homicide	-	-	-	-	-	-
Assault	2	-	-	3	2	7
Robbery	5	-	-	-	3	8
Fraud	-	-	-	-	-	-
Disturbing the peace	27	4	-	17	13	61
Intoxication	22	5	-	6	41	74
Total	**56**	**9**	**-**	**26**	**59**	**150**

1878: Male

Crime:	Italian No.	'Inglés' No.	German No.	Spanish No.	French No.	Total No.
Homicide	4	2	-	-	1	7
Assault	160	8	7	61	18	254
Robbery	247	12	12	177	66	514
Fraud	1	-	-	1	1	3
Disturbing the peace	879	126	66	391	234	1,696
Intoxication	748	142	78	409	202	1,579
Total	**2,039**	**290**	**163**	**1,039**	**522**	**4,053**

1878: Female

Crime:	Italian No.	'Inglés' No.	German No.	Spanish No.	French No.	Total No.
Homicide	1	-	-	-	-	1
Assault	5	-	-	1	2	8
Robbery	6	-	1	3	4	14
Fraud	-	-	-	-	-	-
Disturbing the peace	27	3	1	20	6	57
Intoxication	19	21	-	17	22	79
Total	**58**	**24**	**2**	**41**	**34**	**159**

Appendx V Cont

1881: Male

Crime:	Italian No.	'Inglés' No.	German No.	Spanish No.	French No.	Total No.
Homicide	53	8	-	30	-	91
Assault	131	41	24	44	14	254
Robbery	275	71	59	149	54	608
Fraud	2	-	-	-	-	2
Disturbing the peace	411	144	58	386	158	1,157
Intoxication	949	490	227	657	490	2,813
Total	**1,821**	**754**	**368**	**1,266**	**716**	**4,925**

1881: Female

Crime:	Italian No.	'Inglés' No.	German No.	Spanish No.	French No.	Total No.
Homicide	-	-	-	1	1	2
Assault	3	-	-	1	4	8
Robbery	-	-	-	-	-	-
Fraud	-	-	-	-	-	-
Disturbing the peace	25	-	-	-	25	50
Intoxication	19	-	-	-	19	38
Total	**47**	**-**	**-**	**2**	**49**	**98**

1882: Male

Crime:	Italian No.	'Inglés' No.	German No.	Spanish No.	French No.	Total No.
Homicide	32	2	2	14	8	58
Assault	45	4	-	29	10	88
Robbery	213	24	6	84	38	365
Fraud	-	-	-	-	-	-
Disturbing the peace	776	91	11	342	175	1,395
Intoxication	646	354	52	424	329	1,805
Total	**1,712**	**475**	**71**	**893**	**560**	**3,711**

1882: Female

Crime:	Italian No.	'Inglés' No.	German No.	Spanish No.	French No.	Total No.
Homicide	1	-	-	-	-	1
Assault	-	-	-	-	-	-
Robbery	1	1	-	-	-	2
Fraud	-	-	-	-	-	-
Disturbing the peace	31	-	-	6	2	39
Intoxication	3	6	5	4	4	22
Total	**36**	**7**	**5**	**10**	**6**	**64**

Appendix V Cont

1884: Male

Crime:	Italian No.	'Inglés' No.	German No.	Spanish No.	French No.	Total No.
Homicide	43	6	2	12	5	68
Assault	180	18	-	86	27	311
Robbery	169	22	6	81	33	311
Fraud	1	-	-	-	-	1
Disturbing the peace	886	119	18	252	201	1,476
Intoxication	1,223	498	68	555	411	2,755
Total	2,502	663	94	986	677	7,722

1884: Female

Crime:	Italian No.	'Inglés' No.	German No.	Spanish No.	French No.	Total No.
Homicide	-	-	-	-	-	-
Assault	2	-	-	2	1	4
Robbery	1	-	-	-	1	2
Fraud	-	-	-	-	-	-
Disturbing the peace	15	6	2	21	8	52
Intoxication	6	1	2	7	3	19
Total	24	7	4	30	12	77

1885: Male

Crime:	Italian No.	'Inglés' No.	German No.	Spanish No.	French No.	Total No.
Homicide	34	2	-	19	7	62
Assault	182	6	1	73	28	290
Robbery	122	8	3	86	31	250
Fraud	-	-	-	1	1	2
Disturbing the peace	880	69	16	202	185	1,352
Intoxication	1,156	368	61	400	345	2,330
Total	2,374	453	81	781	597	4,286

1885: Female

Crime:	Italian No.	'Inglés' No.	German No.	Spanish No.	French No.	Total No.
Homicide	2	-	-	-	-	2
Assault	4	-	-	-	-	4
Robbery	1	-	-	-	1	2
Fraud	-	-	-	-	-	-
Disturbing the peace	28	-	1	11	6	46
Intoxication	11	7	-	6	2	26
Total	46	7	1	17	9	80

Appendix V Cont

1886: Male

Crime:	Italian	'Inglés'	German	Spanish	French	Total
	No.	No.	No.	No.	No.	No.
Homicide	44	2	1	15	5	67
Assault	178	15	6	71	36	306
Robbery	196	17	3	85	36	337
Fraud	-	-	-	2	-	2
Disturbing the peace	989	45	12	273	144	1,463
Intoxication	1,288	401	55	444	442	2,630
Total	2,695	480	77	890	663	4,805

1886: Female

Crime:	Italian	'Inglés'	German	Spanish	French	Total
	No.	No.	No.	No.	No.	No.
Homicide	-	-	-	-	2	2
Assault	-	-	-	-	2	2
Robbery	2	-	-	-	1	3
Fraud	-	-	-	-	-	-
Disturbing the peace	27	1	-	5	5	38
Intoxication	7	1	-	2	4	14
Total	36	2	-	7	14	59

Source: Compiled from data in Bibliotecca Senado: *Registro Estadistio, 1872–1886*

APPENDIX VI:

MALE PRISON POPULATION IN BUENOS AIRES PROVINCE BY ETHNIC GROUP AND CRIME, 1872-87

Male: 1872	Italian	'Inglés'	German	Spanish	French	Total
	No.	No.	No.	No.	No.	No.
Crime:						
Homicide	2	-	-	2	-	4
Assault	11	1	-	9	-	21
Robbery	111	9	10	41	19	190
Fraud	-	-	-	-	-	-
Disturbing the peace	1	-	-	-	-	1
Intoxication	-	-	-	-	-	-
Total	125	10	10	52	19	216

1873:	Italian	'Inglés'	German	Spanish	French	Total
	No.	No.	No.	No.	No.	No.
Crime:						
Homicide	25	3	-	11	5	44
Assault	36	3	2	22	3	66
Robbery	175	17	4	106	54	356
Fraud	6	1	1	3	1	12
Disturbing the peace	2	-	-	2	1	5
Intoxication	1	3	2	1	1	8
Total	245	27	9	145	65	601

Male: 1874	Italian	'Inglés'	German	Spanish	French	Total
	No.	No.	No.	No.	No.	No.
Crime:						
Homicide	1	-	-	-	-	1
Assault	49	2	-	22	4	77
Robbery	93	11	3	75	41	223
Fraud	5	-	-	-	2	7
Disturbing the peace	2	-	-	3	1	6
Intoxication	1	-	-	-	1	2
Total	151	13	3	100	49	316

1875:	Italian	'Inglés'	German	Spanish	French	Total
	No.	No.	No.	No.	No.	No.
Crime:						
Homicide	-	-	-	-	-	-
Assault	44	4	-	16	9	73
Robbery	140	6	4	91	43	284
Fraud	1	-	1	1	1	4
Disturbing the peace	3	-	-	5	-	8
Intoxication	2	1	-	-	1	4
Total	190	11	5	113	54	373

Appendix VI Cont

Male: 1876	Italian	'Inglés'	German	Spanish	French	Total	1877: Italian	'Inglés'	German	Spanish	French	Total
Crime:	No.	No.	No.	No.	No.	No.	No.	No.	No.	No.	No.	No.
Homicide	36	1	-	14	12	63	1	-	-	-	-	1
Assault	34	-	-	15	3	52	70	4	-	25	5	104
Robbery	10	1	1	7	8	27	196	9	10	114	50	379
Fraud	3	-	1	3	1	8	-	-	-	-	-	-
Disturbing the peace	12	1	1	8	6	28	20	-	2	10	7	39
Intoxication	1	-	-	-	1	11	3	4	13	4	35	
Total	95	4	3	47	30	179	298	16	16	162	66	568

Male: 1879	Italian	'Inglés'	German	Spanish	French	Total	1880: Italian	'Inglés'	German	Spanish	French	Total
	No.	No.	No.	No.	No.	No.	No.	No.	No.	No.	No.	No.
Homicide	10	3	-	18	2	33	47	2	-	14	2	65
Assault	33	1	1	5	3	43	38	4	-			42
Robbery	44	-	2	30	14	90	60	1	2	30	17	110
Fraud	1	-	-	3	1	5	-	-	-	1	1	2
Disturbing the Peace	n.a.	n.a.	n.a.	n.a.	n.a.	n.a	n.a.	n.a.	n.a.	n.a.	n.a.	n.a
Intoxication	n.a.	n.a.	n.a.	n.a.	n.a.	n.a	n.a.	n.a.	n.a.	n.a.	n.a.	n.a
Total	88	4	3	56	20	171	145	7	2	45	20	219

Appendix VI cont

Male: 1881 / 1882

Crime:	Italian No.	'Inglés' No.	German No.	Spanish No.	French No.	Total No.	1882: Italian No.	'Inglés' No.	German No.	Spanish No.	French No.	Total No.
Homicide	12	3	2	8	2	27	29	5	2	10	6	52
Assault	19	-	2	7	1	29	17	1	-	11	2	31
Robbery	21	-	-	9	10	40	2	-	-	3	2	7
Fraud	-	-	-	-	-	-	-	-	-	-	-	-
Disturbing the peace	n.a.	n.a.	n.a.	n.a.	n.a.	n.a	n.a.	n.a.	n.a.	n.a.	n.a.	n.a
Intoxication	n.a.	n.a.	n.a.	n.a.	n.a.	n.a	n.a.	n.a.	n.a.	n.a.	n.a.	n.a
Total	52	3	4	24	13	96	48	6	2	24	10	90

Male: 1886 / 1887

Crime:	Italian No.	'Inglés' No.	German No.	Spanish No.	French No.	Total No.	1887: Italian No.	'Inglés' No.	German No.	Spanish No.	French No.	Total No.
Homicide	18	5	n.a.	2	5	30	24	3	4	1	-	32
Assault	15	-	n.a.	11	8	34	16	2	11	2	-	31
Robbery	5	-	n.a.	5	2	12	1	-	-	-	-	1
Fraud	-	-	n.a.	-	-	-	-	-	-	-	-	-
Disturbing the peace	n.a.	n.a.	n.a.	n.a.	n.a.	n.a.	n.a	n.a.	n.a.	n.a.	n.a.	n.a.
Intoxication	n.a.	n.a.	n.a.	n.a.	n.a.	n.a	n.a.	n.a.	n.a.	n.a.	n.a.	n.a.
Total	38	5	n.a	18	15	76	41	5	n.a	15	3	64

Source: Compiled from data in Bibliotecca Senado: *Registro Estadistio, 1872–1886*

APPENDIX VII: MALE POLICE CELL ARRESTS FOR ROBBERY AND THEFT BY ETHNIC GROUP, 1882–6*

	Italian	'Inglés'	German	Spanish	French	Total
1882						
Robbery	213	24	6	84	38	365
Theft	45	4	-	22	10	81
1884						
Robbery	169	22	6	81	33	311
Theft	50	6	-	24	13	93
1885						
Robbery	122	8	3	86	31	250
Theft	41	6	-	18	26	91
1886						
Robbery	196	17	3	85	36	337
Theft	30	3	3	13	15	64
Total	866	90	21	413	202	1,592

*
These crimes were not recorded separately in 1883.

Source: Compiled from data in Bibliotecca Senado: *Registro Estadistio, 1872–1886*

APPENDIX VIII:
PATIENTS ADMITTED TO THE HOSPITAL FOR 'DEMENTED WOMEN' BY ETHNIC GROUP, 1858-86

Nationality	Year: 1858	%	1861	%	1862	%	1863	%	1864	%	1865	%	1866	%	1867	%
Spanish	8	36.36	6	21.43	10	27.78	10	25.64	30	37.04	10	24.39	28	28.00	8	32.00
French	5	22.73	10	35.71	10	27.78	11	28.21	15 1	8.52	10	24.39	20	20.00	2	8.00
'Inglés'	-	-	7	25.00	-	-	7	17.95	4	4.94	-	-	10	10.00	7	28.00
Irish	2	9.09	-	-	8	22.22	-	-	-	-	8	19.51	-	-	-	-
Italian	7	31.82	4	14.29	8	22.22	9	23.08	29	35.8	12	29.27	33	33.00	7	28.00
German	-	-	1	3.57	-	-	2	5.13	3	3.70	1	2.44	9	9.00	1	4.00
Total	22	100%	28	100%	36	100%	39	100%	81	100%	41	100%	100	100%	25	100%

Nationality	1868	%	1870	%	1872	%	1873	%	1874	%	1875	%	1876	%	1877	%
Spanish	4	14.81	8	21.00	11	24.44	9	16.07	10	20.00	13	21.31	12	21.43	13	22.03
French	3	11.11	10	26.00	7	15.56	17	30.36	10	20.00	11	18.03	11	19.64	12	20.34
'Inglés'	10	37.04	2	5.00	3	6.67	7	12.50	6	12.00	6	9.84	5	8.93	3	5.08
Irish	-	-	5	13.00	-	-	-	-	-	-	-	-	-	-	-	-
Italian	10	37.04	12	32.00	23	51.11	23	41.07	22	44.00	22	36.07	24	42.86	27	45.76
German	-	-	1	3.00	1	2.22	-	-	2	4.00	9	14.75	4	7.14	4	6.78
Total	27	100%	38	100%	45	100%	56	100%	50	100%	61	100%	56	100%	59	100%

Source: Biblioteca Senado: Registo Estadistio and Sociedad de Beneficiencia, Hospital Nacional de Aliendas, Legajo 218, 1858–86

APPENDIX IX:
PATIENTS ADMITTED TO HOSPITAL SAN BUENA VENTURA (FOR 'DEMENTED MEN') BY ETHNIC GROUP, 1863-9

Ethnic Group	Year 1863	%	1864	%	1865	%	1866	%	1867	%	1868	%	1869	%
Spanish	29	28.71	30	38.46	25	25.00	28	30.77	15	30.00	27	25.96	40	26.85
French	24	23.76	15	19.23	17	17.00	20	21.98	9	18.00	28	26.92	39	26.17
'Inglés'	1	0.99	4	5.13	10	10.00	10	10.99	3	6.00	8	7.69	12	8.05
Italian	47	46.53	29	37.18	48	48.00	33	36.26	23	46.00	41	39.42	58	38.93
German	3	2.97	3	3.85	4	4.00	9	9.89	5	10.00	73	70.19	5	3.36
Total	101	100%	78	100%	100	100%	91	100%	50	100%	104	100%	149	100%

Source: Bibliotecca Senado: Registro Estadistio, 18963–69

APPENDIX X:
TOTAL POLICE CELL ARRESTS (MALE AND FEMALE) BY ETHNIC GROUP, 1872-86

Ethnic group	1872	1874	1875	1877	1878	1881	1882	1883	1884	1885	1886
Argentine	3,581	4,822	5,131	5,564	4,760	3,290	8,851	9,191	9,942	10,044	10,114
Italian	2,003	2,822	3,526	3,569	3,318	3,743	2,843	2,349	3,541	3,473	3,665
Spanish	1,289	1,664	2,160	1,864	1,562	2,344	1,253	1,454	1,388	1,375	1,322
French	676	649	1071	967	769	1,155	816	896	929	851	852
'Inglés'	323	519	576	452	386	1,082	602	574	754	530	537
German	165	186	232	223	216	532	112	79	122	103	101
The Americas	789	491	911	836	584	1,404	418	371	436	459	539
Other	475	969	595	126	633	2,941	232	242	188	219	273
Total	**9,301**	**12,122**	**14,202**	**13,601**	**12,228**	**16,491**	**15,127**	**15,156**	**17,300**	**17,054**	**17,403**
The Americas:											
Uruguayan	547	219	621	521	328	717	185	193	247	248	260
Paraguayan	87	121	107	103	109	108	111	74	91	115	125
Chilean	46	54	67	86	76	131	66	59	68	58	86
Brazilian	109	97	116	126	71	448	56	45	30	38	68
Total	**789**	**491**	**911**	**836**	**584**	**1404**	**418**	**371**	**436**	**459**	**539**

Source: Compiled from *Registro Estadístio, 1872–86*

Sources and Bibliography

PRIMARY SOURCES

A. Manuscripts

1. Argentina

Buenos Aires

Archivo General Nacionál (AGN)

Cárcel Pública, Listas de Presos, 1849–1850 (Sala X, 43–7–6)
Depósito de Policia, 1845–1852 (Sala X, 31–11–4)
Juez de la Paz de Campaña, 1874 (Sala X, 35–5–6)
Juez de la Paz, Criminales Profugos, 1853–59 (Sala X, 32–3–7)
Ministerio de Gobierno de Buenos Aires, 1881–1884 (Legajo 181)
Provincia Gobierno de Buenos Aires, 1881–1884 (Colección Dardo Rocha: Legajo 179)
Sociedad de Beneficencia, Hospital Nacionál de Alienados (Sala X, Legajos 218, 220)

Archivo Provincial de la Congregación Passionista Holy Cross Church [Unsorted Collection]

Acta de la Asociación Católica Irlandesa, 1925
Acta de la Sociedad Irlandés–Argentina, 1920
Chronica Recessus Sancti Pauli a Cruce, 1887–1898
Platea Chronicle of the Holy Cross Church, 1880–1901
Subscriptions and Donations to Irish–Argentine Society, 1919

The Hurling Club
Avenida Gdor. Vergara 5415
Hurlingham

'El Titulo' – La Compra de la Tierra del Club Hurling, n.d.

The Jockey Club
Avenida Alvear 1345

Acta de la Sesión de Instalación del Jockey Club, 1882

San Antonio de Areco

Pallottine Fathers

Libro de Bautismo de la Parroquia, 1863–1874
Libro de Matrimonios del Partido, 1870–1883

Private Collections

Buenos Aires

Memoirs of Tom Garraghan, 1864–1924
By kind permission of the Garraghan family
Rattigan family letters, c. 1890s
By kind permission of the Rattigan family

2. Ireland

Dublin

All Hallows College [Unsorted Collection]

Incoming correspondence from Buenos Aires,
1855–1873 (c. 100 letters)

Dublin Archdiocese

Daniel Murray Papers, AB3/33/13/1–13
Paul Cullen Papers, 332/2/I (2); 339/6/II/1–3

National Library of Ireland (NLI)

William Bulfin Papers, Ms.13,802–823
Parliamentary Papers:

- (1909, CII)
- (1872, 35, vol. LXX),

University College Dublin

Eamon de Valera Papers:
P150/113, 1124, 1131, 1145, 1148, 1398

3. United Kingdom

Kew

National Archives

Foreign Office Records
General Correspondence:
Registers of General Correspondence, 1817–1920 (F.O. 566)
Argentine Republic, 1823–1905 (F.O.6)
Embassy and Consular Archives:
Argentine Republic, 1820–1941 (F.O. 118, 119, 347)
Buenos Aires, 1826–1900 (F.O. 446)

B. Official Publications

1. Argentina

Buenos Aires

Censo de la Ciudad de Buenos Aires, 1855
Primer censo nacional de la República Argentina, 1869
Segundo censo nacional de la República Argentina, 1895
Tercer censo nacional de la República Argentina, 1914
Registro de contribución directa, 1860 (Sala III, 33–6–10)

Ciudad de la Plata

Registro estadistico (Published Annual Reports for the Years
   1858–1887)
Indice de escribanos (Legajos 26/ 81/ 94/ 251/ 254/ 283/ 284/
   303)
*Dirección de geodesia catastro y mapa de la Provincia de Buenos
   Aires, 1855–1900*
*Fichero de inscripción de dominio de compradores y vendores,
   1883–1907*

2. United Kingdom

Census of Ireland for the Years 1841, 1851, 1861 (General Reports)

House of Commons Papers [Command Papers]

Emigration Statistics of Ireland (Published Annual Reports for the years 1876–1910)

Report of the Registrar General of Births, Deaths and Marriages (Published Annual Reports for the years 1864–1920)

Report to the Secretary of the Department of Agriculture and Technical Instruction for Ireland: HCP 1909 [cd. 53], cll

Remarks on the River Plate Republics as a Field for British Emigration: HCP 1872 [cd. 35], lxx

Returns Relating to Emigration from the United Kingdom, 1858–1867: HCP 1868–1869 [cd. 17], l

Tables Relating to Agricultural Returns for the Year 1849 (HCP 1850, li); *1850* (HCP 1851, l); *1851* (HCP 1854, lvii)

Treatment of British Subjects in the Argentine Republic, 1870–72: HCP 1872 [cd.35], lxx

3. United States

Senate Documents on Immigration and Crime (Washington, 1910: 61st Congress, 3rd Session)

C. Newspapers and Periodicals

Argentina

Buenos Aires

El Diario, 1887–1902
La Nación, 1872–1882
La Prensa, 1869–1905
La Tribuna, 1872–1885
The British Packet and Argentine News, 1850–1854
The Buenos Aires Herald, 1878–1889
The Standard, 1861–1920
The Southern Cross, 1875–1920
The Southern Cross, Centenary Edition, 1875–1975
The Southern Cross, Anniversary Edition, 1875–2000

2. Ireland

Dublin

Dublin University Magazine, 1854–1865
Irish Ecclesiastical Record, 1882–1890
Irish Times, 1890–1899
Longford Independent and Westmeath Examiner, 1868–1874
Westmeath Herald and General Advertiser, 1859–1860
Westmeath Independent, 1846–1868
Wexford Guardian, 1847–1855
Wexford People, 1853–1869

3. United Kingdom

The Times 1841; 1842; 1849; 1868; 1875; 1878; 1891;
    1894–1901; 1906; 1909; 1910

D. Printed Primary

Argentina

Buenos Aires

**Archivo Provincial de la Congregación Passionista
Holy Cross Church**

Annals of St Brendan's College: First Report, 1869
Statutes of Irish–Argentine Society, 1919
Statutes of the Knights of the White Cross, n.d.

**Jockey Club
Avenida Alvear 1345**

Plano Catastral, 1901

**Hurling Club
Avenida Gdor. Vergara 5415
Hurlingham**

Estatutos del Club Hurling, n.d.
50th Anniversay of the Hurling Club, 1922–1972

**Colegio Santa Brígida
Avenida Gaona 2068**

Centenario de la Associación Catolica Irlandesa, 1883–1983

E. Contemporary Publications

Anon. 'Hadfield's South America' in *Dublin University Magazine*, vol. 44 (August 1854), pp. 204–222

Bulfin, William. *Tales of the Pampas* (London, 1900)

Bunge, Alejandro E. *La desocupación en la Argentina: Actual crisis del trabajo* (Buenos Aires, 1917)

Daireaux, Emilio. *Vida y costumbres de la Plata* (Buenos Aires, 1888)

Denvir, John. *The Irish in Britain* (London, 1894)

Every, Edward F. *The Anglican Church in South America* (London, 1915)

Farrell, James P. *Historical Notes of County Longford* (Dublin, 1886)

Fraser, Robert. *Statistical Survey of the County of Wexford* (Dublin, 1807)

Gálvez, Manuel. *El solar de la Raza* (Madrid, n.d.)

Garratt, Rev. S. *The Irish in London* (London 1852)

Gibson, Herbert. *The History and Present State of the Sheep Breeding Industry in the Argentine Republic* (Buenos Aires, 1893)

Hadfield, William. *Brazil, the River Plate, and the Falkland Islands* (London, 1854)

Jeridein, Arthur. *The Argentine Republic as a Field for the Agriculturist, the Stock Farmer, and the Capitalist* (London, 1870)

Latham, Wilfrid. *The State of the River Plate: Their Industries and Commerce* (London, 1866)

Lewis, Samuel. *Topographical Dictionary of Ireland*, 2 vols (London, 1837)

McCann, William. *Two Thousand Miles' Ride through the Argentine Provinces* (London, 1853)

MacDonnell, P. *Remarks on the River Plate Republics as a Field for British Immigration* (Buenos Aires, 1872)

Mayhew, Henry. *London Labour and the London Poor* (London, 1861)

Mayhew, Henry and Binney, John. *The Criminal Prisons of London* (London, 1862)

Mulhall, M.G. *The English in South America* (Buenos Aires, 1878)

——*Handbook of the River Plate: Comprising Buenos Ayres, The Upper Provinces, Banda Oriental, and Paraguay*, 2 vols (Buenos Aires, 1869)

——*Manuel de las Repúblicas del Plata: Datos topográficos, históricos, y Económicos* (Buenos Aires and London, 1876)

Murray, Thomas. *The Story of the Irish in Argentina* (New York, 1919)

Napp, Ricardo. *La República Argentina* (Buenos Aires, 1876)

O'Brien, C.M. 'Catholics and Freemasonry' in *The Irish Ecclesiastical Record*, vol.VI (1899), pp. 309–326

Parish, Sir Woodbine. *Buenos Aires and the Provinces of the Rio de la Plata: From their Discovery and Conquest by the Spaniards to the Establishment of their Political Independence* (London, 1838)

Piaggio, Monsignor Agustín. *Influencia del clero en la independencia Argentina, 1810–1820* (Barcelona, 1912)

Ramos Mejía, José M. *Las neurosis de los hombres célebres en la historia, Argentina, 1878–1882* (Buenos Aires, 1915)

Robertson, J.P. and W.P. *Letters on South America*, 3 vols (London, 1843)

Sheehan, P.A. 'The Effect of Emigration on the Irish Churches' in *Irish Ecclesiastical Record*, vol. III (1882), pp. 605–615

Young, Arthur. *A Tour in Ireland*, 2 vols (Dublin, 1780)

SECONDARY SOURCES

A. Ireland and Irish Emigration:

Adams, William Forbes. *Ireland and Irish Emigration to the New World from 1815 to the Famine* (New Haven, 1932)

Akenson, Donald Harman. *Half the World from Home: Perspectives on the Irish in New Zealand, 1860–1950* (Wellington, 1990)

—— *If the Irish Ran the World: Montserrat, 1630–1730* (Liverpool, 1997)

—— *Occasional Papers on the Irish in South Africa* (Grahamstown, 1991)

—— *Small Differences: Irish Catholics and Irish Protestants, 1815–1921: An International Perspective* (Kingston, 1988)

—— 'The Historiography of the Irish in the Unites States of America' in O'Sullivan, Patrick. (ed.), *The Irish in the New Communities* (Leicester, 1992), pp. 99–127

—— *The Irish Diaspora: A Primer* (Toronto and Belfast, 1993)

—— *The Irish in South Africa* (Grahamstown, 1991)

—— *The United States and Ireland: Ecclesiastical Reform and Revolution, 1880–1855* (New Haven and London, 1971)

Arensberg, Conrad M. *The Irish Countryman: An Anthropological Study* (London, 1937)

Arensberg, Conrad M. and Kimball, Solon T. *Family and Community in Ireland* (rev. ed., Cambridge, 1968)

Bales, Robert F. 'Attitudes Toward Drinking in the Irish Culture' in Pitman, David J. and Snyder, Charles R. (eds), *Society, Culture and Drinking Patterns* (Carbondale, 1962), pp. 157–187

Bayor, R.H. and Meagher, T.J. *The New York Irish* (Baltimore, 1996)

Bhugra, Dinesh. *Mental Health of Ethnic Minorites: An Annotated Bibliography* (London, 1999)

Bielenberg, A. (ed.), *The Irish Diaspora* (Harlow, 2000)

Black, R.D. Collison. *Economic Thought and the Irish Question, 1817–1870* (Cambridge, 1960)

Bossy, John. *The English Catholic Community, 1570–1850* (3rd ed., London, 1979)

Boyce, George D. *Nineteenth-Century Ireland: The Search for Stability* (Dublin, 1990)

Boyce, D.G. 'The Marginal Britons: The Irish' in Colls, Robert and Dodd, Philip. (eds), *Englishness: Politics and Culture, 1880–1920* (Kent, 1986), pp. 230–253

Boyle, J.W. 'The Marginal Figure: The Irish Rural Labourer' in Clark, S. and Donnelly, J.S. (eds), *Irish Peasants: Violence and Political Unrest, 1780–1914* (Wisconsin & Manchester, 1983), pp. 311–338

——'The Rural Labourer' in *Threshold*, vol. III, no. 1 (1959), pp. 29–40

Boyle, K. 'The Irish Immigrant in Britain' in *Northern Ireland Legal Quarterly*, vol. XIX, no. 4 (1968), pp. 418–445

Bracken, Patrick J., Greenslade, Liam., Griffin, Barney and Smyth, Marcelino. 'Mental Health and Ethnicity: An Irish Dimension' in *British Journal of Psychiatry*, vol. 172 (1998), pp. 103–105

Burchell, Robert A. *The San Francisco Irish, 1848–1880* (Manchester, 1979)

Campbell, Malcolm, *Ireland's New Worlds: Immigrants, Politics and Society in the United States and Australia, 1815–1922* (Wisconsin, 2008)

Clarke, Brian P. *Piety and Nationalism: Lay Voluntary Associations and the Creation of an Irish–Catholic Community in Toronto, 1850–1895* (Montreal & Kingston, 1993)

Collins, B. 'Proto–Industrialisation and Pre–Famine Emigration' in *Social History*, vol. VII, no. 2 (1982), pp. 127–146

Collins, E.J.T. 'Harvest Technology and Labour Supply in Britain, 1790–1870' in *Economic History Review*, vol. XXII, no. 3 (1969), pp. 453–473

Connell, K.H. *The Population of Ireland, 1750–1845* (Oxford, 1950)

Connolly, Gerard. 'Irish and Catholic: Myth or Reality–' in Swift, R. and Gilley, S. (eds), *The Irish in the Victorian City* (London, 1985), pp. 225–254

Connolly, S.J. *Religion in Nineteenth–Century Ireland* (Dundalk, 1985)

Comerford, R.V. 'Ireland, 1850–70: Post–Famine and Mid Victorian' in Vaughan, W.E. (ed.), *A New History of Ireland: Ireland Under the Union, I, 1801–70*, vol. V (Oxford, 1989), pp. 372–395

—— *Priests and People in Pre–Famine Ireland, 1780–1845* (Dublin, 1982)

Cousens, S.H. 'The Regional Variations in Population Changes in Ireland, 1861–1881' in *Economic History Review*, vol. XVII, no. 2 (1964), pp. 301–321

—— 'Population Trends in Ireland at the Beginning of the Twentieth Century' in *Irish Geography*, vol. V (1964–8), pp. 387–401

—— 'The Regional Variations in Emigration from Ireland between 1821–1841' in *Transactions and Papers of the Institute of British Geographers*, vol. XXXVII (1965), pp. 15–30

—— 'Regional Variations in Population Changes in Ireland, 1861–1881' in *Economic History Review*, vol. XVII, no. 2 (1964), pp. 301–321

—— 'Emigration and Demographic Change in Ireland, 1851–1861' in *Economic History Review*, vol. XIV, no. 2 (1961), pp. 275–288

Cowan, Helen I. *British Emigration to British North America* (rev. ed., Toronto, 1961)

Crotty, R.D. *Irish Agricultural Production: Its Volume and Structure* (Cork, 1966)

Cullen, L.M. *An Economic History of Ireland since 1660* (London, 1972)

—— 'Ireland and France, 1600–1900' in Cullen, L.M. and Furet, F. (eds), *Ireland and France 17th–20th Centuries: Towards a Comparative Study of Rural History* (Paris, 1980), pp. 9–20

—— *The Emergence of Modern Ireland, 1600–1900* (London, 1981)

Cullen, L.M. and Furet, F. (eds), *Ireland and France 17th–20th Centuries: Towards a Comparative Study of Rural History* (Paris, 1980)

Cullen, L.M. and Smout, T.C. (eds), *Comparative Aspects of Scottish and Irish Economic and Social History, 1600–1900* (Edinburgh, 1977)

Curtis, L.P. *Anglo–Saxons and Celts* (Connecticut, 1968)

—— *Apes and Angels: The Irishman in Victorian Caricature* (Washington, 1997)

Daly, Mary E. *Social and Economic History of Ireland since 1800* (Dublin, 1981)

Davis, Graham. *The Irish in Britain, 1815–1914* (Dublin, 1991)

Dickson, David and Ó Gráda, Cormac. (eds), *Refiguring Ireland: Essays in Honour of L.M. Cullen* (Dublin, 2003)

Dickson, D., Ó Gráda, C. and Daultrey, S. 'Hearth Tax, Household

Size and Irish Population Change, 1672–1821' in *Proceedings of the Royal Irish Academy*, vol. 82, c, no. 6 (1982), pp. 125–181

Dolan, J.P. *The American Catholic Experience: A History from Colonial Times to the Present* (New York, 1985)

Donnelly, James S. *The Land and the People of Nineteenth–Century Cork* (London and Boston, 1975)

Donnelly, James S. and Miller, Kerby A. (eds), *Irish Popular Culture 1650–1860* (Dublin, 1998)

Doyle, David Noel. *Irish Americans, Native Rights, and National Empires* (New York, 1976)

—— 'The Remaking of Irish–America, 1845–1880' in Lee, J.J. and Casey, Marion J (eds), Making the Irish American: History and Heritage of the Irish in the United States (New York, 2006)

—— 'The Irish in North America, 1776–1845' in W.E Vaughan (ed.), *A New History of Ireland: Ireland under the Union, I, 1801–70*, vol. V (Oxford, 1989), pp. 682–725

Elliott, Bruce. *Irish Migrants in the Canadas* (Kingston & Montreal, 1988)

Erickson, Charlotte. 'Emigration from the British Isles to the U.S.A. in 1831' in *Population Studies*, vol. XXXV, no. 2 (1981), pp. 175–197

Fernando, S. (ed.), *Mental Health in a Multi–Ethnic Society* (New York 1995)

Finnane, Mark. *Insanity and the Insane in post–Famine Ireland* (London, 1981)

Finnegan, F. *Poverty and Prejudice: A Study of Irish Immigrants in New York* (Cork, 1982)

Fitzgerald, M., McLennan, G. and Pawson, J. *Crime and Society* (London, 1981)

Fitzpatrick, David. 'A Curious Middle Place: The Irish in Britain, 1871–1921' in Swift, Roger and Gilley, Sheridan. (eds), *The Irish in Britain, 1815–1939* (London, 1989), pp. 10–59

—— 'A Peculiar Tramping People: The Irish in Britain, 1801–70' in Vaughan, W.E. (ed.), *A New History of Ireland: Ireland under the Union, I, 1801–70*, vol. V (Oxford, 1989), pp. 623–660

—— 'Flight from Famine' in Póirtéir, C. (ed.), *The Great Irish Famine* (Cork, 1995), pp. 174–184

—— *Irish Emigration, 1801–1921* (Dublin, 1984)

—— 'Irish Emigration in the Later Nineteenth Century' in *Irish Historical Studies*, vol. XXII, no. 86 (1980), pp. 126–143

—— 'Irish Farming Families before the First World War' in *Comparative Studies in Society and History*, vol. XXV, no. 2 (1983), pp. 339–374

—— *Oceans of Consolation: Personal Accounts of Irish Migration to Australia* (Cork, 1995)

——'The Disappearance of the Irish Agricultural Labourer, 1841–1912 in *Irish Economic and Social History*, vol. VII (1980), pp. 66–92

—— 'The Irish in Britain, 1871–1921' in Vaughan, W.E. (ed.), *A New History of Ireland: Ireland under the Union, I, 1801–70*, vol. V (Oxford, 1989), pp. 653–702

Foster, R.F. *Modern Ireland* (London, 1988) (ed.), *The Oxford Illustrated History of Ireland* (Oxford, 1988)

Freeman, T.W. *Pre–Famine Ireland: A Study in Historical Geography* (Manchester, 1957)

Fried, A. and Elman, Richard M. (eds), *Charles Booth's London* (London, 1969)

Gailey, Alan. 'Changes in Irish Rural Housing, 1600–1900' in Flanagan, P., Ferguson, P. and Whelan, K. (eds), *Rural Ireland, 1600–1900: Modernisation and Change* (Cork, 1987), pp. 86–103

Gillespie, Raymond and Moran, Gerard. (eds), *Longford: Essays in County History* (Dublin, 1991)

Gilley, Sheridan. 'The Roman Catholic Church and the Nineteenth Century Irish Diaspora', in *Journal of Ecclesiastical History*, vol. 35, no. 2 (1984), pp. 188–207

—— 'English Attitudes to the Irish in England, 1780–1900' in Holmes, C. (ed.), *Immigrants and Minorities in British Society* (London, 1978)

——'The Garibaldi Riots of 1862' in *Historical Journal*, vol. XVI, no. 4 (1973), pp. 697–732

Gilley, Sheridan and Shiels, W.J. (eds), *A History of Religion in Britain: Practice and Belief from pre–Roman Times to the Present* (Oxford & Cambridge, Mass., 1994)

Grigg, David. *Population Growth and Agrarian Change* (Cambridge, 1980)

Guinnane, T.W. *The Vanishing Irish* (Princeton, 1997)

Gwinnell, Mary. 'The Famine Years in County Wexford' in *Journal of Wexford Historical Society*, no. 9 (1983–84), pp. 36–53

—— 'Some Aspects of the Economic Life of County Wexford in the Nineteenth Century' in ibid., no. 10 (1984–85) pp. 5–23

Handley, James E. *The Navvy in Scotland* (Cork, 1970)

Handlin, Oscar. *Boston Immigrants, 1790–1865* (Cambridge, Mass., 1941)

—— *Race and Nationality in American Life* (Boston, 1957)

Hansen, Marcus Lee. *The Atlantic Migration, 1607–1860* (Cambridge, Mass., 1940)

Holmes, C. (ed.), *Immigrants and Minorities in British Society* (London, 1978)

Hoppen, Theo K. *Ireland since 1800: Conflict and Consent* (New York, 1972)

—— *Elections, Politics and Society in Ireland, 1832–1885* (Oxford, 1984)

Jackson, J.A. *The Irish in Britain* (London, 1963)

Johnson, Stanley C. *History of Emigration from the United Kingdom to North America, 1763–1912* (London, 1913)

Jones, David. *Crime, Protest, Community and Police in Nineteenth–Century Britain* (London, 1982)

Jones Hughes, T. 'Continuity and Change in Rural County Wexford in the Nineteenth Century' in Whelan, Kevin. (ed.), *Wexford: History and Society, Interdisciplinary Essays on the History of an Irish County* (Dublin, 1987), pp. 342–372

—— 'Landholding and Settlement in County Tipperary in Nineteenth Century Ireland' in Nolan, W. (ed.), *Tipperary History and Society* (Dublin, 1985), pp. 339–336

Kennedy, Liam. *Colonialism, Religion and Nationalism in Ireland* (Belfast, 1996)

Kennedy, L., Ell, P.S., Crawford, E.M. and Clarkson, L.A. *Mapping the Great Famine* (Dublin, 1999)

Kennedy, Liam, Miller, Kerby A., with Graham, Mark. 'The Long Retreat: Protestants, Economy, and Society, 1660–1926', in Raymond Gillespie and Gerard Moran (eds), *Longford: Essays in County History* (Dublin, 1991), pp. 31–61

Kennedy, R.E. 'Farm Succession in Modern Ireland: Elements of a Theory of Inheritance' in *Economic History Review*, vol. XLIV, no. 3 (1991), pp. 477–499

—— *The Irish: Emigration, Marriage, and Fertility* (California, 1973)

Kenny, Kevin. *The American Irish: A History* (Harlow, 2000)

Keogh, Dermot. *Ireland and Europe* (Cork and Dublin, 1990)

Kerr, Barbara M. 'Irish Seasonal Migration to Great Britain, 1800–1838' in *Irish Historical Studies*, vol. III, no. 1 (1943), pp. 365–380

Kiberd, Declan. *Inventing Ireland* (London, 1995)

Kiev, A. and Argandoña, M. *Mental Health in the Developing World* (New York, 1972)

King, Seamus J. *The Clash of the Ash in Foreign Fields: Hurling Abroad* (Tipperary, 1998)

Larkin, Emmet. 'The Devotional Revolution in Ireland, 1850–75' in *American Historical Review*, vol. 77, no. 3 (1972), pp. 625–652

——'Church, State and Nation in Modern Ireland', in ibid., vol. 80, no. 5 (1975), pp. 1244–1276

Lawton, R. 'Irish Migration to England and Wales in the Mid-Nineteenth Century' in *Irish Geography*, vol. IV (1959–63), pp. 35–54

Lee, J.J. 'The Irish Diaspora in the Nineteenth Century' in Laurence M. Geary and Margaret Kelleher (eds), *Nineteenth–Century Ireland* (Dublin, 2005), pp. 182–222

—— *The Modernisation of Irish Society, 1848–1918* (Dublin, 1973)

Lees, Lynn Hollen, *Exiles of Erin: Irish Migrants in Victorian London* (New York, 1979)

Light, Dale B. Jr. 'The Role of Irish–American Organisations in Assimilation and Community Formation' in Drudy, P.J. (ed.), *The Irish in America: Emigration, Assimilation and Impact* (Cambridge, 1985), pp. 113–141

Lowe, W.J. *The Irish in Mid–Victorian Lancashire* (New York, 1989)

Lyons, F.S.L. *Ireland Since the Famine* (London, 1971)

MacDonagh, Oliver. 'The Irish Catholic Clergy and Emigration during the Great Famine' in *Irish Historical Studies*, vol. V, no. 18 (1946), pp. 287–302

—— 'Irish Emigration to the United States and British Colonies during the Famine' in Dudley Edwards, R. and Williams, T. Desmond (eds), *The Great Famine* (Dublin, 1956), pp. 317–388

—— *States of Mind: A Study of Anglo–Irish Conflict, 1780–1980* (London, 1983)

—— 'The Irish Famine Emigration to the United States' in *Perspectives in American History*, vol. 70 (January, 1990), pp. 105–106

MacDonagh, Oliver and Mandle, W.F. (eds), *Ireland and Irish–Australia* (Beckenham, 1986)

Malcolm, Elizabeth. *Ireland Sober, Ireland Free: Drink and Intemperance in Nineteenth–Century Ireland* (Dublin, 1986)

—— 'The Rise of the Pub: A Study in the Disciplining of Popular Culture' in Donnelly, James S. and Miller, Kerby A. (eds), *Irish Popular Culture 1650–1860* (Dublin, 1998)

Miles, Robert. *Racism and Migrant Labour* (London, 1982)

Miller, Kerby A. *Emigrants and Exiles* (Oxford, 1985)

—— 'Emigrants and Exiles: Irish Culture and Irish Emigration to North America, 1790–1922' in *Irish Historical Studies*, vol. XXII, no. 86 (1980), pp. 97–125

Millward, Pauline. 'The Stockport Riots of 1852: A Study of Anti–

Catholic and Anti–Irish Sentiment', in Swift, R. and Gilley, S. (eds), *The Irish in the Victorian City* (London, 1985), pp. 207–224

Mokyr, Joel. *Why Ireland Starved: A Quantitative and Analytical History of the Irish Economy, 1800–1850* (London, 1983)

Mokyr, Joel and Ó Gráda, Cormac. 'New Developments in Irish Population History, 1700–1850' in *The Economic History Review*, 2nd ser., vol. XXXVII, no. 4 (1984), pp. 473–488

Moody, T.W. and Martin, F. X. *The Course of Irish History* (Cork, 1984)

Moran, Gerard. 'A Passage to Britain: Seasonal Migration and Social Change in the West of Ireland, 1870–1890' in *Saothar*, vol. 13 (1988), pp. 22–31

Murphy, Daniel. *A History of Irish Emigrant and Missionary Education* (Dublin, 2000)

Murtagh, A. *Portrait of a Westmeath Tenant Community, 1879–85: The Barbavilla Murder* (Dublin & Portland, 1999)

Mulkern, Paul. 'Irish Immigrants and Public Disorder in Coventry, 1845–1875' in *Midland History*, no. 21 (1996), pp. 119–135

Neal, Frank. 'A Criminal Profile of the Liverpool Irish' in *Historic Society of Lancashire and Cheshire*, no. 140 (1991), pp. 161–199

Nolan, W. (ed.), *Tipperary History and Society* (Dublin, 1985)

O'Connor, Emmet. *A Labour History of Ireland, 1824–1960* (Dublin, 1992)

—— *Reds and The Green: Ireland, Russia and the Communist Internationals, 1919–43* (Dublin, 2004)

Ó Gráda, Cormac. 'Across the Briny Ocean: Some Thoughts on Irish Emigration to America, 1800–1850' in Devine, T.M. and Dickson, David (eds), *Ireland and Scotland, 1600–1850* (Edinburgh, 1979), pp. 118–130

—— *Before and After the Famine: Explorations in Economic History, 1808–1925* (Manchester, 1993)

—— 'A Note on Nineteenth Century Emigration Statistics' in *Population Studies*, vol. 29, no. 1 (1979), pp. 143–149

—— 'Demographic Adjustment and Seasonal Migration in Nineteenth–Century Ireland' in Cullen, L.M and Furet, F. (eds), *Ireland and France 17th–20th Centuries: Towards a Comparative Study of Rural History* (Paris, 1980), pp. 181–193

—— 'Fertility and Population in Ireland, North and South' in *Populations Studies*, vol. 49, no. 2 (1995), pp. 259–270

—— *Ireland: A New Economic History, 1780–1939* (Oxford, 1994)

—— 'Irish Agricultural History: Recent Research' in *Agricultural History Review*, vol. 38, no. II, (1990), pp. 165–173

—— *Ireland Before and After the Famine: Explorations in Economic History, 1808–1925* (Manchester, 1993)

—— *Ireland's Great Famine: Interdisciplinary Perspectives* (Dublin, 2006)

—— 'Poverty, Population and Agriculture' in Vaughan, W.E. (ed.), *A New History of Ireland: Ireland under the Union, I, 1801–70*, vol. V (Oxford, 1989), pp. 108–136

—— 'Seasonal Migration and Post–Famine Adjustment in the West of Ireland' in *Studia Hibernica*, vol. 13 (1973), pp. 48–76

—— 'Some Aspects of Nineteenth–Century Irish Emigration' in Cullen, L.M. and Smout, T.C. (eds), *Comparative Aspects of Scottish and Irish Economic and Social History, 1600–1900* (Edinburgh, 1977), pp. 65–73

O'Sullivan, Patrick (ed.), *The Irish World: History, Heritage, Identity*, 2 vols. (London, 1992)

Ó Tuathaigh, M.A.G. *Ireland Before the Famine, 1798–1848* (Dublin, 1972)

—— 'The Irish in Nineteenth–Century Britain: Problems of Integration' in *Transactions of the Royal Historical Society*, 5th ser., vol. XXXI (1981), pp. 149–173

Petersen, William. *Malthus* (London, 1979)

Póirtéir, C. (ed.), *The Great Irish Famine* (Cork, 1995)

Prior, Pauline M. 'Prisoner or Patient– The Official Debate on the Criminal Lunatic in Nineteenth–Century Ireland' in *History of Psychiatry*, vol. XV, no. 2 (2004), pp. 177–192

Richardson, C. 'The Irish in Victorian Britain' in *Bradford Antiquary*, vol. XI (1976), pp. 294–316

Russell, M. 'The Irish Delinquent in England' in *Studies*, vol. 53 (Summer, 1964), pp. 136–148

Schrier, Arnold. *Ireland and the American Emigration, 1850–1900* (rev. ed., New York, 1970)

Sheehan, J. (ed.), *Westmeath: As Others Saw It* (Kilkenny, 1982)

Solar, Peter M. 'Agricultural Productivity and Economic Development in Ireland and Scotland in the Early Nineteenth Century' in Devine, T.M. and Dickson, David (eds), *Ireland and Scotland, 1600–1850* (Edinburgh, 1979), pp. 70–88

Stivers, Richard. *A Hair of the Dog* (Pennsylvania, 1976)

Swift, Roger E. 'Anti–Catholicism and Irish Disturbances' in *Midland History*, vol. IX (1984), pp. 87–108

—— 'Another Stafford Street Row: Law and Order and the Irish Presence in Mid–Victorian Wolverhampton' in *Immigrants and*

Minorities, vol. III, no. 1 (1984), pp. 5–29

—— 'Crime and the Irish in Nineteenth–Century Britain' in Swift, Roger E. and Gilley, Sheridan. (eds), *The Irish in Britain, 1815–1939* (London, 1989), pp. 163–182

Swift, Roger E. and Gilley, Sheridan. (eds), *The Irish in Britain, 1815–1939* (London, 1989)

Taylor, David. *Crime, Policing and Punishment in England* (London, 1998)

Treble, J.H. 'The Navvies' in *Scottish Labour History Society Journal*, no. 5, pp. 34–54

—— 'Irish Navvies' in *Transport History*, vol. VI, pp. 227–247

Vaughan, W.E. (ed.), *A New History of Ireland*, vols V, VI (Oxford, 1989, 1996)

—— 'Agricultural Outputs, Rents and Wages in Ireland, 1850–1880' in Cullen, L.M and Furet, F. (eds.), *Ireland and France 17th–20th Centuries: Towards a Comparative Study of Rural History* (Paris, 1980), pp. 85–97

—— 'Ireland c. 1870' in Vaughan, W.E. (ed.), *A New History of Ireland: Ireland under the Union, I, 1801–70*, vol. V (Oxford, 1989), pp. 727–800

—— *Landlords and Tenants in Mid–Victorian Ireland* (Oxford, 1994)

Vaughan, W.E. and Fitzpatrick, A.J. (eds), *Irish Historical Statistics: Population, 1821–1971* (Dublin, 1978)

Whelan, K. 'The Famine and Post–Famine Adjustment' in Nolan, W. (ed.), *The Shaping of Ireland: The Geographical Perspective* (Cork & Dublin, 1986)'Pre and Post–Famine Landscape Change' in Póirtéir, C. (ed.), *The Great Irish Famine* (Cork, 1995), pp. 19–33

—— 'An Account of the Baronies of Forth and Bargy in 1814' in *Journal of Wexford Historical Society*, no. 11 (1986–7), pp. 14–31

B. Argentina and South America:

Ablard, Jonathan. 'The Limits of Psychiatric Reform in Argentina, 1890–1946' in Porter, Roy and Wright, David (eds.), *The Confinement of the Insane: International Perspectives, 1800–1965* (Cambridge, 2003), pp. 226–247

Albert, Bill. *South America and the World Economy from Independence to 1930* (London, 1983)

Alonso, Paula. *Between Revolution and the Ballot Box: The Origins of the Argentine Radical Party in the 1890s* (Cambridge, 2000)

Anna, Timothy E. *Spain and the Loss of America* (Lincoln, Nebr., 1983)

Archetti, E. and Stolen, K. *Explotación familiar y acumulación de capi-*

tal en el campo (Buenos Aires, 1975)

Arnols, Samuel. *Viaje por America del Sur* (Buenos Aires, 1951)

Avellando, Nicolas. *Estudios en las leyes de tierra publicas* (Buenos Aires, 1865)

Bakewell, Peter J., Johnson, John J. and Dodge, Meredith D. (eds), *Readings in Latin American History: The Modern Experience* (Durham, 1985)

Barros, Alvaro. *Indios, fronteras y seguridad interior, 1872–1876* (Buenos Aires, 1975)

Bertoni, Lilia Ana. *Patriotas, cosmopolitas y nacionalistas: La construcción de la nacionalidad Argentina a fines del siglo XIX* (Buenos Aires, 2001)

Bethell, Leslie (ed.), *The Cambridge History of Latin America*, 11 vols (Cambridge, 1986)

Birschoff, E. *Historia de Córdoba* (Buenos Aires, 1979)

Blanksten, George. I. *Peron's Argentina* (Chicago, 1974)

Brown, Jonathan C. *A Socio–Economic History of Argentina, 1776–1860* (Cambridge, 1979)

Burgin, Miron. *The Economic Aspects of Argentine Federalism, 1820–1852* (Cambridge, Mass., 1946)

Burnet–Merlin, Alfredo R. *Cuando Rosas quiso ser inglés* (Buenos Aires, 1974)

Bushnell, David and Macaulay, Neill. *The Emergence of Latin America in the Nineteenth Century* (Oxford, 1988)

Cansenello, Carlos. 'Domiciliarios, transeúntes en el proceso de formación estadal Bonaerense, 1820–1832' in *Entrepasados*, vol. IV, no. 6 (1994), pp. 7–22

Carlson, M. *Feminismo, The Women's Movement: Argentina from its Beginnings to Eva Peron* (Chicago, 1988)

Carretero, Andrés M. *El pensamiento politico de Juan Manuel de Rosas* (Buenos Aires, 1970)

Cayetano, Bruno. *Historia de la iglesia en la Argentina* (Buenos Aires, 1976)

Chiaramonte, José C. *Nacionalismo y liberalismo económicos en la Argentina, 1860–1880* (Buenos Aires, 1971)

Cortés Conde, Roberto. 'The Growth of the Argentine Economy, c. 1870–1914' in Bethell, Leslie (ed.), The *Cambridge History of Latin America*, vol. V (Cambridge, 1986), pp. 327–357

Cortés Conde, Roberto and Stein, Stanley J. (eds), *Latin America: A Guide to Economic History, 1830–1930* (Berkeley, 1977)

Cortés Conde, Roberto and Hunt, Shane J. (eds), *The Latin American*

Economies: Growth and the Export Sector, 1880–1830 (New York, 1985)

De Lucía, Daniel Omar. 'Iglesia, estado y secularización en la Argentina (1800–1890)' in *El Catoblepas*, no. 16 (June, 2003), pp. 13–45

De Torres, Haydeé Gorostegui. *La organización nacional* (Buenos Aires, 2000)

Devoto, Fernando J. *Historia de la inmigración en la Argentina* (Buenos Aires, 2003)

Di Tella, Guido and Zymelman, Manuel. *Las etapas del desarrollo económico Argentino* (Buenos Aires, 1967)

Díaz Alejandro, Carlos F. *Essays on the Economic History of the Argentine Republic* (New Haven & London, 1970)

Dodds, Klaus John. 'Geography, Identity and the Creation of the Argentine State' in *Bulletin of Latin American Research*, vol. XII, no. 3 (1993), pp. 311–331

—— Entraigas, R. *Historia de los Salesianos en la Argentina* (Buenos Aires, 1972)

Ferns, H.S. *The Argentine Republic* (Newton Abbot, 1973)

—— *Argentina* (London, 1969)

—— *Britain and Argentina in the Nineteenth Century* (Oxford, 1960)

—— 'Investment and Trade between Britain and Argentina in the Nineteenth Century' in *Economic History Review*, 2nd ser., vol. III, no. 2 (1950), pp. 203–218

—— 'Beginnings of British Investment in Argentina' in *Economic History Review*, 2nd ser., vol. IV, no. 3 (1951), pp. 341–352

Ferrari, Gustavo and Gallo, Ezequiel (eds), *La Argentina del ochenta al centenario* (Buenos Aires, 1980)

Furlong Cardiff, Guillermo. 'El catolicismo Argentina entre 1860 y 1930' in R. Levene (ed.), *Historia de la Nación Argentina*, vol. III (Buenos Aires, 1937), pp. 595–622

—— *Nacimiento y desarrollo de la filosofia en el rio de la Plata*, 1536–1810 (Buenos Aires, 1952)

Galeano, Eduardo. *Las venas abiertas de America Latina* (rev. ed., Madrid, 2003)

Gallo, Ezequiel. 'Argentina: Society and Politics, 1880–1916' in Bethell, Leslie (ed.), *The Cambridge History of Latin America*, vol. V (Cambridge, 1986), pp. 359–391

Gálves, Lucia. *Historias de inmigración* (Buenos Aires, 2003)

Garavaglia, Juan Carlos. *Poder, conflicto y relaciones sociales: El río de la Plata, XVIII–XIX* (Rosario, 1999)

Gayol, Sandra. *Sociabilidad en Buenos Aires: Hombres, honor y cafés,*

1862–1910 (Buenos Aires, 2000)

Gerbi, Antonello. *The Dispute of the New World: The History of a Polemic, 1750– 1900*, trans. by Jeremy Moyle (Pittsburgh, 1973)

Godio, J. *Historia del movimiento obrero Argentino: Immigrantes, asalariados y lucha de clases, 1880–1910*(Buenos Aires, 1973)

Gongora, Mario. *Studies in the Colonial History of Spanish America* (Cambridge, 1975)

Goodrich, Carter, 'Argentina as a New Country' in *Comparative Studies in Society and History*, 7 (Oct, 1964), pp. 70–88

Hale, Charles A. 'Political and Social Ideas in Latin America, 1870–1930' in Bethell, Leslie (ed.), *The Cambridge History of Latin America*, vol. IV (Cambridge, 1986), pp. 367–526

Halperín–Donghi, Tulio. 'Economy and Society in post–Independence Spanish America' in Bethell, Leslie (ed.), *The Cambridge History of Latin America*, vol. III (Cambridge, 1986), pp. 299–345

—— *Historia Contemporánea de America Latina* (5th ed., Madrid, 2004)

—— *Politics, Economics and Society in Argentina in the Revolutionary Period* (Cambridge, 1975)

—— *Revolución y guerra* (Buenos Aires, 1972)

—— *The Aftermath of Revolution in Latin America* (New York, 1973)

Ivereigh, Austen. *Catholicism and Politics in Argentina, 1810–1960* (New York and London, 1995)

—— 'The Shape of the State: Liberals and Catholics in the Dispute Over Law 1420 of 1884 in Argentina' in Ivereigh, Austen (ed.), *The Politics of Religion in an Age of Revival* (London, 2000), pp. 166–187

Lewis, Colin M. 'La consolidación de la frontera Argentina a fines de la década del setenta: Los indios, Roca y los ferrocarriles' in Ferrari, Gustavo and Gallo, Ezequiel (eds), *La Argentina del ochenta al centenario* (Buenos Aires, 1980)

Link, Paul. *Sheep Breeding and Wool Production in the Argentine Republic* (Buenos Aires, 1934)

Lynch, John. *Argentine Dictator: Juan Manuel de Rosas, 1829–1852* (Oxford, 1981)

—— 'The Catholic Church in Latin America, 1830–1930' in Bethell, Leslie (ed.), *The Cambridge History of Latin America*, vol. IV (Cambridge, 1986), pp. 527–595

—— 'The Origins of Spanish American Dependence' in Bethell, Leslie. (ed.), *The Cambridge History of Latin America*, vol. III (Cambridge, 1986), pp. 3–50

—— 'The River Plate Republic from Independence to the Paraguayan War' in Bethell, Leslie (ed.), *The Cambridge History of Latin America*, vol. III (Cambridge, 1986), pp. 615–676

—— The Spanish American Revolutions, 1808–1826 (New York, 1965)

Lynch, John; Cortés Conde, Roberto; Gallo, Ezequiel; Rock, David; Torre, Juan Carlos; and De Riz, Liliana, *Historia de la Argentina* (Barcelona, 2001)

Masur, Gerhard, *Nationalism in Latin America* (London, 1966)

Mecham, J. Lloyd. *Church and State in Latin American History: A History of Politico–Ecclesiastical Relations* (Chapel Hill, 1966)

O'Donnell, Guillermo. *Modernization and Bureautic Authoritarianism: Studies in South American Politics* (Berkeley, 1973)

Ortiz, Ricardo M. *Historia económica de la Argentina* (Buenos Aires, 1955)

Page, Joseph A. *Peron: A Biography* (New York, 1983)

Parry, J.H. *The Spanish Seaborne Empire* (Harmondsworth, 1973)

Payne, Stanley G. *El catolicismo español* (Barcelona, 1984)

Peloso, Vincent C. and Tennenbaum, Barbara (eds), *Liberals, Politics and Power: State Formation in 19th Century Latin America* (London, 1996)

Pike, Frederick (ed.), *Freedom and Reform in Latin America* (Notre Dame, 1967)

Platt, D.C.M. *Latin America and British Trade, 1806–1914* (London, 1972)

Potash, Robert A. *The Army and Politics in Argentina, 1928–1945* (Stanford, 1969)

Rock, David. *Argentina, 1516–1982: From Colonization to the Falklands War* (London, 1986)

—— *Authoritarian Argentina: The Nationalist Movement, its History and its Impact* (Berkeley & Oxford, 1993)

—— *Politics in Argentina, 1890–1930: The Rise and Fall of Radicalism* (London, 1975)

Romero, José Luis. *A History of Argentine Political Thought* (London, 1963)

Rosa, José Maria. *Historia Argentina*, vol. VIII (Buenos Aires, 1969)

Rosoli, Gianfranco. 'Las escuelas de las sociedades italianos en la Argentina, 1866–1914' in Devoto, Fernando J. and Rosoli, G. (eds), *La inmigración en la Argentina* (Buenos Aires, 1988), pp. 165–207

Sábato, Hilda. 'Citizenship, Political Participation and the Formation of the Public Sphere in Buenos Aires, 1850s–1880s' in *Past and*

Present, no. 136 (August 1992), pp. 139–163

—— *La política en las calles: Entre el voto y la movilización, 1862–1880* (Buenos Aires, 1998)

Sáenz Quesada, María. *La Argentina: Historia del país y de su gente* (Buenos Aires, 2001)

Sampay, Arturo Enrique. *Las ideas políticas de Juan Manuel de Rosas* (Buenos Aires, 1970)

Sánchez–Albornoz, Nicolás. 'The Population of Latin America, 1850–1930' in Bethell, Leslie (ed.), *The Cambridge History of Latin America*, vol. IV (Cambridge, 1986), pp. 121–152

Sánchez Alonso, Blanca. *La inmigración española en Argentina, siglos XIX y XX* (Barcelona, 1992)

Sarmiento, Domingo Faustino. *Facundo: Civilización y barbarie* (2nd ed., Madrid, 1993)

Scobie, James R. *Argentina: A City and a Nation* (2nd ed., New York, 1971)

—— *Revolution on the Pampas: A Social History of Argentine Wheat* (Austin, 1967)

—— *Buenos Aires: Plaza to Suburb, 1870–1910* (New York, 1974)

Smith, Peter H. *Politics and Beef in Argentina* (New York, 1969)

Socolow, Susan Midgen. 'Economic Activities of the Porteño Merchants: The Viceregal Period' in *Hispanic American Historical Review*, vol. 55, no. 1 (1975), pp. 1–24

Solberg, Carl. *Immigration and Nationalism in Argentina and Chile, 1890–1914* (Austin & London, 1970)

—— 'Immigration and Urban Social Problems in Argentina and Chile, 1890–1914' in *Hispanic American Historical Review*, vol. 49, no. 2 (1969), pp. 215–232

Stavenhagen, R. *Las clases sociales en las sociedades agrarias* (Mexico, 1971)

Vallier, Ivan. *Catholicism, Social Control, and Modernization in Latin America* (New Jersey, 1970)

Vogel, Hans. 'New Citizens for a New Nation: Naturalization in Early Independent Argentina' in *Hispanic American Historical Review*, vol. 71, no. 1 (1991), pp. 107–131

Williamson, Edwin. *The Penguin History of Latin America* (London, 1992)

—— *Argentina and the Failure of Democracy: Conflict Among Political Elites* (Madison, 1974)

Woodward Jr., Ralph Lee. (ed.), *Passivism in Latin America, 1850–1900* (Lexington, Mass., 1971)

Wynia, Gary W. *Argentina: Illusions and Realities* (New York, 1986)

Zimmerman, A.F. 'The Land Policy of Argentina: With Particular Reference to the Conquest of the Southern Pampas' in *Hispanic American Historical Review*, vol. XXV, no. 1 (1945), pp. 3–26

Zimmermann, E.A. *Los liberals reformistas: La cuestión social en la Argentina 1890–1916* (Buenos Aires, 1995)

—— 'Racial Ideas and Social Reform: Argentina, 1890–1916' in *Hispanic American Historical Review*, vol. 72 (1992), pp. 23–46.

C. Irish Immigration to Argentina:

Alsina, Juan. *La inmigración en la Republica Argentina* (Buenos Aires, 1903)

Batolla, O. *Las primeras ingleses en Buenos Aires* (Buenos Aires, 1865)

Caillet–Bois, Ricardo R. *Nuestros corsarios: Brown y Bouchard en el Pacifico, 1815–1816* (Buenos Aires, 1930)

Carcana, Miguel A. *Evolución historia del régimen de la tierra, 1810–1916* (Buenos Aires, 1917)

Carreño, Virginia. *Estancias y Estancieros* (Buenos Aires, 1968)

Carretero, Andrés. *La propiedad de la tierra en la época de Rosas* (Buenos Aires, 1972)

Coghlan, Eduardo A. *Andanzas de un irlandés en el campo porteño, 1845–1864* (Buenos Aires, 1981)

—— *El aporte de los irlandeses a la formación de la nación Argentina* (Buenos Aires, 1982)

—— *Fundadores de la segunda época: Los irlandeses* (Buenos Aires, 1967)

—— *Los irlandeses en la Argentina* (Buenos Aires, 1987)

—— 'Origines y evolución de la colectividad hiberno argentina' in *The Southern Cross, Numero de Centenaria* (Buenos Aires, 1975), pp. 29–31

De Courcy Ireland, John. 'Admiral Brown at Martin Garcia and Montevideo 1814' in *The Irish Sword*, vol. III, no. 23 (1957), pp. 20–24

—— 'Admiral William Brown', in *The Irish Sword*, vol. VI, no. 23 (1962), pp. 119–121

—— *Ireland and the Irish in Maritime History* (Dublin, 1986)

—— 'Irish Soldiers and Seamen in Latin America' in *The Irish Sword*, vol. I, no. 4 (1952–53), pp. 296–303

—— *The Admiral from Mayo: A Life of Admirante William Brown from Foxford* (Dublin, 1995)

Delaney, Juan José, *Moira Sullivan* (Buenos Aires, 1999)

—— *Treboles del Sur* (Buenos Aires, 1994)

Ferns, Henry. *Argentina y Gran Bretaña en el siglo XIX* (Buenos Aires, 1968)

Gately, Sister Mary Josephine. *The Sisters of Mercy* (New York, 1931)

Gaynor, Rev. John. *Memoir of Father Dolan* (Buenos Aires, 1958)

—— *Memoir of Father Patrick O'Grady* (Buenos Aires, 1959)

—— *The English–Speaking Pallottines* (Buenos Aires, 1962)

—— *The History of St Patrick's College in Mercedes* (Buenos Aires, 1958)

Graham–Yooll, Andrew. *The Forgotten Colony: A History of English Speaking Communities in Argentina* (London, 1981)

Harrington, Isabel. *Un crillo irlandés* (Buenos Aires, 1976)

Hennessey, Alistair and King, John (eds), *The Land that England Lost: Argentina and Britain, a Special Relationship* (London, 1992)

Hinchcliff, Thomas. *Viaje a la Plata en 1861* (Buenos Aires, 1955)

Izarra, Laura. 'The Irish Diaspora in Argentina' in *British Association for Irish Studies*, bulletin 32 (October 2002), pp. 5–9

Julianello, Maria Theresa and Silvana, Maria. 'The Story of Camilla O'Gorman' in *Irish Roots*, no. 3 (1996), pp. 18–19

—— *The Scarlet Trinity* (Cork, 2000)

Kiely, Benedict. 'Man from the Pampas', in *The Capuchin Annual* (1948), pp. 428–436

Kirby, Peadar, *Ireland and Latin America* (Dublin, 1992)

Korol, Juan Carlos and Sábato, Hilda. *Cómo fue la inmigración irlandesa en Argentina* (Buenos Aires, 1981)

Landaburu, Roberto E. *Irlandeses: Eduardo Casey, vida y obra* (Santa Fe, 1995)

Levine, Ricardo. *Historia de la nación Argentina* (Buenos Aires, 1936)

—— 'The Personality of Admiral Brown' in *The Irish Sword*. vol. III, no. 23 (1957), pp. 25–27

Lynch, Ricardo and Lynch, Patricio. *Novela historica* (Buenos Aires, 1929)

MacLoughlin, Guillermo. 'Argentina: The Forgotten People' in *Irish Roots*, no. 4 (1993), pp. 6–7

—— 'The Forgotten People: The Irish in Argentina and other South American Countries' in *Celtic News* (Buenos Aires), March, April, and May/June, 1998

—— 'Los primeros irlandeses vinieron con Magellanes' in T*he Southern Cross* (August–September, 1991), p. 6

—— 'The Irish in South America' in Evans, M.D. and O'Duill, Eileen (eds), *Aspects of Irish Genealogy* (Dublin, 1993), pp. 170–177

Marshall, Oliver. *English, Irish and Irish–American Pioneer Settlers in*

Nineteenth–Century Brazil (Oxford, 2005)

—— (ed.), *English–Speaking Communities in Latin America* (Houndsmills, 2000)

—— *The English–Language Press in Latin America* (London, 1996)

McGinn, Brian. 'The Lynch Family of Argentina' in *Irish Roots*, no. 2 (1993), pp. 11–14

—— 'The South American Irish' in Irish Roots, nos. 25–28 (1998)

—— 'The Irish in South America: A Bibliography' in O'Sullivan, Patrick (ed.), Irish Diaspora Studies website, at http://www.brad-ford.ac.uk/acad/diaspora/guides/samerica.shtml

McKenna, Patrick. 'Irish Migration to Argentina', in O'Sullivan, Patrick (ed.), *The Irish Worldwide, History, Heritage, Identity: Patterns of Migration*, vol. 1 (Leicester, London & New York, 1992), pp. 63–83

—— 'Irish Migration to Argentina: A Different Model' in Bielenberg, Andy (ed.), *The Irish Diaspora* (Harlow, Essex, 2000), pp. 195–212

—— 'The Formation of Hiberno–Argentine Society,' in Oliver Marshall (ed.), *English-Speaking Communities in Latin America* (New York, 2000), pp. 81–103

Murray, Edmundo. *Devenir irlandés* (Buenos Aires, 2004)

Murray, John. 'The Irish and Others in Argentina' in Studies, no. 38 (1949), p. 377–388

Nally, Pat. 'Los irlandeses en la Argentina' en *Familia: Ulster Genealogical Review*, vol. II, no. 8 (1992), pp. 69–77

Nevin, Kathleen, *You'll Never Go Back* (Maynooth, 1937)

Petit de Murat, Ulises. *Genio y figura de Benito Lynch* (Buenos Aires, 1968)

Pyne, Peter. *The Invasions of Buenos Aires, 1806–1807: The Irish Dimensions* (University of Liverpool: Institute of Latin American Studies, Research Paper 20, 1996)

Ready, William, B. 'The Irish and South America' in *Eire–Ireland*, vol. I, no. 1 (1996), pp. 50–63

Ratto, Hector R. *Historia del Almirante Brown* (3rd ed., Buenos Aires, 1985)

Saez–Germain, Alejandro. 'Siempre al frente los Lynch: Casi mil años de Historia' in *Noticias* (March, 1994), pp. 44–51

Ussher, Mons. Santiago M. *Father Fahy: A Biography of Anthony Dominic Fahy, O.P.* (Buenos Aires, 1951)

—— 'Irish Immigrants in Argentina' in Irish Ecclesiastical Record (Dublin, 1948), 5th ser., vol. 70, pp. 385–392

—— *Las Hermanas de la Misericordia, 1856–1956* (Buenos Aires, 1955)

—— *Los capellanes irlandeses en la colectividad hiberno Argentina durante el siglo XIX* (Buenos Aires, 1953)

Walsh, Edward. 'The Irish in the Argentine Republic: John Cullen's 1888 Report' in *Collectanea Hibernica*, vol. 43 (2001), pp. 239–246

Walsh, Michelin. 'Unpublished Admiral Brown Documents in Madrid', in *The Irish Sword*, vol. III, no. 23 (1957), pp. 17–19

White, Arden C. 'The Irish Immigration to Argentina: An Historical Focus' in *The Irish at Home and Abroad*, vol. 4, no. 3 (1997), pp. 133–134

D. General Immigration to Argentina:

Baily, Samuel L. *Immigrants in the Lands of Promise: Italians in Buenos Aires and New York City, 1870–1914* (New York, 1999)

—— 'Italian Immigrants in Buenos Aires and New York City, 1870–1914: A Comparative Analysis of Adjustment' in Baily, Samuel L. and Míguez Eduardo José (eds), *Mass Migration to Modern Latin America* (Wilmington, 2003)

Baily, Samuel L. and Miguez, Eduardo José. *Mass Migration to Modern Latin America* (Wilmington, 2003)

—— 'Sarmiento and Immigration: Changing Views on the Role of Immigration in the Development of Argentina' in Criscenti, Joseph, T. (ed.), *Sarmiento and his Argentina* (London and Colorado, 1993), pp. 31–142

—— 'The Role of Two Newspapers in the Assimilation of Italians in Buenos Aires and Sao Paulo, 1893–1913' in *International Migration Review*, vol. 12, no. 3 (1978), pp. 321–340

Clementi, Hebe (ed.), *Inmigración española en la Argentina* (Buenos Aires, 1991)

Cortés Conde, Roberto. 'Migración, cambio agrícola y políticas de protección: El caso Argentino' in Clementi, Hebe (ed.), *Inmigración española en la Argentina* (Buenos Aires, 1991), pp. 17–32

Da Orden, Maria Liliana. 'Liderazgo étnico y redes socials: Una approximación a la participación política de los españoles en la Argentina, 1880–1912' in Fernández, Alejandro Enrique and Moya, José C. (eds), *La inmigración española en la Argentina* (Buenos Aires, 1999), pp. 167–187

Devoto, Fernando J. *Estudios sobre la emigración italiana a la Argentina en la segundo mitad del siglo XIX* (Rome, 1991)

—— *Historia de la inmigración en la Argentina* (Buenos Aires, 2003)

—— 'Las condiciones de posibilidad de los movimientos migratorios: Notas sobre el caso español en una perspectiva comparada' in Clementi, Hebe (ed.), *Inmigración española en la Argentina* (Buenos Aires, 1991), pp. 35–57

Devoto, Fernando J. and Gianfranco Rosoli (eds), La inmigración italiana en la Argentina (Buenos Aires, 1988)

Di Tella, Torcuato S. 'El impacto inmigratorio sobre el sistema politico Argentino' in Jorrat, Jorge Raul and Sautu, Ruth. (eds), *Después de Germani* (Buenos Aires, 1992), pp. 86–104

—— *Historia Social de la Argentina Contemporánea* (Buenos Aires, 1998)

Dore, Grazia. 'Un periodico italiano en Buenos Aires, 1911–1913' in Devoto, Fernando J. and Rosoli, Gianfranco (eds), La inmigración italiana en la Argentina (Buenos Aires, 1998), pp. 127–140

Duarte, Ángel. *La república del emigrante* (Buenos Aires, 1998)

Favero, Luigi 'Las escuelas de las sociedades italianas en la Argentina, 1866–1914' in Devoto, Fernando J. and Rosoli, G. (eds), *La inmigración italiana en la Argentina* (Buenos Aires, 1998), pp. 165–205

Fernández, Alejandro Enrique. 'Los españoles de Buenos Aires y sus asociaciones en la época de inmigración masiva' in Clementi, Hebe (ed.), *Inmigración española en la Argentina* (Buenos Aires, 1991), pp. 59–83

Fernández, Alejandro Enrique and Moya, José C. (eds.), *La inmigración española en la Argentina* (Buenos Aires, 1999)

Halperín–Donghi, Tulio. 'La integración de los inmigrantes italianos en Argentina: Un comentario' in Devoto, Fernando J. and Rosoli, Gianfranco (eds), *La inmigración italiana en la Argentina* (Buenos Aires, 1998), pp. 87–93

Klein, Herbert S. 'The Integration of Italian Immigrants into the United States and Argentina: A Comparative Analysis' in *The American Historical Review*, vol. 88, no. 2 (1983), pp. 306–329

Kleiner, Alberto. *Inmigración inglesa en la Argentina: El informe, 1875* (Buenos Aires, 1983)

Moya, José C. *Cousins and Strangers: Spanish Immigrants in Buenos Aires, 1850–1930* (Berkeley & London, 1998)

—— 'La fiebre de la emigración: El proceso de diffusion en el éxodo transatlantico español, 1850–1930' in Fernández, Alejandro Enrique and Moya, José C (eds), *La inmigración española en la Argentina* (Buenos Aires, 1999), pp. 20–41

Newton, Ronald C. *German Buenos Aires, 1900–1933: Social Change and Cultural Crisis* (Austin & London, 1977)

Ogelsby, J.C.M. '"Who are we?" The Search for a National Identity in Argentina, Australia and Canada, 1870–1950' in Platt, D.C.M. and Di Tella, Guido (eds), *Argentina, Australia and Canada: Studies in Comparative Development, 1870–1965*, (London, 1985), pp. 110–122

Recchini de Lattes, Z. and Lattes, Alfredo E. *Migración en la Argentina* (Buenos Aires, 1969)

Rodino, Hugo José. *Inmigrantes españoles en Argentina: Adapción e identidad* (Buenos Aires, 1999)

Rosoli, Gianfausto 'Las organizaciones y la inmigración italiana en la Argentina' in Devoto, Fernando and Rosoli, Gianfranco (eds), *La inmigración italiana en la Argentina* (Buenos Aires, 1998), pp. 209–239

Seeber, Francisco. *Ensayo sobre inmigración y colonización en la Provincia de Buenos Aires* (Buenos Aires, 1971)

Wiedman, Ingrid. 'La colonización alemaña y alemaño' in Wiedman, Ingrid, et al., *La colonizacion alemaña en misiones* (Posados, 2001), pp. 12–32

Williams, Glyn. *The Welsh in Patagonia: Critical Bibliographic Review* (Cardiff, 1979)

D. International Studies:

Anderson, Benedict. *Imagined Communities* (London, 1936)

Baines, D. *Emigration from Europe, 1815–1930* (Macmillan, 1991)

—— *Migration in a Mature Economy* (Cambridge & New York, 1985)

Becker, G.S. *Altruism in the Family and Selfishness in the Market Place* (Discussion Papers, Centre for Labour and Economics, London School of Economics, 1980) no.73

—— *A Treatise on the Family* (Cambridge, Mass., & London, 1981)

Becker, G.S. and Becker, G.N. *The Economics of Life* (New York, 1997)

Bhugra, Dinesh. *Mental Health of Ethnic Minorities: An Annotated Bibliography* (London, 1999)

Boneva, B.S. and I.H. Frienze, 'Toward a Concept of Migrant Personality' in *Journal of Social Issues*, vol. 57, no. 3 (2001), pp. 477–491

Cloward, Richard A. and Ohlin, Lloyd E. *Delinquency and Opportunity* (London, 1961)

Colls, Robert and Dodd, Philip (eds), *Englishness: Politics and Culture, 1880–1920* (Kent, 1986)

Davar, Bhargavi V. *Mental Health from a Gender Perspective* (New Delhi and London, 2001)

David, P.A. and Reder, M.W. (eds), *Nations and Households in*

Economic Growth (New York & London, 1974)

De Jong, G.F. and Gardner, R.W. (eds), *Migration Decision Making: Multidisciplinary Approaches to Micro Level Studies in Developed and Developing Countries* (New York & Oxford, 1981)

Ernst, Robert. *Immigrant Life in New York City* (New York, 1949)

Fairburn, Miles and Haslett, Stephen. 'Violent Crime in Old and New Societies: A Case Study Based in New Zealand, 1853–1940', in *Journal of Social History*, vol. XX, no. 1 (1986), pp. 89–126

Faist, T. *The Volume and Dynamics of International Migration and Transnational Social Space* (Oxford, 2000)

Fernando, Susan. *Mental Health in a Multi–Ethnic Society* (New York, 1995)

Finnane, Mark. *Insanity and the Insane in Post–Famine Ireland* (New Jersey, 1981)

Foster, J. Class *Struggle and the Industrial Revolution* (London 1974)

Gellner, Ernest. *Encounters with Nationalism* (Oxford, 1994)

—— *Nationalism* (London, 1997)

—— *Nations and Nationalism* (Oxford, 1983)

Ghosh, Bimal. 'Economic Migration and the Sending Countries' in Broeck, J. Van Den (ed.), *The Economics of Labour Migration* (Cheltenham & Vermont, 1996), pp. 77–113

Giddens, Anthony. *The Constitution of Society* (Cambridge, 1984)

Glazer, Nathan and Moynihan, Daniel Patrick. *Beyond the Melting Pot* (2nd ed., Cambridge, Mass., 1963)

Gould, J.D. 'European Inter–Continental Emigration: The Road Home: Return Migration from the U.S.A.' in *Journal of European Economic History*, vol. IX, no. 1 (1980), pp. 55–60

Grabosky, P. *Sydney in Ferment: Crime, Dissent and Official Reaction, 1788–1973* (Canberra, 1977)

Grinberg, L. and Grinberg, R. *Psychoanalytic Perspectives on Migration and Exiles* (New Haven & London, 1989)

Grob, Gerald N. *The State and the Mentally Ill* (North Carolina, 1966)

—— *Managing Migration: Time for a New International Regime?* (Oxford, 2000)

Hajnal, J. 'Age at Marriage and Proportions Marrying' in *Population Studies*, vol.VII, (November 1953), pp. 111–136

Hannan, D. *Rural Exodus* (London, 1970)

—— 'European Marriage Patterns in Perspective' in Glass, D.V. and Everseley, D.E.C. (eds), *Population in History* (London, 1965), pp. 101–143

Hiesel, D.F. 'Theories of *International Migration*' in *International*

Migration in the Arab World, vol. II (Beirut, 1982), pp. 653–684

Hobsbawn, E.J. Nations and Nationalism since 1780 (Cambridge, 1990)

Homes, Colin. *Immigrants and Minorities in British Cities* (London, 1978)

Houghton, W.E. (ed.), *The Wellesley Index to Victorian Periodicals, 1824–1900*, 5 vols (Toronto, 1987)

Hvidt, Kristian. *Flight to America: The Social Background of 300,000 Danish Emigrants* (New York, 1975)

Isaac, Julius. *Economics of Migration* (London, 1947)

Jackson, J. *Migration* (London and New York, 1986)

Jellinek, E.M. 'Cultural Differences in the Meaning of Alcoholism' in Pittman, David J. and Synder, Charles R. Society, *Culture and Drinking Patterns* (Carbondale, 1962), pp. 382–388

Kiev, A. and Argandoña, M. *Mental Health in the Developing World* (New York, 1972)

Kidd, Alan J. and Roberts, K.W. (eds), *City, Class and Culture* (Manchester, 1985)

Knafla, L.A. (ed.), *Crime and Criminal Justice in Europe and Canada* (Waterloo, 1981)

Knodel, J. *The Decline of Fertility in Germany* (Princeton, 1974)

Kohn, Hans. Nationalism, its Meaning and History (New York, 1955)
—— *The Idea of Nationalism* (New York, 1944)

Kosa, J, 'A Century of Hungarian Migration' in *American Slavic and East European Review*, vol. XVI (1957), pp. 501–514

Lane, Roger. 'Murder in America: A Historian's Perspective' in Tonry, Michael. (ed.), *Crime and Justice: A Review of Research*, vol. 25 (Chicago & London, 1999), pp. 191–224
—— *Policing the City: Boston, 1822–1885* (Harvard, 1967)

Longmate, Norman. *The Waterdrinkers* (London, 1968)

Mitchell, B.R. *International Historical Statistics: The Americas, 1750–1988* (2nd ed., New York, 1993)

Monkkonen, Eric H. *The Dangerous Class* (Harvard, 1975)

Nann, R.C. (ed.), *Uprooting and Surviving* (Holland & Boston, 1982)

Nugent, Walter. *Crossings: The Great TransAtlantic Migrations, 1970–1914* (Bloomington & London, 1992)

Papasterigiadis, N. *The Turbulence of Migration* (Cambridge, 2000)

Phinney, Jean S.; Horenczyk, Gabriel; Liebkind, Karmela; and Vedder, Paul. 'Ethnic Identity, Immigration, and Well Being: An Interactional Perspective' in *Journal of Social Issues*, vol.57, no. 3 (2001), pp. 493–510

Pittman, David, J. and Snyder, Charles R. *Society, Culture and*

Drinking Patterns (Carbondale, 1962)

Porter, Roy and Wright, David (eds), *The Confinement of the Insane: International Perspectives, 1800–1965* (Cambridge, 2003)

Pozetta, George E. *American Immigration and Ethnicity: Law, Crime, Justice, Naturalization and Citizenship* (New York, 1991)

Richardson, James F. *The New York Police* (Oxford, 1970)

Room, Robin. 'Cultural Contingencies of Alcoholism: Variations between and within Nineteenth Century Urban Ethnic Groups' in *Journal of Health and Social Behaviour*, vol IX, no. 2 (1968), pp. 99–113

Savitz, Leonard. *Delinquency and Migration* (Philadelphia, 1960)

Sexton, J.J. *The Economics and Social Implications of Emigration* (Dublin, 1991)

Stoep, Ann Vander and Link, Bruce. 'Social Class, Ethnicity, and Mental Illness: The Importance of being more than Earnest' in *American Journal of Public Health*, vol. 88, no. 9 (1998), pp. 1396–1402

Sutherland, Edwin H. and Cressey, Donald R. (eds), *Criminology* (9th ed., Philadelphia & New York, 1970)

Thomas, Brinley. *International Migration and Economic Development* (Paris, 1961)

Tonry, Michael. *Ethnicity, Crime and Immigration: Comparative Cross–National Perspectives* (Chicago and London, 1997)

Walker, R.B. 'Bush Ranging in Fact and Legend', in *Historical Studies of Australia and New Zealand*, vol. XI, no. 42 (1964), pp. 206–221

White, R. and Haines F. *Crime and Criminology: An Introduction* (Oxford, 1996)

Wilbanks, William. *Murder in Miami* (Florida, 1984)

Willcox, Walter F. (ed.), *International Migrations: Statistics*, vol. I (New York, 1929)

—— *International Migrations: Interpretations*, Vol. II (New York, 1931)

Winchie, D.B. and Carment, D.W. 'Migration and Motivation: The Migrants' Perspective' in *International Migration Review*, vol. XXIII, no. 1 (1989), pp. 96–99

Wolfgang, M. and Ferracatti, P. *The Subculture of Violence: Towards an Integrated Theory in Criminology* (London, 1967)

E. Unpublished Dissertations and Articles:

Bailey, John Paul. *The British Community in Argentina* (PhD dissertation, University of Surrey, 1976)

Cox, David. *From Intransigence to Integration: English–speaking Communities and the Emergence of the National Self in Post–Colonial Argentina* (MA dissertation, University of Helsinki, 2004)

Keep, G.R.C. *The Irish Migration to North America in the Second Half of the Nineteenth Century* (PhD dissertation, Trinity College Dublin, 1951)

McKenna, Patrick. *Nineteenth–Century Irish Migration to, and Settlement in, Argentina* (MA dissertation, St. Patrick's College, Maynooth, 1994)

Murray, Edmundo. *How the Irish became 'Gauchos Ingleses': Diasporic Models in Irish–Argentine Literature* (M.A. dissertation, University of Geneva, 2003)

Norbeto Marquiegui, Dedier. *Circularidad y Permanencia: La Inmigración Irlandesa en Luján, Provincia de Buenos Aires, Rep. Argentina, 1830–1895* (article, 2005)

Sábato, Hilda. *Wool Production and the Agrarian Structure in the Province of Buenos Aires, North of The Salado, 1840s–1880s* (Ph.D dissertation, University of London, 1980)

Web Sites:

Irish Migration Studies in Latin America
http://www.irishargentine.org
Edited by Edmundo Murray (2003)

Index